ROUTLEDGE LIBRARY EDITIONS:
WORK & SOCIETY

Volume 18

THE IMPACT OF RECESSION

THE IMPACT OF RECESSION

On Industry, Employment and the Regions, 1976–1981

ALAN R. TOWNSEND

LONDON AND NEW YORK

First published in 1983 by Croom Helm Ltd.

This edition first published in 2024
by Routledge
4 Park Square, Milton Park, Abingdon, Oxon OX14 4RN

and by Routledge
605 Third Avenue, New York, NY 10158

Routledge is an imprint of the Taylor & Francis Group, an informa business

British Library Cataloguing in Publication Data
A catalogue record for this book is available from the British Library

ISBN: 978-1-032-80236-7 (Set)
ISBN: 978-1-032-82075-0 (Volume 18) (hbk)
ISBN: 978-1-032-82080-4 (Volume 18) (pbk)
ISBN: 978-1-003-50283-8 (Volume 18) (ebk)

DOI: 10.4324/9781003502838

Publisher's Note
The publisher has gone to great lengths to ensure the quality of this reprint but points out that some imperfections in the original copies may be apparent.

Disclaimer
The publisher has made every effort to trace copyright holders and would welcome correspondence from those they have been unable to trace.

The Impact of Recession

On Industry, Employment and the Regions, 1976–1981

Alan R. Townsend

CROOM HELM
London & C

Croom Helm Ltd, Provident House, Burrell Row,
Beckenham, Kent BR3 1AT
Croom Helm Australia, PO Box 391,
Manuka, ACT 2603, Australia
First paperback edition 1984

British Library Cataloguing in Publication Data

Townsend, Alan R.
The impact of recession.
1. Great Britain – Economic conditions – 1945-
I. Title
330.941'0857 HC256.6

ISBN 0-7099-2433-X

Typeset by Leaper & Gard, Bristol

CONTENTS

FIGURES

New preface to the Reissue of 2024

The Impact of Recession
On Industry Employment and the Regions, 1976-1981

This book turned out to have a misleading title. "Recession" is normally accompanied by cyclical recovery, sometimes rapid. After 1981, I looked in vain for any re-opening of the many closed or partly closed factories which it records. Statistically, there have since barely been any periods when manufacturing employment as a whole, or even individual sectors, showed more than the most marginal increases in employment.

Thus, employment was plunged into its major change of the century, the faster replacement internationally of manufacturing jobs by those in services and service centres. The book's central thesis was that British areas suffered differentially from employment decline in proportion to their dependence on manufacturing in 1980.

The recession of 1980-1 (which followed lesser ones of 1973-5) was due to deflationary government policies including high interest rates to combat 20% inflation. It led to a mountain of unemployment for much of the decade, long-lasting benefit dependency and a combined legacy of very significant social, political and geographical change. Elliott (*Guardian,* 26th February, 2024) wrote that while 1980 was "the start of Britain's rapid de-industrialisation" (Martin and Rowthorn, 1986), the end of the Miners' strike in 1984 concluded a shift of power "in favour of capital over labour".

The differential effect then tended to be forgotten under a less interventionist state, and in years of relative *overall* national prosperity. But recognition of the "peripheral areas", particularly Tyneside, Merseyside and Clydeside, as in 1976-9 in the book, extended to embrace the whole of Yorkshire and the Humber, the North West and the West Midlands in the "North" in analysis of the "North-South Divide".

However, the identity of "de-industrialised" and "left-behind" towns eventually re-emerged when former Labour-voting areas outside the country's cities voted for BREXIT in 2016, and for the Conservatives in the 2019 election, overturning the "Red Wall" of hitherto Labour industrial towns in England and Wales.

How recession unfolded after publication of the book

Although national production as a whole was restored from 1984, and then took off strongly in other sectors including financial and business services and North Sea oil, manufacturing *production* failed to recover its 1980 levels until 1988, using technical change to increase productivity.

The 1980-1 recession turned out to be the second largest in terms of lost production compared with the two major later ones, of 1990-1 and 2008-9, but to have double the manufacturing job losses. The reader is able to compare them by "Googling" UK historic recessions.

Unemployment peaked after each recession but was at its highest a*verage* in 1984 at 12%, including continued decline in the public sector in steel, and the heavy loss of jobs in the National Coal Board. There was later some arrival of factories in ex-coalmining areas but, during the period of globalisation experienced strongly under Labour governments, 1997-2010, many of these closed again.

With only a modest impact from "re-shoring" of production from abroad, Great Britain's factory employees dropped over the 46 years from 1976 to 2022 from nearly 7.1 to 2.3 million, i.e. from nearly a third of the workforce (32.2%) to one in 13 (7.6%). The period of the book, 1976-81 saw it drop by more than a million and below **30%,** from 32.2% to 28.4%. The 1990-1 recession saw it drop below **20%,** but only by half a million, and that of 2008-9 below **10%,** and again by half a million. The distinction between manufacturing and other industries has been lost amidst firms' IT, research and repair functions.

What about the policy reaction (Part Three)?

One reason that I wrote was to express shock. As a government regional Research Officer in the 1960s, I was used to a "Butskellite" concern for full employment, which led to government assistance to areas with 4.5% or more unemployment, or the threat of it from closures. Conservative governments sought to transfer expansions of major firms, including car production, to the assisted areas, with the help of controls on new factories or extensions in prosperous areas.

Only recently has there been much realisation of the lack of any policy by Conservative governments, 1979 to 1997, for declining coal and manufacturing areas. The party line was that previous regional policy had been relatively unsuccessful, if not a zero sum game. Thus, intervention was confined to Urban Development Corporations in conurbations and local Enterprise Zones.

The Labour governments from 1997 to 2010 established relatively powerful Regional Development Agencies, but with no particular remit to transfer investment from richer to poorer Regions, although a belated programme for "Coalfield Regeneration" was established.

Left behind towns today

At the time of the book, diversification of the economy was largely confined to London and its outflow of research laboratories and private offices to the greater South East. Over time, service jobs in health and education increased very widely, and the claims of provincial cities to be leading growth came true after 2010, in financial and business services and universities (Townsend and Champion, 2020).

The central issue is that, in social and cultural terms, areas adjust only slowly to the economy. It is debated whether surrounding "left behind towns" can enjoy growth independently of the larger cities and commuting to them. A key aspect is their dependence mainly on Further Education Colleges, not universities, for their training needs. Their "economic base" remains mainly dependent on a mixture of incoming call centres, warehousing and distribution depots. The modest "Levelling Up" programme of the Conservative government since 2019 has also to fight other battles like the decline of town centres and seaside resorts. Both parties' policy of devolution to "Combined Authorities", for conurbations and other areas, relies somewhat on the possible scale of endogenous growth.

Alan R. Townsend, March 2024.
Alan.Townsend1939@gmail.com

References

Martin, R. and Rowthorn, B. *The geography of de-industrialisation* (Macmillan, 1986)

Champion, A.G. and Townsend, A.R, Contemporary Britain (Edward Arnold, London, 1990)

Townsend, A. and Champion, T. 'Core Cities' strong growth in the 2010s: Were they leaving behind the rest of their regions?' Local Economy, vol. 35, (2020) pp.,566-585

PREFACE

The impact of recession has been felt by everyone in the industrialised West at the beginning of the 1980s. It is perhaps in the United Kingdom that the shock has been greatest, from the sheer scale of change in manufacturing industry; nothing less than war could displace recession, redundancies and riots from pre-eminence in the media. National life and regional prospects have been deeply and permanently altered.

Social scientists, planners, geographers, trades unionists and politicians need an account of the impact in time and space. Several valuable books exist on national unemployment: I shall trace recession from its industrial and company origins to its impact on places, on the map of unemployment and on the home regions where people must search for jobs.

Since 1976 I have been recording data on redundancies and closures in a study of industrial and employment change, and have therefore seen a large recession unfold. This book deals with a major period of change, 1976-9, and a massive loss of jobs in 1979-81 between two 'plateau levels' of unemployment. Data extend up to the end of 1981, although results from the 1981 Census of Employment are still awaited when going to press. Now the pace of redundancy has been almost halved in a year, although the prospects of a significant decline in unemployment are remote. New redundancies in 1982 are tending to occur in the same corporations recorded in my text and tables for 1976-81; change is marking time and the precedent of the 1930s would indicate no further widening of regional differences.

Acknowledgements are due to many colleagues, in Durham and elsewhere: to Dick Morley for reading Chapters 2 and 3 in draft; to Doreen Massey for reading Chapter 4 and permitting sight of *The Anatomy of Job Loss*, written jointly with Richard Meegan, before publication; to three research students for stimulus and insights – Colin Crouch, Alun Adler and Ian Leveson; to Peter Dodds, Ian Leveson and Bob Nelson for preparing data in Chapter 10; and to the Central Electricity Generating Board, Department of Employment, English Industrial Estates, Manpower Services Commission and several County Councils for unpublished data.

Thanks are due to David Hume for preparing the Figures, and to Mrs Rita Hart and Mrs Mary Coffield for excellent typing. Above all I am grateful to Miss Hope Page, supported by my wife and father, for proposing many changes to the expression. All remaining errors and misunderstandings are my own responsibility.

Alan R. Townsend
Willington, near Crook,
Co. Durham

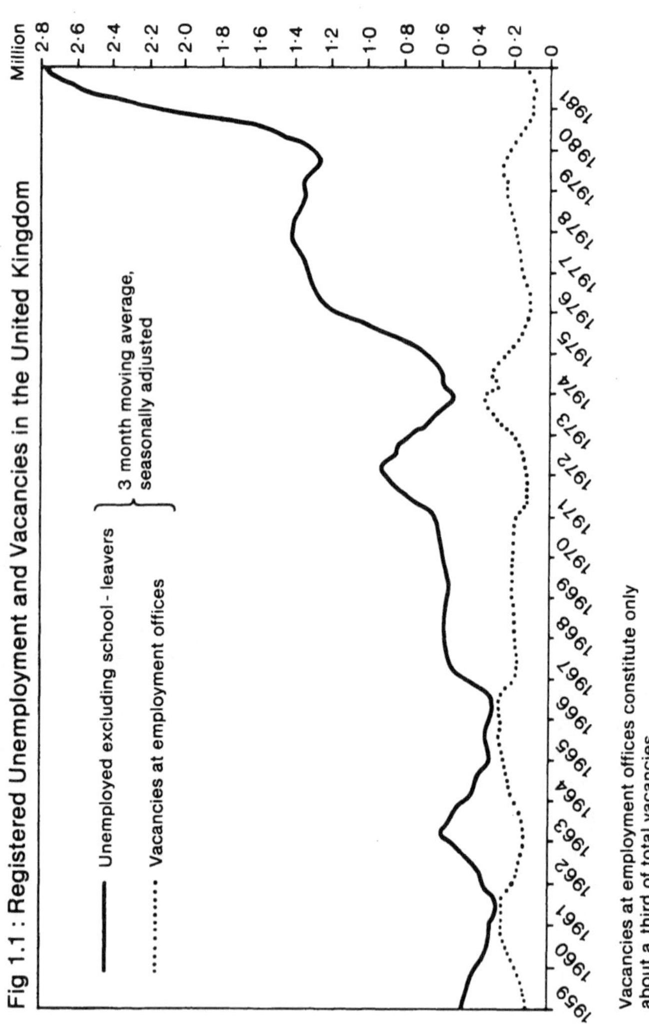

Fig 1.1 : Registered Unemployment and Vacancies in the United Kingdom

Source : Employment Gazette, vol. 90, no. 1 (1982), vol. 81, no. 1 (1973)

1 INTRODUCTION

'We want jobs!' is a slogan now heard in Britain very often indeed. Most rich industrial countries entered the 1980s harried by mass unemployment, but Britain seemed particularly stricken. Riots and marches were accompanied by talk of 'a generation without work' and 'the total collapse of the economy'. Since average real earnings in the UK continued to rise until 1981, how significant were these phenomena? Britain is not unique. In January 1982, unemployment in Britain officially passed three million, after doubling in less than two years; in West Germany, numbers out of work approached two million after doubling in 14 months; levels were already at two million in France and Italy and reached ten million in the USA.[1] Virtually everywhere youth unemployment loomed large and pressures bore heavily on minorities – on migrant workers in West Germany, on blacks in the USA, on blacks and on inner-city populations in England. Everywhere tensions, crime and distress have many causes, but are inseparable from unemployment and in turn from the unprecedented loss of manufacturing jobs. The hitherto stable bases of many local economies collapsed, often it would seem for good.

In creating these levels of unemployment, demographic and economic factors combined. Simultaneously the labour force expanded – more women were seeking work and the number of teenagers reached a peak – and labour demand contracted. In some countries imports discernibly replaced home production; in others, automation and the micro-processor alarmed unions. A new international division of labour may be developing a more restricted role for industrialised countries. But throughout there were repercussions from events in the world economy.

This book takes the view that in the United Kingdom changes of permanent significance were precipitated by recession. The post-1979 recession was felt more deeply and immediately than in other countries, and, unlike many, more sharply than that of 1974–5.

Registered unemployment, as shown in Figure 1.1, not only failed to decline after the 1974–5 recession, but continued to grow (though output was increasing) till the end of 1977. There was then a slight improvement to 1979, before the figures doubled in two years. Most forecasters (at the time of writing) expected them to stay at around three million until 1985,[2] but there were fears of four million when manufacturing output failed to recover in the year-ending May 1982. Not only is there now an accepted time lag before unemployment itself responds at all to economic change, but the pattern of all recent precedents is for only a limited response when it does come.

Economically the period 1976–81 was a turning point in the balance of production and employment. Whatever happened in the rest of the UK economy – in North Sea oil, in banking, or in services – manufacturing employment sustained a lasting setback. It is easy to realise that the closure of steelworks and motor car factories in the period meant a permanent loss in the nation's productive capacity and employment. It was even more ominous that few large factories were built or effectively re-used, and that manufacturing output was not expected to recover sufficiently to require any appreciable re-expansion of its work force.[3] The manufacturing work force in Great Britain was given as 5.7 million at the beginning of 1982, compared with 7.2 million in 1977 and 8.4 million in 1966[4] – a steep acceleration of the decline dating back to the mid–1960s. It is notable that *no less than 1.2 million factory jobs* were lost within a period of two years, which therefore must surely deserve as much study as many longer ones for its impact on places and society.

Aims and Background

Our aim is to study the period 1976–81 as a formative one for the 1980s' distribution of employment and unemployment, particularly through the impact of redundancies and closures within the UK on individual regions and sub-regions. Our analysis must be placed in a different policy context from any previous post-war work on regional economic change, since this period is also a watershed in political attitudes towards full employment and the distribution of industry. The Labour government of 1974–9 found itself placing less weight than before on the post-war ideal of full employment. The Conservative government elected in May 1979 questioned many of the planning mechanisms and assumptions built up since the war, and particularly since 1963.

For most of the post-war period the western industrialised countries were assured of economic growth. It was the focus of economic policy and the basis of a long period of full employment, and provided the public funds for expanded welfare services and for 'infrastructure' such as motorways. In the UK the peak birth-rate of 1964 increased the organised location of new housing in a second generation of New Towns, and in 'overspill towns'; planning was to do with the location and distribution of growth, whose existence was often taken for granted. This led universities and polytechnics to build up urban and regional planning and the locational science of understanding where new investments would and should be developed: factories, offices, retailing complexes, housing and recreational facilities. There were, it was realised, locational and cyclical variations in the incidence of growth, but some of these could be alleviated through regional policy, which was given a basic description by McCrone.[5]

With hindsight we can say that the conditions necessary for 'growth-planning' ended well before 1976. In fact the ten years 1956–66 were the last sustained period of full employment in Britain. It was the severe decline of that decade in the 'primary sector' of the economy (chiefly in mining but also agriculture) which stimulated an active period in the evolution of regional policy. It is since 1966 that manufacturing employment in the country as a whole fell into decline, together with parts of the service sector. Gradually it came to be realised that this decline was systematically biased to the detriment of the conurbations (in whichever Region[6] they were located). But the logic of more recent views, Hall[7] considers, is now pulling away from a direct geographical focus on, say, the 'inner city' of the conurbations, and towards one which sees the city as a symptom or even a caricature of wider changes in British society.

The understanding of selective spatial decline, in published research available in 1982, mainly focused on the late 1960s and the first half of the 1970s. Keeble (1980)[8] shows how the increasing dominance of industrial decline, up to 1976, accentuated location tendencies evident in his earlier book.[9] Fothergill and Gudgin (1982) bring together a lot of their analyses in a study of *Unequal Growth*,[10] mainly in the period up to 1975. Massey and Meegan (1982)[11] write an extensive and innovative interpretation of industrial change based on studies covering the years 1968–1973, while Healey (1982)[12] reports on plant closures in multi-plant enterprises from 1967 to 1972. More radically, Carney, Hudson and Lewis (1980)[13] present a range of European Marxist views on *Regions in Crisis*, while Lloyd and Dicken[14] incorporate recent Anglo-American perspectives on trends and prospects for employment. The growth of British unemployment has made it a larger focus of study in its own right, as is shown by the publication of works by Hawkins (1979),[15] Creedy (1981)[16] and Sinfield (1981).[17] However, most of these volumes treat the location of unemployment as just one variable among several, and this present work represents the first extensive approach to the impact of recession on places within the UK.

In our present period of study events at their worst, in 1980 and 1981, showed that almost any type of locality faced the risk of losing its principal sources of employment (Townsend, 1981).[18] This might be through the dying gasps of traditional 'school-textbook' industries (say, Lancashire cotton or Chatham Dockyard), through the decline of industries developed in the inter-war period (say, Coventry motor vehicles production, or bus manufacture in London), or through the failure of post-war, even post-1966, factory investments in their new environments (for example, TV factories in several coastal towns, or artificial fibres in Northern Ireland). Physical geography shows that, in the evolution of the natural landscape, the occasional severe storm may have a greater effect than continuous processes: so too a severe 'storm' in the manufacturing economy, the worst since the Second World War, has effected some changes of an irreversible character. In 1979–81 the factory output of the country fell below its lowest levels of the 1970s and many areas lost as many jobs as they had patiently gained *in the whole decade*. It is important to survey and understand the incidence of decline, i.e. the selective 'denudation' in periods of disinvestment of various past patterns of development. Why is it not as important as understanding the patterns of new factory investment in periods of growth?

This volume attempts to identify and interpret the effects of recession on the various parts of the UK, including a variety of changes in the period 1976–9 before deep recession set in (1979–81). As the causes are national and international, Part One is concerned with post-war trends at the national level. It introduces the fashionable concept of British 'de-industrialisation', and considers the possible roles of large national corporations in distributing decline to different areas. Two classes of data are introduced which only the present author has hitherto used as the basis of published academic work. These are government statistics of 'redundancies occurring' (Townsend, 1982)[19] and a five-year collection of job losses reported under employers' names from the *Financial Times* (Townsend, 1981).[20] These sources form the basis of succinct analyses in Part Two which consider the consequences of recession in each Region.

The media will have given us certain impressions: that recession has worsened the endemic employment difficulties of, say, Liverpool or Glasgow; that the severe problems of the British Steel Corporation have caused distress in most dependent communities in the North-East or South Wales; or that the West Midlands has joined the first rank of problem regions of Britain. We will systematise the available information in Part Two, firstly at the regional level, to ask whether the difficulties are indeed concentrated in particular industrial corporations or types of areas. But the question 'Is recession national?' is still in many ways an open one (Chapter 8).

In Part Three, we relate the results to a variety of crucial policy issues, though decline allows only limited conditions for any effective future spatial policies. National and local finances have naturally reflected the economic problems since the 1974–5 recession. In 1976 the Labour government three times cut back on expenditure. At first it avoided curbing the public sector's own large demands for manpower; the problem of widespread redundancies was passed on to the heavily depressed construction industry, through reductions concentrated on capital expenditure. This contributed to a steady decline over the decade in house-building, and to successive cuts in road-building (which in 1980 reached its lowest level for 15 years). The Conservative government of 1979 renewed this policy towards capital spending, and made a more determined attempt to contain the (previously very important) growth of public sector employment (Chapter 10). Both parties altered the balance of financial support between conurbations ('metropolitan' counties) and other counties, but individual local authorities receive no compensation for the loss of rates when businesses fall vacant.

Before proceeding to our main analysis it will be valuable, in the rest of this chapter, to consider some of the wider implications of reduced production, employment and investment for the environment and for planning.

The Implications of Recession for the Environment and Society

The *social scientist*, whether dedicated to social administration, sociology, or social geography, can see the impact of recession as a terrible working model of the relationships he studies. The impact of job losses is cushioned for many workers by redundancy pay (see below, Chapter 3). But it is widely suggested that there are direct relationships between unemployment and crime. The eruptions of violence in many English cities in the fortnight ending 28 July 1981 were attributed by Lord Scarman's report[21] to a mixture of factors which included unemployment and deprivation among minority groups. Clearly sub-regional problems rebound markedly on under-privileged groups within an individual urban area.

The reader may perhaps have difficulty reconciling the reasonable prosperity of the majority of the British nation with the picture which is being painted. A student aged between 17 and 21 is likely to come from a family which has enjoyed a rising standard of living throughout his or her lifetime. The British student's own 'life prospects' probably still offer security, given some adaptation to the openings available in the labour market and a willingness to move between Regions. It is his or her contemporaries, the great majority who left school at 16, who face the full employment problem of the 1980s. Many have had few job opportunities and no chance of real training. The possibility of moving to another area offered little escape because of the pressure on jobs everywhere and the costs of moving. In early 1982 nearly 1.2 million individuals under 25 were registered as unemployed in the UK (Chapter 10). They made up two-fifths of the total numbers unemployed in the country.[22]

The situation has been similar throughout Western Europe, with the under 25s accounting for up to 40 per cent of the unemployed in most individual countries. The conclusion drawn in nearly every official study was that unless major changes were made in social, educational and working habits, Western Europe faced a further decade of continuing high unemployment among its youth. But governments cannot focus on youth to the detriment of other parts of the population: those who are obliged to retire early because of the redundancy of their skills, married women who may have fewer chances of a return to full employment after bringing up their children, and many whose choice of jobs is very restricted in their home areas.

Deep recession has far-reaching implications beyond the immediate fields of employment and unemployment. In *environmental conservation* the deferment of production growth due to recession has dealt a blow which the environmental movement itself would be proud of. The demands of heavy industry for water have often been put back by several years. The national demand-curve for energy has been recalculated (for instance by Economic Models, 1981[23]) to show a problem unique in the development world – a considerable surplus of home-produced fuel, at least till 1990. In 1981 there were higher estimates than before of the period for which North Sea oil was expected to meet net domestic demand, and the government was able to defer till 1982 its decision – eventually a planning compromise – over the National Coal Board's controversial proposals to mine coal in the Vale of Belvoir, Leicestershire. The closure of major plants such as oil refineries (for example, BP, Isle of Grain, Kent, late 1982), or iron and steel plants (e.g. Consett, Co. Durham, 1980) leaves expensive clearance and landscaping probems; even general-purpose factories when they fall vacant need maintenance to avoid dereliction, pending the establishment of a new use. But industrial closures can also open up planning opportunities, for instance in allowing plans for the recreational use of vacated riverside sites, or even in the conservation of industrial buildings themselves (an opportunity lost in the demolition of the Firestone Tire Factory, West London, held to be a classic model of inter-war architecture).

For the *town planner* many of the changes which result from recession are less visible; they are changes in the *intensity* with which commercial floor-space is used, and may long remain undetectable on air photographs, in 'remote sensing' or on maps. Many factory job losses occur as reductions in the use of machinery through natural wastage and redundancy in the work force, rather than total closures; the planner must make due allowance in re-calculating their role in the 'activity system' of their surrounding sub-region, in terms of traffic generation and their support of a certain size of population with direct income. Decline in employment at large industrial sites (such as the Trafford Park Industrial Estate, Manchester, or large steelworks) had its predictable effects in reducing traffic congestion and the demand for peak-hour bus services; the increased unemployment of 1980–1 was given as the direct cause of redundancies in municipal bus staffs in several conurbations, and was one of several multiplier effects in the 'service sector'.

Growing Difficulties Obscured in the 1970s; Other Issues of the Decade

In the 1970s it was still common to write off increases of unemployment as mainly cyclical events, temporary aberrations to be endured pending the resumption of economic growth. Three serious recessions did occur in the level of economic activity of the rich industrial countries. The first, in 1971, was followed by buoyant recovery, and the second, beginning in 1973, was readily attributable at the time to the 'special' effects of the October Middle East War on the price of oil. Only after 1976 was it undeniable that the underlying trend of industrial production was slower and faltering, and that the *balance* of effects (after allowing for modest gains in productivity) was insufficient to demand more industrial labour. The post–1979 recession confirmed that there had been a relative deterioration in Britain's economic performance within Europe. Only with this *third* recession after 1970 did the majority of commentators perceive that unemployment and youth unemployment were likely to be the leading issue of the 1980s in the UK. There is an element of fashion among politicians, academics and publishers in the selection of leading issues. There were other real and less real issues in the 1970s which masked that of unemployment, or rivalled it for attention:

(1) Wide areas of the UK enjoyed growth during the 1970s. Plans laid for the building of motorways and New Towns between 1963 and 1973 came to fruition; New Towns and official overspill towns provided some of the highest rates of poulation growth in the overall period 1971–81. Many areas of the Home Counties had unemployment under three per cent as late as mid–1979,[24] and this no doubt influenced thinking in the new Conservative government, with its main support in the South.

(2) Non-manufacturing employment was growing virtually throughout the period in the UK; the *total* number of people at work in the summer of 1979 (25.1 million) was almost as high as its

previous peak in 1974, prior to falling to 23.0 million before the end of 1981.[25] It was easy to miss the point that the employable population was growing even more quickly. The 'working population' (employed plus unemployed) increased by nearly one million between 1971 and 1979, before recession encouraged workers to leave the labour market. The birth-rate had been increasing till 1964, influencing school-leaving most up to 1980, and an increasing proportion of women were seeking employment. Much of the increase of employment achieved in many areas was in part-time work in schools, hospitals and other establishments in the public sector (where economies could later be demanded). The proportion of women who were 'economically active' was such that, even in 1981, Eversley could calculate that Britain still had a higher proportion of its population at work (after subtracting the unemployed) than most European countries.[26]

(3) In the 1970s price inflation replaced full employment as the first target of economic policy. Inflation exceeded ten per cent per annum in all years after 1973 (except 1978), and was over 20 per cent in 1975 and 1980. The Labour government of 1974–79 sacrificed some of its prior concern for full employment to exert tighter financial discipline, and its Conservative successors, more single-mindedly espousing 'monetarist' policies, explicitly rejected a policy of short-term relief of unemployment, as being a diversion from the path to recovery through reduced inflation. Thus unemployment was accepted as a necessary temporary evil, in the public mind at least till mid–1980, and in the government's stance at least till mid–1981.

(4) Several special features gave promise of renewed growth. Entry into the European Economic Community (EEC) in 1973 appeared to offer some prospect of change, before the Community too was more clearly trapped in the problems of 'stagflation'. The development of North Sea oil reserves, which provided the equivalent of all the UK's net needs by 1980, seemed to promise much direct and indirect employment, till Forsyth and Kay[27] pointed in 1980 to the possible *negative* effects on manufacturing exports of having a buoyant 'petro-currency' in world exchange markets. The Labour government's 'industrial strategy'[28] included substantial fresh investment in the National Coal Board (creating few additional jobs); the British Steel Corporation based plant expansion on highly optimistic expectations of demand till late 1979 (see Chapter 4).

(5) Politicians were, for much of the decade, distracted by the intricacies of constitutional questions: local government reform, achieved in England and Wales in 1974 (in Scotland in 1975); the proposals for devolution to Scotland and Wales; and fundamental political violence in Northern Ireland. The origins of constitutional problems in all three areas lay partly in persistent high unemployment, but many of the niceties of the devolution proposals were irrelevant to it.

(6) Regional policy remained on the statute book under the 1972 Industrial Development Act, but as the main official remedy for areas of higher unemployment it declined in practical significance even more than politicians and academics realised at the time (Chapter 9).

The politics and theory of redistribution had worn threadbare by mid–decade. Chisholm, in 1976, explored the constraints on *Regional Policies in an Era of Slow Population Growth and Higher Unemployment*,[29] and House, 1977, summed up the position as follows:

> In a situation of national non-growth, one region can grow only if another is in decline. Redistribution to prevent decline will be possible only by taking away any growth which one region might have and transferring it to a region where contraction is occurring. Such a policy, which requires fossilization of the distribution of economic activity, is unlikely to be acceptable politically.
>
> J.W. House, 1977[30]

The difference between 'non-growth' and actual deterioration was another matter. Although there were forecasts of actual deterioration in the *Cambridge Economic Policy Review* as early as 1975, these were largely disregarded.

The Need for a Fresh Appreciation of Industrial Decline

The 'growth ideology' of much of the available literature from the 1960s does not help in considering the employment situation of the 1980s. It is true that *cyclical variation* has been well explored in economic statistics. From work initiated in Britain by Brechling,[31] developed by geographers including Bassett and Haggett,[32] and applied to the period 1963–76 by Frost and Spence,[33] it is possible to see how different Regions vary in their response to a recession. But the models tend to assume 'symmetrical' change over time, a return by each areal unit to its previous relative position. This is a different field from the understanding of possible *permanent* changes occasioned by deep recession. The tendency of past appraisals has been to identify permanent decline as occurring in 'pockets', such as mining areas, textile towns or inner cities.

Much of the theoretical literature in Human Geography and Planning is however concerned with the location of new elements of activity, and with regional variations in the distribution of growth, as it was experienced before say 1973. One of the central questions here is whether the principles and models of this writing can be 'thrown into reverse' to predict, describe and explain negative changes in the space economy. For example, the 'growth-pole' model originated by Perroux[34] presumed that the development of a leading industry in a given area would attract further development. This concept, much in vogue in the mid–1960s, was more fashionable than useful chiefly because in an era of much reduced transport costs it placed too much of a premium on short-distance communication in the location of new plants. It may be, however, that the opposite process, the withdrawal of a major plant (as in a 'contraction-pole') may have more observable effects on its historic network of surrounding plants, such as engineering sub-contractors.

Theory for the location of individual new industries (as of Weber,[35] Hoover[36] or Lösch[37]) is more complex than any existing separate theories for the closure of plants. Traditional location theory suggests that firms are more likely to close plants in areas where either costs rise relatively quickly or market prospects deteriorate and sales revenue falls. Smith's[38] concept of 'spatial margins' for profitable production is applicable. A rise in costs or a fall in demand results in a contraction of margins, and this will lead to plant closures. The survey of plant closures undertaken for this study does show some that were related to the location of relevant markets, both through decline in locationally linked industries and through adjustments in market-oriented networks of production. Other work on closures is on new plants in assisted areas of development, for instance the Republic of Ireland (by O'Farrell[39]). It would however be wrong to jump to the conclusion that the causes – as opposed to the effects – of job losses are geographical. As we shall see in Chapter 4, Massey and Meegan[40] (and others) have shown how many features of job loss are national in origin and *aspatial* in character. A large part of regional economics is applicable to problems of regional decline. The technique of shift-share analysis has been successfully applied during the 1970s to the unequal growth of different UK sub-regions; Fothergill and Gudgin[41] thereby questioned the distinctions between Regions (as such) which are traditionally made in the British literature. The question can be illuminated from shift-share analyses of *decline* conducted below in Chapter 8.

Earlier British geographical literature is relevant, ironically, just because it dwelt on the development of those earlier industries which are now among those vulnerable to decline. A well-known textbook, Stamp and Beaver (first edition 1933; fifth edition 1963)[42] may be taken as an illustration. In its 26 chapters there are five on agriculture, forestry and fishing, two on mining, and eight on manufacturing industries. This example shows an academic time-lag in the appreciation of change. Long after the Industrial Revolution writers still tend to stress the small primary industries (agriculture, forestry, fishing and mining); within manufacturing there is a tendency to stress *primary-processing* industries, the activities which process raw materials directly – whether metal ores, fibres or chemicals – though it is the secondary use of these products that make up the great weight of surviving industrial employment. Stamp and Beaver clearly had difficulty in keeping up with the diversification of British industry since the 1930s, both in the 'secondary' metal-using activities of engineering and in the 'miscellaneous' industries. Estall and Buchanan (1961)[43] give more space to the examples of motor vehicles and oil refining together than to iron and steel. But the point is that substantive and theoretical development appropriate to post-war industry was long delayed.

The possible conclusions are startling. First, it may be that decline in the 1980s is focused on some of these leviathans of the old textbooks – iron and steel, textiles and motor vehicles; the textbooks may provide valuable background for unintended reasons. Secondly, it may be that school and university teaching about an out-of-date industrial structure itself both exemplifies and contributes to the national problem. It is sometimes alleged that there is insufficient emphasis in British culture and among craft trades unions on technological change and the need for rapid adjustment to new commercial opportunities:

> English culture and the British State never liked industry, or thoroughly adapted to it. They benefited from the great cuckoo of the Industrial Revolution, of course. But in the long, quiet struggle which ensued they proved themselves far stronger than it. The 'workshop of the world' never remade the nest to suit its own long-term interests; on the contrary, it was first of all contained, then coddled and weakened by empire, and finally run down into 'de-industrialisation'.
>
> Nairn, 1981[44]

Here we do not favour a 'single-cause' explanation of the accelerating decline of manufacturing employment in the 1970s. It does not appear to be due solely, for instance, to our accession to the EEC, nor to the consequent weakening of Commonwealth trading links, nor indeed to our peripheral spatial position within the EEC; nor is it due to the decline in the birth-rate since 1964, because only a small part of the previous increase of production was linked with the natural increase of population (Reddaway,[45] Eversley and Köllmann[46]). A part of the laying-off of labour in 1980 was certainly due to the financial circumstances of that year and the particular balance of Conservative government policy; yet, as the next chapter will show, there was already a well-established decline in Britain's competitive position, under both Labour and Conservative governments. This volume deals both with industrial failure in the period 1976–9, when there was a partial cyclical recovery from the recession of 1974–5 in some areas, and with the severe conditions of 1979–81. It notes all reported redundancies and closures in both periods affecting more than 1,000. There are relatively few 'success stories' of industrial development to report, as new technological investment was increasingly overtaken by more straightforward rationalisation and closures in the period. Many of the redundancies and closures reported in these pages are due to national trading circumstances and pre-date the much-heralded fuller application of microelectronic technology. That itself, as Sleigh *et al.*[47] point out, must wait a period of new investment. A point to consider in reading this volume is whether this further displacement of jobs, or the new workplaces it may also create is itself predictable. Will it help at all the places we identify as having experienced the worst job losses since the Second World War?

Notes

1. *Employment Gazette*, vol. 90, no. 4 (1982), Table 2.18.

2. A *Financial Times* survey of 15 forecasts for the UK economy in 1982 showed an average expansion of output of 1.2 per cent in 1982 compared with 1981, whereas unemployment would continue to rise, from 2.9 to 3.1 million at end-1983 (excluding school leavers). *Financial Times*, 5 July 1982.

3. In 1981 no forecasts (or government statements) were available which would indicate any expansion of the manufacturing labour force, except over a period of years. 'This is a major difference from previous recessions, or from beliefs and behaviour in the current recession in other countries . . . The low investment plans of all industries and the virtual disappearance of investment to expand capacity are also an indication that no strong expansion is expected. Much of the reduction in labour is adjustment to lower output, but a continued fall may be part of the adaptation to an indefinite period in which the only way of increasing profits will be through further productivity rises at constant output. Some apparent falls, however, represent a different, structural form of long-term adaptation, of which there are indications in such industries as motor vehicles.' National Institute of Economic and Social Research, *National Institute Economic Review*, no. 97 (August, 1981), p. 9.

4. Department of Employment, 'continuous series' of employees in employment, including official estimates for February in *Employment Gazette*, vol. 90, no. 4 (1982), Table 1.2.

5. G. McCrone, *Regional Policy in Britain* (Allen & Unwin, London, 1969).

6. The standard statistical Regions adopted in this text are shown at Figure 5.1, page 88.

7. P. Hall, 'The Geographer and Society', *The Geographical Journal*, vol. 147, pt. 2 (1981), p. 151.

8. D. Keeble, 'Industrial Decline, Regional Policy, and the Urban-rural Manufacturing Shift in the UK', *Environment and Planning A*, vol. 12, no. 8 (1980), pp. 945–62.

9. D. Keeble, *Industrial Location and Planning in the United Kingdom* (Methuen, London, 1976).

10. S. Fothergill and G. Gudgin, *Unequal Growth: Urban and Regional Employment Change in the UK* (Heinemann, London, 1982).

11. D.B. Massey and R.A. Meegan, *The Anatomy of Job Loss* (Methuen, London, 1982).

12. M.J.Healey, 'Plant Closures in Multi-Plant Enterprises – the Case of a Declining Industrial Sector', *Regional Studies*, vol. 16, no. 1 (1982), pp. 37–51.

13. J. Carney, R. Hudson and J. Lewis (eds.), *Regions in Crisis* (Croom Helm, London, 1980).

14. P.E. Lloyd and P. Dicken, *Modern Western Society: a Geographical Perspective on Work, Home and Wellbeing* (Harper & Row, London, 1981).

15. K. Hawkins, *Unemployment* (Penguin, Harmondsworth, 1979).

16. J. Creedy (ed.), *The Economics of Unemployment in Britain* (Butterworths, London, 1981).

17. A. Sinfield, *What Unemployment Means* (Martin Robertson, Oxford, 1981).

18. A.R. Townsend, 'Geographical Perspectives on Major Job Losses in the UK, 1977–80', *Area*, vol. 13, no. 1 (1981), pp. 31–8.

19. A.R. Townsend, 'Recession and the Regions in Great Britain, 1976–80: Analyses of Redundancy Data', *Environment and Planning A*, vol. 14 (1982), forthcoming.

20. Townsend, 'Geographical Perspectives on Major Job Losses in the UK,

1977–80', pp. 31–8.
21. Report of an Inquiry by the Rt. Hon. The Lord Scarman, OBE, *The Brixton Disorders, 10–12 April 1981* (HMSO, London, 1981), Cmnd. 8427.
22. *Employment Gazette*, vol. 90, no. 4 (1982), Table 2.5.
23. Economic Models, *European Energy Forecasts Report* (Economic Models, London, June, 1981).
24. *Department of Employment Gazette*, vol. 87, no. 7 (1979), p. 684.
25. *Employment Gazette*, vol. 90, no. 4 (1982), Table 1.1
26. D. Eversley, reported in *Planner News* (November, 1981), p. 6.
27. P. Forsyth and J. Kay, *The Economic Implications of North Sea Oil Revenues* (Institute of Fiscal Studies, London, 1980).
28. Government White Paper, *An Approach to Industrial Strategy* (HMSO, London, 1975), Cmnd. 6315.
29. M.D.I. Chisholm, 'Regional Policies in an Era of Slow Population Growth and Higher Unemployment', *Regional Studies*, vol. 10, no. 2 (1976), pp. 201–13.
30. J.W. House, *The UK Space: Resources, Environment and Future*, 2nd edn. (Weidenfeld and Nicolson , London, 1977), p. 510.
31. F. Brechling, 'Trends and Cycles in British Regional Unemployment', *Economic Papers*, vol. 19, no. 1, (1967), pp. 1–21.
32. K. Bassett and P. Haggett, 'Towards Short-term Forecasting for Cyclic Behaviour in a Regional System of Cities', in M. Chisholm and A.E. Frey (eds.), *Regional Forecasting* (Butterworths, London, 1971), pp. 389–413.
33. M. Frost and N. Spence, 'The Timing of Unemployment Response in British Regional Labour Markets, 1963–1976', in R.L. Martin (ed.), *Regional Wage Inflation and Unemployment* (Pion, London, 1981).
34. F. Perroux, *l'Economie du XXe Siècle* (PUF, Paris, 1964), pp. 123–276.
35. A. Weber, English translation with notes by C.F. Friedrich, *Alfred Weber's Theory of the Location of Industries* (University Press, Chicago, 1929).
36. E.M. Hoover, *The Location of Economic Activity* (McGraw-Hill, New York, 1948).
37. A. Lösch, translated into English as *Economics of Location* (Yale University Press, New Haven, 1954).
38. D.M. Smith, 'A Theoretical Framework for Geographical Studies of Industrial Location', *Economic Geography*, vol. 42, no. 2 (1966).
39. P.N. O'Farrell, 'An Analysis of Industrial Closures: Irish Experience, 1960–73', *Regional Studies*, vol. 10, no. 4 (1976), pp. 433–48.
40. Massey and Meegan, *The Anatomy of Job Loss*, pp. 123–40.
41. Fothergill and Gudgin, 'Regional Employment Change: a Sub-regional Explanation', *Progress in Planning*, vol. 12, part 3 (1979), pp. 155–219.
42. L.D. Stamp and S.H. Beaver, *The British Isles*, 5th edn. (Longman, London, 1963), p. xi.
43. R.C. Estall and R.O. Buchanan, *Industrial Activity and Economic Geography* (Hutchinson, London, 1961).
44. T. Nairn, 'The Strange Death of Industrial England', *Guardian*, 9 April 1981.
45. W.B. Reddaway, 'The Economic Consequences of Zero Population Growth', *Lloyds Bank Review*, no.124 (1977), pp.14–30.
46. D. Eversley and W. Köllman, *Population Change and Social Planning*, (Arnold, London, 1982).
47. J. Sleigh, B. Boatwright, P. Irwin and R. Stanyor, *The Manpower Implications of Micro-electronic Technology* (HMSO, London, 1979).

PART ONE

THE DEVELOPMENT OF A CRISIS IN UK INDUSTRY AND EMPLOYMENT

2 THE POST-WAR RISE AND FALL OF MANUFACTURING EMPLOYMENT

The main focus of this volume is on the pattern of UK events after 1975, in which difficulties were concentrated in the manufacturing sector of the economy. However, it may readily be held that these events represented a deep accentuation of existing trends. Some of these were shared with other rich industrial countries, including a fundamental slowing-down in post-war economic growth and a decline in manufacturing's share of total employment. These and other aspects were peculiarly emphasised in the UK after 1975. To appreciate this study in overall perspective it will be valuable to review the international context and the British historical context in turn.

The International Context; Production and Unemployment

'In the midst of so many controversies about national economic policies it is easy to forget that the recession is world-wide and that the specific policies of different governments are responsible for variations around a common theme' (Brittan, 1980[1]). The international focus of attention was oil. At the time it certainly seemed that the quadrupling of oil prices in 1973–4 by the Organisation of Petroleum Exporting Countries (OPEC) was the cause of the 1974–5 recession, and it is little realised that oil prices declined in real terms after that date. Likewise an official statistical source speaks of the 'recession induced by the second major oil price rise'[2] (150 per cent between end–1978 and mid–1980). The effects of oil price increases in inducing recession are to raise the general price level and invite deflationary action by governments.

There has been an increased tendency to see OPEC action as a trigger rather than a cause of recession. Marxist writers saw the international recession of 1974–5 in a still longer-term perspective, in fact as one of the major periodic crises of capitalism in which the relations between industries, the labour force and technology produce a widespread reduction in the rate of profit. Mandel, writing *The Second Slump*[3] originally in German in 1977, saw the

1974–5 recession as marking the end of a long period of post-war expansion. This is often seen as a 'long boom', between 1945 and 1965, fuelled by high post-war investment in the rich industrialised countries and a markedly expanding volume of world trade. During that period many large firms became multinational and established factories in different countries. With hindsight this 'long boom' is naturally and not infrequently identified with the re-exhumed 1926 article of the Russian, Kondratieff, on *The Long Waves in Economic Life*.[4] He posited cycles of about 50 years in the world economy, with long upswings of economic activity characterised by the application of technological change, and less dynamic periods characterised by more marked recessions. He identified three 'long waves', with periods of rising growth from the 1780s to 1810–17, from the 1840s to the 1870s, from the 1890s to 1914–20; it is not difficult to extend this sequence through the depression of the 1930s to see a further rise from the 1940s to the 1960s, followed by the present period of more marked recessions.

Mandel[5] agreed that oil prices advanced the moment at which inflation had critical negative effects, but calculated that OPEC hoarding of profits was very small in relation to the size of the western economy. Rather he stressed that the western economy had suffered 20 cyclical troughs ('over-production crises') since 1825, there being no need to adduce special extraneous political factors on that last occasion. If the 1974–5 crisis was more serious it was partly because a long post-war boom was exhausting itself for inherent reasons, a reversal he had predicted as early as 1964.[6] Mandel affirmed that the recession in 1974–5 was felt more severely because it occurred simultaneously in many countries. Decreases in industrial production varied between seven per cent in Canada and twenty per cent in Switzerland, with a below average reduction of ten per cent in the UK.[7] The recession could be described internationally as beginning in the automobile and construction industries, and then spreading to a wide range of other activities, till finally it reduced orders in industries such as telecommunications which had seemed to be enjoying constant expansion.

International organisations predicted firm expansion out of that recession, but with hindsight Mandel was right to stress the recovery's 'unevenness by country and sector, and hence its non-cumulative and hesitant character'.[8] (Later we shall find that we can add unevenness by region.) Unevenness by sector was exemplified both in certain older industries – witness persistent international

Table 2.1: Percentage Unemployment Rates, Standardised According to International Definitions

	USA	Japan	W. Germany	France	Italy	UK
1974	5.4	1.4	1.6	2.8	5.3	2.9
1975	8.3	1.9	3.7	4.1	5.8	3.9
1976	7.5	2.0	3.7	4.4	6.6	5.5
1977	6.9	2.0	3.7	4.7	7.0	6.2
1978	5.9	2.2	3.5	5.2	7.1	6.1
1979	5.7	2.1	3.2	5.9	7.5	5.7
1980	7.0	2.0	3.1	6.3	7.4	7.4
1981	7.5	2.2	4.6	7.6	8.3	11.2

Source: *National Institute Economic Review*, no. 99 (1982), p. 108; 1981 data are provisional estimates.

problems in iron and steel – and in some recent growth industries, as seen in the acute excess capacity in artificial fibres. 'All the projects for the consolidation and extension of the Common Market were hit full force by the recession.'[9] Evidence increased of manufacturing firms diverting more of their actual production capacity to Third World countries (such as Brazil, Tunisia and Taiwan). Some radical economists such as Gunder Frank[10] asserted that this was a principal symptom of recession in the rich industrialised world. A major research study in West Germany[11] saw this 'new international division of labour' as significant for domestic levels of unemployment. These levels continued to rise for several years in industrialised countries (save in the United States) as we can see in Table 2.1. Recovery was insufficient to re-absorb newly displaced workers. Nowhere did unemployment fall back to the levels of 1974; in fact there was a considerable time-lag before rates of unemployment reached their peak. For example, in the UK the peak came in 1977, leaving only a short period before this country was disproportionately involved in a renewed increase in 1980. International unemployment series for 1981, however, showed how the USA, West Germany and France followed the UK into worse recession conditions in that year. The West German data showed a particularly rapid deterioration in the second half of 1981.

Were the events of 1980 in the British economy due more to its own deterioration than to renewed 'world recession'? The volume of world trade, which dropped by five per cent from 1974 to 1975, expanded by 31 per cent to 1979, and then stagnated before showing signs of expansion in mid–1981.[12] Industrial growth had been slowing down in most countries, and in some the economy contracted. But output fell unusually fast in the UK, and only there fell back to its low 1975 level. This is shown by indices of industrial production for the fourth quarter of three years:

	1975	1979	1980	1981
United Kingdom	100	115	103	104
OECD total excluding UK	100	126	124	124

Source: *National Institute Economic Review*, no. 99 (1982), p. 31.

UK foreign trade performance is an obvious area to examine:

> It should be emphasised how staggering a deterioration opened up simply between 1977 and 1979. Between these years the volume of manufactured exports ceased to grow (and finished manufactures fell by 2 per cent); the volume of manufactured imports rose by 29 per cent (finished manufactured imports by 39 per cent).
>
> Hughes, 1981[13]

The UK's long-term loss of competitiveness became more and more worrying in this period. Private sector profits, which had stood at ten per cent per annum in 1966–8, resumed their downward falling trend and reached the level of three per cent or less by 1980.[14] Various quoted factors in the overall situation may now be summarised:

(1) Industrial relations and wage levels, particularly in large plants; Brittan[15] calculated how UK unit labour costs relative to those of seven major competitors rose by 40 per cent from 1975 to 1980 (although exchange rate movements concentrated most of the effect after 1978).

(2) 'Poor management' and 'lack of engineering expertise', attributed to a British middle-class snobbishness about manufacturing and an anti-business culture in schools and universities.[16]

(3) Diversion of resources to the 'non-market sector', as interpreted by Bacon and Eltis[17] (see also p. 39).

(4) Failure by British financial institutions to provide sustained

support for the needs of manufacturing (Lever and Edwards, 1980[18]).

(5) Inappropriate and inconsistent action by government and civil servants, specified repeatedly by the *Cambridge Economic Policy Review*. Their charge against successive governments throughout the 1970s was that, in their differing preoccupations with finance and inflation, they failed to come to grips with the loss of international competitiveness.

Inflation was the first priority for governments of the 1970s. This included the 1974–9 Labour government which compromised its traditional concern with employment levels. Whatever the precise emphasis on and use of monetary theory by different governments in attempting to control inflation, it is an international fact that the 'trade-off' between inflation and unemployment has disappeared in nearly all the major western countries since the late 1960s.

The International Context; Manufacturing and Service Employment

The UK employment crisis of the early 1980s is the more serious because it represents a breakdown in the gradual *net* transfer of workers from the manufacturing industries to the service sector. The factory workforce contracted far faster than before and the service sector itself ceased to grow; in fact, it fell into unprecedented (if modest and possibly temporary) decline, as shown in Figure 2.1. This changed the previous relationship between the sectors, which we must now explore in Britain and abroad. Services here are taken to include all activities of the economy other than agriculture, forestry, fishing, mining and extractive industries and manufacturing. They include the distributive trades, transport and communication, professional and government services, utilities and construction.

Manufacturing increased its share of total employment between 1950 and 1955[19]; then the share was reduced but the absolute number of workers in manufacturing continued to grow, reaching a peak in 1966.[20] The share of manufacturing in the total of national output (measured at constant prices) showed a gentle peak around 1970.[21] The decline in manufacturing employment was welcomed to the extent that it reflected improved productivity. Only in the

Figure 2.1: Manufacturing and Other Employees in Employment, Great Britain

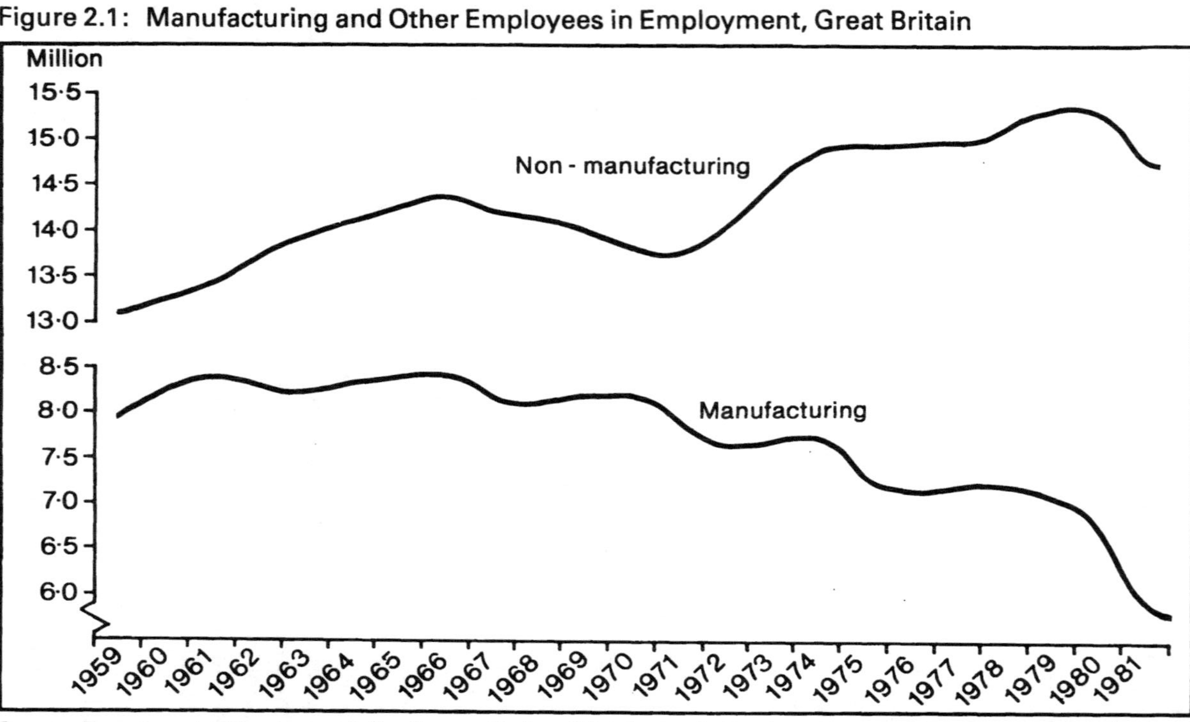

Source: Department of Employment, Continuous Series of Employees in Employment, provisional seasonally adjusted data from mid-1978.

1970s was there concern over the *possible excessive speed* of the relative transfer of resources out of manufacturing, before the trend was heavily exaggerated in 1979 to 1981.

The service sector was belatedly a focus of increasing work in the early 1970s among geographers, with emphasis on the information processing activities of offices and research laboratories (as instanced in the work of Goddard[22] or Buswell and Lewis[23] respectively). The growth of non-manufacturing employment as a whole was a remarkable feature of the 1960s and 1970s, normally offsetting significant decline in manufacturing employment (see Figure 2.1). For individual areas it was the most reliable source of employment gains, but it could also be the deciding factor in the relative labour market trends of different areas. Lloyd and Reeve[24] established that the relative prosperity of the Merseyside and Greater Manchester conurbations in the 1970s depended chiefly on their respective service sectors' performance. Townsend[25] suggested that unemployment levels in smaller labour market areas were inversely related to their status as service centres; the principal feature of many provincial Regions was the growth of jobs in 'professional and scientific services', chiefly that is in schools and hospitals. Conversely, a marked dependence on manufacturing was a liability from the mid–1960s if we are thinking at the level of statistical probabilities; decline was then rarely as sudden or as dramatic as in 1980 and 1981.

A swing from manufacturing to service employment is the post-war pattern in rich industrialised countries. A study of all statistical regions of the EEC was undertaken by a planning team for South East England in 1976, but they found nothing disturbing about that Region's high and growing dependence on service employment.[26] In the USA Gottmann had established in 1961 that a decline in the proportion of workers in manufacturing was entirely compatible with the continued growth of income in *Megalopolis*, the urbanised North-Eastern Seaboard.[27] In more recently industrialised countries it is clear that Japan, Italy and much of France drew their post-war economic growth from a net transfer of workers from agriculture into manufacturing. However, the OECD countries as a whole showed no change in the overall share of their workers in manufacturing (36 per cent) from 1961 to 1974, because the proportion in the more advanced constituent countries began to fall in this period. Between 1950 and 1975 the proportion in the USA fell from 34 per cent to 29 per cent, in the Netherlands from 30 per cent to 24 per cent, in Belgium from 33 per cent to 30 per cent, and in the UK from 35 per cent to 31 per cent.[28] The changes appeared to be a function of increased wealth; indeed, it was generally accepted (as by Fuchs[29]) that improvements in manufacturing productivity generated increased national wealth for distribution through the service sector, where the automation of tasks was generally less feasible. Bell[30] and others coined the notion of a post-industrial 'service society', in which the ratio of workers in the service sector might increase to a level of 70 per cent.

In the 1970s it was realised that many service sector jobs were uncongenial and poorly paid, that corporations were finding it more profitable to invest in the automation of certain services,[31] and that the declining trend of manufacturing employment was becoming more marked. In the USA, total manufacturing employment in the 'manufacturing belt' had reached a 'historical breakpoint' in 1966 (Norton and Rees[32]) and went into absolute decline from 1969. In Japan and Italy, the rate of growth of the manufacturing share of the labour force slackened significantly in the early 1970s. In the earlier industrialised nations there was generally a reduction between 1970 and 1975 in the relative contribution of manufacturing to total output and to total employment. In an international analysis of the ratio of manufacturing to total output, Brown and Sheriff[33] therefore suggest that 'the UK's experience is by no means unique . . . the difference in the UK (and the US and the Netherlands) has been in the extent of decline since 1970'.

The Historical Context; Growth in British Manufacturing Employment to 1966

We must now set the UK's experience in a longer-run perspective. Figures assembled by Marquand[34] indicate that services had around 30 per cent of the UK labour force by the middle of the nineteenth century, a figure which had grown to 45 per cent by 1921. Over the next 40 years the growth in the services' share of employment was relatively slow and by 1961 it was surpassed by Canada and the USA and more or less equalled by Australia and New Zealand. In fact the total workforce grew in both manufacturing and services; the trend of absolute levels of employment in manufacturing is shown in Table 2.2, though the figures for different years are not strictly comparable.

Table 2.2: Employment in Manufacturing, United Kingdom, 1907–81, thousands

1907	4,950	1951	7,830
1924	5,380	1959	8,070
1930	5,440	1966	8,580
1935	5,690	1976	7,250
1948	7,310	1981	6,038

Source: A.R. Thatcher in F. Blackaby (ed.), *De-industrialisation* (Heinemann, London, 1979), p. 32.

In absolute terms the national peak of manufacturing employment in the late 1960s may be seen as the culmination of a long-term trend of growth, which was only checked in the inter-war period and continued after World War II. In individual areas of the country, of course, the picture was very different, especially in areas that suffered from the decline of coal-mining after 1924. Manufacturing employment fluctuates normally as factories open and close, expand and contract, causing repercussions in time and space. The identification of periods of net expansion provides a broad locational typology of the stock of establishments which survived till 1976, as the starting point of more detailed studies from the next chapter onwards:

(1) Production patterns of 1907 were still concentrated to a remarkable extent on coalfield areas, larger ports (including Belfast and the London riverside and East End), railway workshops and naval dockyards.

(2) Inter-war growth was characterised by areas such as Coventry, Oxford and Middlesex suburbs of London, though most English conurbations saw some diversification of their metal-using industries. Thus the effects of severe economic depression in older, export-oriented industries were offset nationally by recovery in the 1930s in the South East and Midlands, with notable growth of international factory investment in West London.[35]

(3) The 1940s saw growth of industries such as electronics and aircraft production in the South East, but also considerable dispersal of strategic industries and Royal Ordnance Factories to provincial areas, and a concentration of immediate post-war factory investment in government Development Areas.

(4) 'Various evidence agrees that the 1950s witnessed massive

absolute and relative manufacturing growth in and around the central industrial conurbations of London and Birmingham' (Keeble, 1976[36]).

(5) In its last period of overall growth in employment, from 1960 to 1966, manufacturing showed a novel preference for dispersal to relatively unindustrialised sub-regions and to the peripheral 'assisted areas'.

These stages may be read as a set of successive 'layers' of investment, superimposed on each other over the map of the UK. This idea of 'layers' was first presented by Massey.[37] (Any one industry may take part in different 'layers' of location decisions, but the work of each theoretician tends for practical purposes to be restricted to a single layer). It will be of great importance (particularly in Chapters 7 to 9) to establish whether all 'layers' are involved in post–1976 disinvestment. Of course some growth continued after 1966, but in the two successive quinquennia[38,39] mapped by Keeble net growth in manufacturing employment was increasingly confined to smaller and less industrialised sub-regions. Gross expansion of employment occurred in a few individual establishments even in 1981. West Yorkshire County Council (Chapter 6) attempted to collate reports of favourable developments along with those of closures and job losses. Their resulting 'job replacement ratios' fell as low as 0.16 in the worst recorded year, 1980.[40]

If a few areas had growth after 1966, in areas of structural decline such as Lancashire and Yorkshire, and in the larger conurbations, the net decline in employment in manufacturing clearly began before 1966. The former London County Council area showed a fall in manufacturing employment between the 1951 and 1961 Censuses of Population[41]; Greater London and the Manchester, West Yorkshire and Clydeside sub-regions had all followed by 1959–66.[42] Indeed, at about that time, the total of *all employment* began to fall in those areas; Lever shows that in seven out of eight conurbations total employment was in decline by the period 1963–8, though this was concentrated in his 'inner cities'.[43]

Figure 2.1 showed the peak of manufacturing employment in 1966. But it is clear that this is only an average turning-point. Manufacturing employment fell into decline earlier in some critical areas, and the strong further national growth of service employment, at least until 1972, was not shared by all areas sufficiently to offset this decline; indeed Townsend[44] shows how some parts of the service sector itself, such as transport and distribution, also showed net employment decline as well after 1966. Further, Gudgin *et al.*[45] demonstrate particular reductions in manual work. Manual production jobs in manufacturing were declining in relation to the rest of the sector. By 1971 only 54 per cent of Greater London 'manufacturing jobs' were actually classified as work on production, compared with a GB average of 65 per cent, a feature of great significance for the effects of later *production* recessions.

The Role of Factory Closures in the Decline of Employment, mid-1960s to mid 1970s

So far, we have been concerned almost exclusively with *net* statistical change, without reference to the actual role of closures and employment reductions as gross contributors to the net change. Methodological developments enable us to study manufacturing decline in the period to 1976 with reference to the different components of change, including closures and reductions in the workforce at individual factories. They are a normal part of the complex processes of job turnover, especially in the areas of conurbations which contain a large population of medium and small-scale plants.

Table 2.3 summarises six such sub-regional studies: it comprises areas of varying size in several Regions, and the periods covered are not uniform. It is clear still that, in the decade ending in the mid-1970s, plant closures were often responsible for a gross reduction of manufacturing employment of the order of 20 per cent. The exception is Cleveland (Teesside and Hartlepool), with its industrial structure of large establishments. In very large establishments it is possible for a corporation to close and/or replace individual plants within the curtilage; no closure is recorded unless the whole establishment shuts down. In Greater London the ratio of closures to openings was the decisive factor in a heavy manufacturing decline.

Marquand, who in her official capacity in the Department of Industry was able to assess unpublished preliminary information on the 'births' and 'deaths' of establishments, 1971–5, on a regional basis, concluded:

Table 2.3: Components of Manufacturing Change; Selected Areas in England

Area	Openings	Closures	In-situ Change	Total Change	Years	Base Year Employment
	Employment change as a percentage of base year employment					
Cleveland	+ 13%	– 9%	– 15%	– 11%	1965–76	114,500
Outer Merseyside	+ 28%	– 14%	+ 12%	+ 26%	1966–75	96,500
East Midlands	+ 26%	– 28%	+ 23%	+ 25%	1948–67	479,800
Inner Merseyside	+ 10%	– 22%	– 12%	– 24%	1966–75	76,100
Inner Manchester	+ 13%	– 50%	– 6%	– 43%	1966–75	91,500
Greater London	+ 1%	– 22%	– 7%	– 28%	1966–74	1,290,000

Source: J.F. Robinson and D. Storey, 'Employment Change in Cleveland, 1965–76', *Regional Studies*, vol. 15, no. 3 (1981), p. 165.

(1) Regional variations in the net birth rates of establishments arose from variations in closure rates rather than from variations in crude birth rates.

(2) In four out of the five conurbations examined, contraction in employment through closures, together with a lesser job loss from transfers out of the area where these were separately identified, greatly outweighed net *in situ* loss of employment. Not even the closures were offset by new jobs from plant openings and transfers.

(3) 'We conclude not only that closures are an important ingredient in the changing location of jobs but it appears probable that they exhibit marked spatial characteristics'.[46]

Unfortunately, further published studies of the 'components of change' do not take us very far into the period 1976–81. But by 1976 the extent of industrial difficulties had given rise to earnest discussion of their origins and implications at a national level, and we must now give a view of this discussion.

The Nature and Merits of 'De-industrialisation'

The doubling of national unemployment from 1974 to 1976 formed the background to a debate about 'de-industrialisation'. This is a powerful word, but its precise meaning is still subject to dispute. Some clarification was provided by 1978 for instance in discussions published by Blackaby.[47] One possible measure of the term was in the ratio of manufacturing to total employment. The ratio grew from 1950 to 1955, but established a rapid rate of decline in the first half of the 1970s (Table 2.4). The direction and rate of change were remarkably consistent as between different constitutent areas of the country. Precisely comparable data for individual areas were available (at the date of writing) only for the period 1971 to 1977. In that period the proportion of manufacturing was falling in all counties of England and Wales except Durham, Northumberland, Oxfordshire, Gwynedd and Mid-Glamorgan.[48]

According to Bacon and Eltis in *Britain's Economic Problem: Too Few Producers*, 'The fall in industrial employment in relation to non-industrial employment is what has caused Britain's difficulties, and this trend will continue, making the situation worse each year unless investment recovers its pre–1965 levels.'[49] Their analysis was mainly based on the period 1961–75; it drew attention to the persistent growth of employment in public services, suggesting even that workers taken on in recession conditions were unavailable at large to manufacturing in subsequent booms. We share the general scepticism[50] about the role of public services in the apparent relative decline of manufacturing. Constant labour shortages did not prevent West Germany's post-war growth; labour shortages were not general throughout the UK, 1961–75; public services, such as health and education, had frequently recruited workers who were not previously employed, particularly part-time married women. Moore and Rhodes[51] argue that the tax burden on private industry had not increased.

Economists however found cause for concern, *irrespective* of the facts illustrated in Table 2.4 and *before* the post–1976 trend of output and employment was known. A broader definition of 'de-industrialisation' showed that the performance and size of the UK manufacturing sector gave cause for concern. This definition was provided by the Cambridge school of economists, in particular by Singh: 'we may define an efficient manufacturing sector as one which, currently as well as potentially, not only satisfies the demand

Table 2.4: Percentage of Total GB Employees in Manufacturing, June, 1959–81

1959	37.7	1977	32.3
1961	38.4	1978	32.0
1966	36.9	1979	31.4[a]
1971	36.4	1980	30.3[a]
1976	32.2	1981	28.6[a]

Note: a. Provisional estimates subject to revision, *Employment Gazette,* Table 1.2 (monthly).

Source: Department of Employment, continuous series of employees in employment.

of consumers at home, but is also able to sell enough of its products abroad to pay for the nation's import requirements'.[52] This is more than a statement of the familiar British problem of the balance of payments. Among many connotations of the analysis is the picture of a relentless cumulative process reminiscent of Myrdal's[53] economic concepts of cumulative disequilibria in regional economies:

> Within a country, it was not considered surprising that a region which had begun to decline should continue to do so; cumulative processes were clearly set up which tended to perpetuate the decline (unless strong policies were adopted). There could be much the same sort of decline for individual countries in a free trading world.
>
> Blackaby, 1979[54]

The Cambridge school went on to argue for import controls, and in continuing to do so have tended to win support in Labour Party policies. Certainly we shall find in this volume that successive Regions have suffered from international trading difficulties including import penetration, and that these have been accentuated by the relatively slow and unsteady growth of world trade in the 1970s. The further feature associated by radical writers with 'de-industrialisation' was a net outflow to other countries of productive investment by manufacturing firms. This was associated with the increasingly 'multinational' nature of company operations in the 1960s, the improvement of containerisation and other transport techniques for shipping light products between countries, and the lower labour costs achieved by operating in Mediterranean or Third

World countries. In other words, the rich industrialised countries were losing some of their basic historic advantages as sites for production; this led the German researchers, Froebel *et al.*, to hypothesise· *The new international division of labour; structural unemployment in industrialised countries and industrialisation in developing countries.*[55] First published in German in 1977, their work stressed the growth from about 1960 in 'world market factories' owned by West German concerns in other countries; by 1975 they employed 1.5 to 1.6 million workers.[56] Whether at that date their impact on domestic unemployment was very great is to be doubted. For Britain also the merits of the trend of investment are unclear. Morgan[57] noted that the British stake in foreign manufacturing in 1971 was two to three times larger than the German, but it was concentrated on 'white commonwealth' countries, on traditional products and to some extent on local markets. The 1970s saw an increase in the recorded flow of investment from Britain as well as from Germany, particularly to the EEC and USA; Morgan did not however believe there were negative effects for the balance of payments or employment. The emigration of labour-intensive industries she simply regarded as a specific exception, admittedly involving loss of employment, higher imports and possibly a diversion of managerial talent abroad.[58] Holland[59] however stressed how much foreign investment and trade were under the control of multinational firms and that they should not be beyond government influence. Dunning[60] showed that by 1976 nearly one quarter of the profits of UK companies were earned by foreign operations, and that in all activities (and particularly manufacturing) there appeared to have been a generally faster rate of direct investment by UK firms abroad than by foreign firms in the UK.

The pages which follow do therefore include cases where a contraction of activity in Britain was accompanied by expansion abroad in the same corporation; in a few redundancy reports, the transfer of production to Third World countries is cited, but by and large the evidence is lacking on this point. We are inclined to agree with the Latin Americanist, Fitzgerald, on the specific 1981 relations between the 'centre' (the rich industrialised world) and the 'periphery' (the Third World):

> The reaction [to the slowdown in the long boom] it would now appear has taken the form of demand deflation and downward

> pressure on wages at the centre, combined with a concerted effort to restructure metropolitan industry away from traditional branches such as textiles and steel towards more dynamic, high-technology sectors. It is not quite clear how the multinationals have reacted to this: there is evidence that indicates that some production has been transferred to the periphery where labour costs are lower, and also there has been a major renewal of investment in sources of agricultural and mineral raw materials; but the main change appears to be in the elevation of labour productivity in the central economies themselves.
>
> Fitzgerald, 1981[61]

Perhaps the main lesson to be learned from trends in the internationalisation of production is that job losses in Britain are less likely to be replaced in the 1980s than they were in the past. Poorer areas of Britain must face the proven competitive ability of Mediterranean and some Third World countries to undertake repetitive, labour-intensive, semi-skilled operations in a widening range of manufacturing, textiles, clothing and electronics, etc. This makes our task, below, of assessing industrial employment decline between 1976 and 1981 all the more grave. One question remains, however, to be answered. If growth in services largely offset the decline of manufacturing employment in the past, why should it not provide the answer to 'de-industrialisation' in the future? We must be aware of grounds for pessimism. In the first place, the dislocation of manufacturing has itself widespread direct implications for government finance and for the rest of the economy. Secondly, much of the increase of service employment was, as Bacon and Eltis indeed stressed, in the public sector; further growth in the public sector has been checked by both governments in the period 1976–81 (see Chapter 10). Thirdly, experts agree that there is no 'services solution' to the international problems of the economy. Although 'invisible exports' (returns from shipping, banking, finance, insurance, tourism, etc.) were equivalent in 1976 to about half the value of manufacturing exports, their further expansion is not expected to be sufficient. The problem facing the UK is that her exports of services already command a relatively large share of what is still a relatively small market (Sargent, 1979[62]). If the service sector was not to produce much buoyancy after 1976, then perhaps it would be logical to look to the growth of North Sea oil production. Amazingly this too failed to guarantee sustained growth until 1981, so widespread was the eventual incidence of manufacturing recession.

Notes

1. S. Brittan, 'Into and out of the World Slump', *Financial Times*, 17 July 1980, p. 25.
2. *Employment Gazette*, vol. 89, no. 1 (1981), p. S3.
3. E. Mandel, *The Second Slump, A Marxist Analysis of Recession in the Seventies* (New Left Books, London, English translation, 1978).
4. N.D. Kondratieff (translated by W.F. Stolper, 1935, and abbreviated), 'The Long Waves in Economic Life', *Lloyds Bank Review*, no. 129 (1978), pp. 41–60.
5. Mandel, *The Second Slump*, pp. 34–9.
6. Ibid., p. 13.
7. Ibid., p. 14.
8. Ibid., p. 94.
9. Ibid., p. 124.
10. A.G. Frank, *Reflections on the World Economic Crisis* (Hutchinson, London, 1981), pp. 48–52.
11. F. Froebel, J. Heinrichs and O. Kreye, *The New International Division of Labour* (Cambridge University Press, Cambridge, English translation 1980).
12. National Institute of Economic and Social Research, *National Institute Economic Review*, no. 99 (February 1982), p. 110.
13. J. Hughes, *Britain in Crisis* (Spokesman, Nottingham, 1981), p. 16.
14. Pre-tax rates of return on capital employed, private sector industrial and commercial companies excluding North Sea Oil, *Financial Times*, 30 June 1981.
15. S. Brittan, 'Unemployment: the Need to Look Deeper', *Financial Times*, 20 Aug. 1981.
16. See for example M.J. Wiener, *English Culture and the Decline of the Industrial Spirit, 1850–1950* (Cambridge University Press, Cambridge, 1981).
17. R. Bacon and W. Eltis, *Britain's Economic Problem: Too Few Producers* (Macmillan, London, 1976).
18. H. Lever and G. Edwards, *Banking on Britain, Reversing Britain's Economic Decline* (Sunday Times reprint of six articles, London, 1981).
19. C.J.F. Brown and T.D. Sheriff, 'De-industrialisation: a Background Paper', in F. Blackaby (ed.), *De-industrialisation* (Heinemann, London, 1979), p. 234.
20. *Department of Employment Gazette*, vol. 83, no. 3 (1975), p. 196.
21. Brown and Sheriff, 'De-industrialisation: a Background Paper', p. 239.
22. J.B. Goddard, 'Office Linkages and Location. A Study of Communications and Spatial Patterns in Central London', *Progress in Planning*, vol. 1, no. 2 (1973), pp. 109–232.
23. R.J. Buswell and E.W. Lewis, 'The Geographical Distribution of Industrial Research Activity in the UK', *Regional Studies*, vol. 4, no. 3 (1970), pp. 297–306.
24. P.E. Lloyd and D.E. Reeve, 'North West England, 1971–1977: a study in Industrial Decline and Economic Restructuring', Working Paper 11, *North West Industry Research Unit* (School of Geography, University of Manchester, 1981).
25. A.R. Townsend, 'Unemployment Geography and the New Government's "Regional" Aid', *Area*, vol. 12, no. 1, (1980), pp. 9–18.
26. South East Joint Planning Team, *Strategy for the South East: 1976 Review*

(HMSO, London, 1976), p. 11.

27. J. Gottmann, *Megalopolis: The Urbanised Northeastern Seaboard of the United States* (MIT Press, Cambridge, Mass., 1961), p. 449.

28. Brown and Sheriff, 'De-industrialisation: a Background Paper', p. 237. The estimated reference series quoted here is substantially different from official UK data appearing later in this chapter.

29. V.R. Fuchs, *The Service Economy* (Columbia University Press, New York, 1968).

30. D. Bell, *The Coming of Post-Industrial Society, A Venture in Social Forecasting* (Heinemann, London, 1974).

31. E. Mandel, *Late Capitalism* (New Left Books, London, 1975).

32. R.D. Norton and J. Rees, 'The Product Cycle and the Spatial Decentralization of American Manufacturing', *Regional Studies*, vol. 13, no. 2 (1979), pp. 141–51.

33. Brown and Sheriff, 'De-industrialisation: a Background Paper', p. 238.

34. J. Marquand, 'The Service Sector and Regional Policy in the United Kingdom', *Centre for Environmental Studies*, Research Series 29 (Centre for Environmental Studies, London, 1979), p. 1.

35. G. McCrone, *Regional Policy in Britain*, 1st edn. (Unwin, London, 1969), p. 101.

36. D. Keeble, *Industrial Location and Planning in the United Kingdom* (Methuen, London, 1976), p. 14.

37. D.B. Massey, 'In What Sense a Regional Problem?', *Regional Studies*, vol. 13, no. 3 (1979), pp. 233–44.

38. Keeble, *Industrial Location and Planning*, p.18.

39. D. Keeble, 'Industrial Decline, Regional Policy and the Urban-rural Manufacturing Shift in the United Kingdom', *Environment and Planning A*, vol. 12, no. 8 (1980), pp. 945–62.

40. West Yorkshire Metropolitan County Council, *Economic Trends*, no. 18 (November, 1981), p. 30.

41. B.E. Coates and E.M. Rawstron, *Regional Variations in Britain: studies in economic and social geography* (Batsford, London, 1971), p. 52.

42. Keeble, *Industrial Location and Planning*, p. 17.

43. W.F. Lever, 'The Inner-City Employment Problem in Great Britain Since 1952: A Shift-Share Approach', in J. Rees, G.J.D. Hewings and H.A. Stafford (eds.), *Industrial Location and Regional Systems* (Croom Helm, London, 1981), p. 175.

44. A.R. Townsend, 'The Relationship of Inner City Problems to Regional Policy', *Regional Studies*, vol. 11, no. 4 (1977), pp. 225–51.

45. G. Gudgin, R. Crum and S. Bailey, 'White Collar Employment in UK Manufacturing Industry', in P.W. Daniels (ed.), *Spatial Patterns of Office Growth and Location* (Wiley, Chichester, 1979), p. 141.

46. J. Marquand, 'Measuring the Effects and Costs of Regional Incentives', *Government Economic Service Working Paper* No. 32 (Department of Industry, London, 1980), p. 71.

47. F. Blackaby (ed.), *De-industrialisation* (Heinemann, London, 1979).

48. Annual Census of Employment, unpublished data supplied by Department of Employment.

49. Bacon and Eltis, *Britain's Economic Problem*, p. 20.

50. As reported by Blackaby, *De-industrialisation*, p. 264.

51. B. Moore and J. Rhodes, 'The Relative Decline of the UK Manufacturing Sector', *Economic Policy Review*, issue no. 2 (1976), pp. 36–41.

52. A. Singh, 'UK Industry and the World Economy; a Case of De-industrialisation?', *Cambridge Journal of Economics*, vol. 1, no. 2 (1977), p. 128.

53. G. Myrdal, *Economic Theory and Underdeveloped Regions* (Duckworth, London, 1957).
54. Blackaby, *De-industrialisation*, p. 266.
55. Froebel *et al.*, *The new international division of labour.*
56. Ibid., p. 201.
57. A.D. Morgan, 'Foreign Manufacturing by UK Firms', in F. Blackaby (ed.), *De-industrialisation* (Heinemann, London, 1979), p. 81.
58. Morgan, 'Foreign Manufacturing by UK Firms', pp. 92–3.
59. Comment on Morgan (reference no. 43), pp. 95–101.
60. J.H. Dunning, 'The UK's International Direct Investment Position in the Mid–1970s', *Lloyds Bank Review*, vol. 132, no. 1 (1979), pp. 1–21.
61. E.V.K. Fitzgerald, 'The New International Division of Labour and the Relative Autonomy of the State: Notes for a Reappraisal of Classical Dependency', *Bulletin of Latin American Research*, vol. 10, no. 1 (1981), p. 7.
62. J.R. Sargent, 'UK Performance in Services', in F. Blackaby (ed.), *De-industrialisation* (Heinemann, London, 1979), p. 111.

3 INDUSTRIAL RECESSION, 1976–1981: THE NATIONAL INCIDENCE OF REDUNDANCY

This chapter considers two phases of recession in industry, both at a general level and from an original analysis of redundancy data. First, from 1976 to 1979, an expected recovery in manufacturing largely failed to take place. Then, from 1979 to 1981, followed an unprecedented collapse of activity. It will be demonstrated that the period 1976 to 1979 was essentially a 'plateau' in the level of manufacturing output in Britain: the expected recovery proved partial, both sectorally and spatially, and difficulties then spread by 1980 to virtually all parts of manufacturing. World processes interacted with and intensified the longer-term national trends discussed in Chapter 2. There we considered the changing relative shares of manufacturing and other sectors in the economy. We come now to the arrival of a deep recession in the absolute level of manufacturing output, with many permanent effects on manufacturing areas and their employment.

Events in manufacturing were masked by better performance in other sectors – a real source of potential confusion. Figure 3.1 therefore adopts on three statistical series the index value of 100 for 1975, the trough of the mid–1970s recession. The solid black line, for UK manufacturing output, reveals both the limited scale of the 1976–9 recovery, and an overall 1974–81 trend which actually pointed downward, despite a hesitant recovery of output initiated in the second half of 1981. The overall 'index of production' rose to a peak of 115 in mid–1979, because 'production' here includes the extraction of mineral oil and natural gas. Output of North Sea Oil expanded in this very period from virtually nothing to full production, although direct employment in the activity remained remarkably small.[1] The overall index of output for the whole economy, its 'gross domestic product', had expanded by ten per cent up to 1979 because investment and activity in the service sector and oil remained more buoyant than in manufacturing. Average real earnings continued to rise until the year-ended April 1981[2] and it was difficult then to see any real signs of falling spending in the shops, although manufacturing employment had dropped 16 per cent in two years. Thus any widespread effects of recession on non-

Figure 3.1: The Rise and Fall of National Output from 1975 to 1981

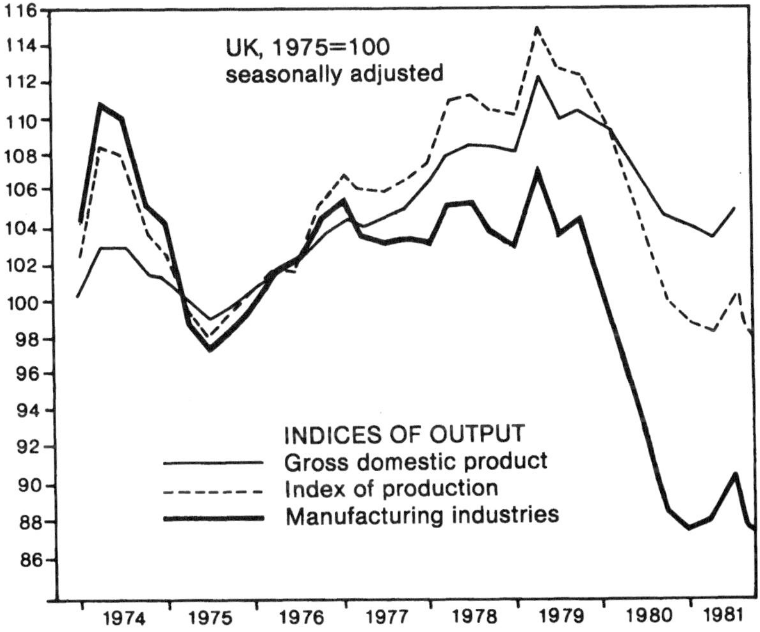

Source: *Employment Gazette*, vol. 90, no. 1 (1982).

manufacturing employment were delayed. The direct effects of recession were concentrated heavily on manufacturing employers and workpeople and it was this impact, together with some demographic factors, which gave Britain such high rates of unemployment at the start of the 1980s. In June 1981, numbers unemployed in GB had doubled in 24 months.

The Impact on the Industrial Workforce

Recession is fairly readily measured through changes in different aspects of employment. It is in this field that it had the strongest and most important direct impacts. The principal labour market impact of industrial trends in the 1970s was to reduce the rate of turnover of the factory workforce. This can be expressed in terms of 'engagement rates', the percentage of the workforce starting work with a fresh employer in a given period. In 1969 the rate for manufacturing was just over three per cent per month; by 1976 it stood at two per cent per month; but it then fell at an increasing rate to stand at just one per cent by mid–1981.[3] Over the period as a whole there was also a reduction in the rate at which people left their jobs, but this normally lagged behind the engagement rate in recessions. From 1976 to end–1980 however the rate of leaving held up at two per cent per month, while the engagement rate declined to its lowest level of the post-war period. At the end the opportunity for workers to move, that is to be engaged elsewhere, was so much reduced that a greater proportion of the increased net job losses was accounted for by compulsory means, in fact by redundancy. The *net* loss of 27 per cent of the GB manufacturing population between mid–1969 and mid–1981 – a large change in its 'stock' of employees – was achieved after much larger changes in its composition, brought about by the 'flows' of workpeople on and off the books of manufacturing establishments, and into and out of other sectors of the economy.

The approach to labour market changes through 'stocks' and 'flows' can also be applied to the official registers of unemployed and vacancies. Between mid-1976 and end-1981 the 'inflow' of workpeople joining the GB unemployment register never averaged less than 264,000 per month. At the end of 1980 it reached a peak of 362,000. The 'outflow' of workpeople leaving the register, principally but not solely to take up employment, varied less, from 254,000 to 314,000 per month.[4] Thus over most of the period changes in the national level of unemployment resulted from a relatively small excess of inflows over outflows from the register of unemployment. From 1976 to 1979 this never exceeded 14,000 per month, but in 1980 the net additions to the register rose rapidly to nearly 90,000 per month at the end of the year. Reports in the media in 1980 tended to understate the number of people affected, in saying that, for instance, 'another 60,000 have joined the dole queues', when this was only the *net* change in the size of the register. On the other hand it was a government need to stress that some recruitment continued, albeit at a reduced level, before some recovery occurred at end-1981.

Such data give a good general description of the national incidence of recession over time, but say little about the source of job losses in different industries. For this purpose data on redundancies prove more instructive. We have details of this particular flow of workpeople out of employment as a by-product of legal and administrative arrangements: in the Redundancy Payments Act of 1965 Parliament introduced a new concept into employer/employee relations by providing for the payment of minimum compensation (up to £3,900 from 1981) to staff dismissed for reason of redundancy. The idea was not to punish the employer or to create a recipe for underemployment (Waud, 1981[5]), but to encourage the employer to keep his staff intact by alternative employment in associated companies or plants. The legislation gave rise to three series of unpublished statistics (Tidsall, 1980;[6] Noble, 1981[7]), 'prior notifications' (series HR1), 'redundancies occurring' (series ES955) and 'redundancy payments made'. None of these series is or is intended to be a total record, but series ES955 is recognised as the most reliable and will be extensively used in the rest of this volume as an indicator of the industrial and regional incidence of larger job losses (see Townsend, 1982,[8] for further details and availability of the figures).

The shape of cyclical recession as expressed in terms of 'redundancies occurring' in thousands (series ES955) is seen below:

1971	336.3	1979	186.8
1972	187.6	1980	493.8
1973	81.4	(1980	191.9 January to June)
1974	127.4	(1980	302.0 July to December)
1975	249.9	*1981	532.0
1976	166.9	*(1981	296.1 January to June)
*1977	158.4	(1981	236.0 July to December)
1978	172.6	(1982	183.0 January to June, provisional)

* break in series involving increased recording.

Source: Manpower Services Commission and Department of Employment.

The 'flow' of 494,000 redundancies of 1980 (including 400,000 from manufacturing) contributed to the estimated net loss in the 'stock' of jobs in the year of 1,047,000 (704,000 in manufacturing). The 'plateau' in redundancies of the period 1976–9 stands in clear contrast from the recession years of 1971, 1975 and 1980–1. These data may be disaggregated to Regions and fairly narrowly defined industries. The national industrial patterns of difficulties, both in hesitant recovery up to 1979 and in deep recession thereafter, are essential inputs to the regional calculations and hypotheses in Part

Table 3.1: Rates of Job Losses by Industry, GB 1976–81; Redundancies Occurring and Net Changes in Employees (percentages of employees in employment, 1976, expressed at annual rates)

Order Totals of Standard Industrial Classification, 1968	Redundancies Occurring (ES955)			Employees in Employment, Net Change[a]		
	1976–79	1980	1981	1976–79	1980	1981
Agriculture etc.	– 0.2	– 0.3	– 0.2	– 1.3	– 0.7	– 1.7
Mining & quarrying	– 0.5	– 0.8	– 1.6	– 0.2	– 1.6	– 4.3
Food, drink, etc.	– 1.9	– 3.1	– 4.2	– 0.5	– 5.5	– 5.8
Petroleum products etc.	– 0.7	– 0.6	– 0.5	+ 0.1	– 3.1	– 6.6
Chemicals etc.	– 0.7	– 2.7	– 4.4	+ 1.3	– 6.8	– 5.9
Metal manufacture	– 1.9	– 13.0	– 10.1	– 2.1	– 18.1	– 12.8
Mechanical engineering	– 2.0	– 5.7	– 6.2	– 0.9	– 10.3	– 10.1
Instrument engineering	– 1.2	– 3.2	– 4.0	+ 0.0	– 11.0	– 7.8
Electrical engineering	– 1.8	– 4.5	– 6.6	+ 0.5	– 8.1	– 7.9
Shipbuilding etc.	– 2.9	– 4.7	– 2.8	– 2.8	– 8.5	– 3.5
Vehicles	– 1.3	– 5.5	– 6.7	+ 0.2	– 8.7	– 11.5
Other metal goods	– 1.1	– 6.4	– 5.9	+ 0.3	– 11.8	– 9.2
Textiles	– 2.7	– 11.7	– 5.4	– 3.0	– 16.2	– 6.3
Leather etc.	– 2.7	– 4.8	– 3.5	– 2.5	– 9.4	– 5.8
Clothing & footwear	– 2.1	– 7.9	– 5.4	– 0.5	– 12.5	– 6.6
Bricks, pottery, etc.	– 1.3	– 6.4	– 5.1	– 0.6	– 12.0	– 8.9
Timber, furniture, etc.	– 1.6	– 4.0	– 4.0	– 0.9	– 8.8	– 5.5
Paper, printing, etc.	– 0.9	– 3.0	– 3.6	+ 0.1	– 6.1	– 4.5
Other manufacturing	– 1.7	– 6.4	– 4.7	– 0.9	– 15.2	– 4.4
Total manufacturing	– 1.7	– 5.7	– 5.6	– 0.5	– 10.1	– 7.8
Construction	– 1.8	– 3.0	– 3.9	– 0.6	– 5.5	– 7.2
Services[b]	– 0.2	– 0.4	– 0.6	+ 1.1	– 1.9	– 2.4
Total	– 0.8	– 2.2	– 2.4	+ 0.4	– 4.6	– 4.5

Note: a. Years ending December. All data are based on official estimates subsequent to June 1978.
b. For further details see Table 10.1.

Source: Unpublished data of Manpower Services Commission, Sheffield; *Employment Gazette*, Table 1.2 (monthly).

Two and will now be summarised. Table 3.1 displays data on industrial job losses through redundancy, compared with changes in the total stock of jobs.

We can see, from the first two columns of Table 3.1, how all but one of the industries presented (petroleum products) showed an increase in job losses in 1980, a steep acceleration in the recorded rate. The fourth column of figures confirms a net increase (0.4 per cent per annum) in total employment 1976–9, principally in services. Some sectors can decline without much 'redundancy' (e.g. agriculture), whereas construction or the food industry can experience disproportionate volumes of 'redundancy' due to the temporal and/or seasonal nature of work.

The primary and service sectors did not however contribute a lot of job losses. Compared with general post-war trends in the primary sector, mining and agricultural areas had relatively little to fear from the main onset of recession, although 1981 showed the highest level of coalmine closures for six years, and a reduction of 12,000 in the industry's labour force.[9] With low levels of investment established in housing, factory-building and 'infrastructure', construction had a lower rate of job losses than manufacturing after 1979. Certain parts of the service sector, notably the statutory undertakings providing gas, electricity and water, continued gradual reductions in employment. By and large, however, the Conservative government were correct to stress that the public sector workforce was carrying a much smaller burden of the recession than manufacturing. That government met difficulties in its aim of reducing total public employment, partly because of the security enjoyed by public servants (many of whom are not catered for in the redundancy payments legislation). We should note that the relative stability of the primary and service sectors (at least till end–1981) may have profound effects on the differential performance of different Regions in our analysis in Part Two. Manufacturing areas in general could be expected to gain least and suffer most from employment trends of this period.

Does the period involve any fresh elements of decline within manufacturing employment? If we refer to the two previous quinquennia, 1966–71 and 1971–6, we find the greatest proportionate declines in the following (industry headings as Table 3.1):

1966–71: Textiles, −17.8 per cent; Leather etc. −13.0 per cent; Metal manufacture, −11.3 per cent; Clothing and footwear, −11.2 per cent; Average −6.2 per cent. All manufacturing industry headings except three showed reductions.
1971–76: Textiles, −17.4 per cent; Metal manufacture, −15.6 per cent; Leather etc, −15.5 per cent; Clothing and footwear, −15.2 per cent; Average, −10.0 per cent. *Manufacturing employment declined in all industry headings and all conurbations* (Keeble[10]).

In the period 1976–9, therefore, four of the five industries of greatest net reduction in employment had been defined by previous experience; they were joined by shipbuilding and marine engineering, while other parts of vehicle manufacture and engineering also deserve comment. We may examine these industry headings in 1976–9, making reference to the trend of redundancies in some principal sectors in Figure 3.2:

(1) Textiles, clothing, leather and footwear continued in structural decline. All parts of these industries showed employment decline including the production of man-made fibres, where a problem of world over-capacity began to emerge. In cotton and allied textiles the inroads made by cheap production by less developed countries were understandable, but increased imports from the EEC represented a real failure by the home industry.[11]

(2) The number of redundancies in iron and steel up to the end of 1979 (see Figure 3.2) understate the growing problems of the British Steel Corporation, many of which were held over until after the general election of May 1979. Production fell each year from 1976, whereas development plans had been based on the previous trend of expansion. The Corporation's gradual programme of closing older, higher-cost works was insufficient to match faltering demand from domestic construction, shipbuilding, vehicle manufacture and engineering.

(3) Shipbuilding shows the highest rate of redundancies, 1976 to 1979, years which included nationalisation in 1977 and the 1978 corporate plan to reduce heavy financial losses in merchant shipbuilding through redundancy and early retirement.

(4) Data for motor vehicle redundancies (Figure 3.2) show a very serious pattern. As in iron and steel domestic production totally failed to recover its 1973 production level; output of

Figure 3.2: Four Leading Industries of Redundancy, Great Britain, 1976–81

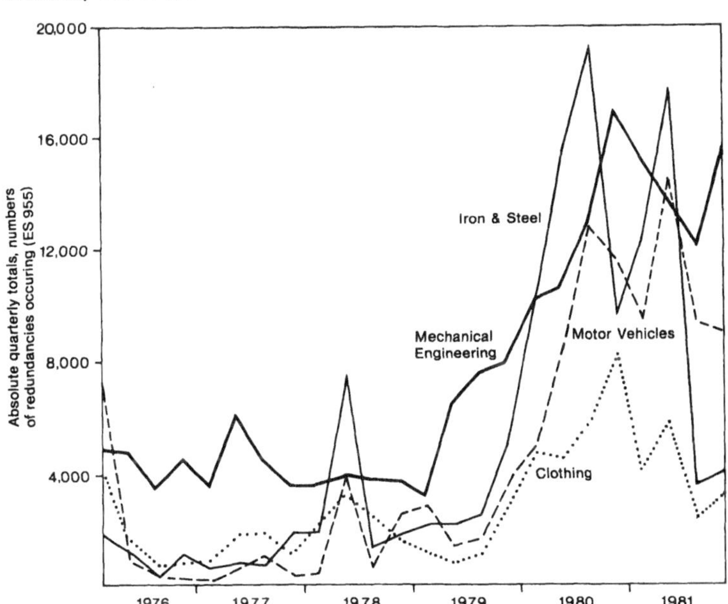

passenger cars fell from 33,600 per week in 1973 to 25,200 in 1976 and 20,600 in 1979.[12] Much of the associated reduction of employment occurred before 1976; the appointment in late 1977 of Mr Michael Edwardes as head of BL (British Leyland)[13] presaged a radical reorganisation in early 1978 which led to the loss of 18,000 jobs, through natural wastage and other means, by the autumn of 1979.[14]

(5) The engineering industry is of crucial importance because of its size, because of its linkages, and because its two main branches – mechanical and electrical engineering – showed a greater than average rate of redundancies over the period 1976–9. Mechanical engineering output declined each year from 1976 to 1979 with record levels of imports reflecting both a long-term trend and reduced UK price competitiveness in 1978 and 1979.[15] Loss of output was marked both in older sub-sectors, like textile machinery and the fabrication of industrial plant and steelwork, and in some newer sectors such as office machinery. Within electrical engineering, growth sectors held the balance, but redundancies appeared in factories producing telecommunications equipment –

radio, musical and electronic components – the result both of technological change and the advance of Japanese imports.

Events in major industries may thus confirm Mandel's prediction (Chapter 2) that recovery from the 1974–5 recession would be patchy. Despite a minor peak of manufacturing output as a whole in 1979, there were several major industries (and many minor ones) whose output in 1979 lay below the cyclical trough level of 1975 (Hughes, 1981[16]). We may now ask whether the more general decline of 1980 was expected.

The Onset of Severe Difficulty in 1980–1

It is an object lesson that 'no forecaster had expected such a devastating slump' (Hughes, 1981[17]) as occurred in 1980. The only certainty in employment prediction was that the number of young people reaching school-leaving age would rise to a peak in 1981, corresponding with the 1964 peak in the birth-rate. Recruitment prospects were less calculable; a number of forecasters saw the slight national improvement in unemployment from 1977 to 1979 as precarious. Two wings of Cambridge economics had foreseen a possibility of 3m unemployed by 1985.[18,19] In 1979 the EEC[20] had forecast an increase in member countries' unemployment from 6.5m to 15m (by 1985); before the UK general election there was a clear expectation of recession, due to a renewed world oil crisis. GB redundancies occurring did not, however, increase much above 1978 levels until September, 1979 (when they rose notably in the iron and steel industry, vehicles and mechanical engineering); only the seasonally adjusted unemployment data showed any increase in the numbers out of work by the end of the year.

In March 1980 one consultancy firm[21] forecast the loss of 575,000 private sector jobs by February 1981, for the reason that very heavy *overstocking* in manufacturing made these workers redundant. This forecast proved an underestimate, but it identified the main factor. Stocks were high because of the success of imports and the stagnation in British exports, due in turn to the rising value of the pound (then especially valued as an 'oil currency'). Particular need to reduce both the workforce and stocks (i.e. to reduce production while stocks of manufactured goods in warehouses were run down) came from severe pressure on company finances from the high level of interest rates and the pound. These were severe measures of adjustment, but they were sufficient to enable British industry to move back into financial surplus in the first quarter of 1981, while the pound (for other reasons) fell back to more normal levels in foreign exchange markets.

Changes in output and stocks were however greatly disproportionate to those of other countries; various factors have been adduced to explain the intensification of recession in Britain. Some Labour Party speeches blamed the whole recession on the Conservative government, but more considered views are perhaps typified by the following quotation:

> The economic problems presented by a rising sterling exchange rate and a worsening of the comparative cost performance of the UK economy preceded the election of the Conservative government. However, it is also evident that the policies pursued by the present government have greatly intensified the problem.
>
> Hughes, 1981[22]

Economists of many schools objected to the strictly monetarist position of the government, when the emphasis on reducing inflation appeared to be at the expense of mounting unemployment figures. Calculations by the Manpower Research Group, University of Warwick, suggested however that if Labour had continued in office the combined effect of their declared policies would have created levels of unemployment exceeding 2.5m by 1985,[23] perhaps 0.5m less than the Group's main projection.

The climate of 1980 enabled firms to implement long-intended reductions in their labour forces; unemployment weakened the negotiating position of unions at all levels, and redundancy became a realisable mode of approach. The effects of all these changes as we saw them in Table 3.1 involved a remarkable similarity of performance in many different manufacturing industries. The average rate was exceeded most heavily in industries discussed above, i.e. metal manufacture, textiles and clothing and footwear. Heavy warning blows from the nationalised sector of industry had arrived in late–1979, notably from the British Steel Corporation and BL (British Leyland) and were soon registered in redundancies occurring (Figure 3.2). The total output of cars and commercial vehicles fell by 24 per cent between the fourth quarters of 1979 and 1980. These reductions also affected the components industry,

Table 3.2: The Range of Variation in the Performance of Major Manufacturing Industries, in the Two Years ending December 1981, thousands

Order Totals of the Standard Industrial Classification, 1968		Employees in Employment, net loss		Redundancies Occurring ES 955
		no.	per cent	no.
	Heaviest percentage losses			
Order				
VI	Metal manufacture	124.1	28.6	104.0
XII	Textiles	92.2	21.4	76.0
XIII	Metal goods	104.5	19.9	60.9
VII	Mechanical engineering	172.4	19.4	107.8
Best percentage performance				
X	Shipbuilding etc.	18.6	11.7	12.3
III	Food, drink & tobacco	74.4	11.0	50.5
XVIII	Paper, printing etc.	55.7	10.4	35.7
IV	Petroleum products etc.	3.7	9.4	2.0
III–XIX	Manufacturing total	1195.3	17.2	797.4

Source: *Employment Gazette*, vol. 90, no. 2 (1982); data for December 1979 to December 1981.

including many metal industries as well as the production of tyres, windscreens and upholstery. Mechanical engineering industries showed a marked and widespread increase in redundancies in mid–1980. But very different industries, for instance pottery, also shed many jobs over the year (ascribed once more to the severe and prolonged squeeze on profits, resulting from high exchange rates and interest rates). Reasons for difficulty in some industries were individual, as with the incidence of high energy costs in paper-making. But the effects of recession were so widespread in different manufacturing sectors as to suggest it was virtually universal in its effects on different industries and Regions.

Closer inspection distinguishes variation in the incidence of recession, both between industries and over time. By end–1981 GB manufacturing employment had fallen by nearly 1.20 million in a period of 24 months, to a level of 5.78 million.[24] Table 3.2 shows that the estimated average decline of 17.2 per cent over two years still included a range of variation in performance, including some perhaps surprising results. The temporarily improved performance of Order X, Shipbuilding and Marine Engineering (a nationalised industry concentrated in peripheral areas), was perhaps little known.

The proper place for locating job losses such as those of BL is at the more precise 'minimum list heading' (MLH) level of the Standard Industrial Classification. Of the 66 main headings the following showed the worst percentage losses of employees in the two years, 1980 and 1981 together:

34.9%;	MLH 311,	Iron and steel (general)
31.3%;	MLH 312,	Steel tubes
27.9%;	MLH 381,	Motor vehicle manufacturing
25.6%;	MLH 463,	Glass
25.0%;	MLH 442,	Mens' and boys' tailored outerwear
24.2%;	MLH 336,	Construction and earth-moving equipment
23.8%;	MLH 412,	Cotton spinning etc.
23.8%;	MLH 332,	Machine tools
23.6%;	MLH 321,	Aluminium
23.0%;	MLH 462,	Pottery

These above average increases suggest biases of possible significance for the spatial pattern of unemployment. The combination of such heavy losses in regions of specialised activity may predict some of the basic differences to be presented in Part Two. It is because of this MLH variation that Chapter 8 examines the industrial impact of recession at the MLH level. The reader who is searching for the 'positive' elements of change might also note that there were three larger MLH groups which were estimated to have *increased* their employment in 1980 (but not thereafter): MLH 367, Radio, radar and electronic capital goods; MLH 383, Aerospace equipment manufacturing and repairing; MLH 485, Printing and publishing of newspapers; all three again imply bias in overall regional performance.

Recession of manufacturing output was most pronounced in the calendar year of 1980, but not all industries were in phase. 'Intermediate goods' such as metals and textiles were the chief industries showing an early peak of job losses before mid–1980. 'Consumer goods' such as clothing and footwear followed. 'Capital goods' production however showed a delayed profile of decline; mechanical engineering showed above average rates of job losses only in the second half of 1980. (Such patterns of change had an effect on the industrial composition of unemployment demonstrated as far as November 1980 by Gillespie and Owen.[25]) In 1981 the average loss of manufacturing jobs (8 per cent) was exceeded most heavily (see Table 3.1) in the metal industries, including metal manufacture itself, vehicles and mechanical engineering, while textiles, clothing and footwear were declining at less than the average rate. Redundancies remained high in mechanical engineering and it was expected that engineering and construction materials would show only moderate and temporary recovery after the reduction in capital investment in 1981, itself an adjustment by industry to lower overall demand.[26]

Net employment decline in the service sector from late 1979 onwards was unprecedented but still not dramatic. The most direct effects of recession were evident in transport (both in road freight and passenger employment) and in various forms of wholesaling. Most other forms of service employment were remarkably stable in 1980, but redundancies increased in the first half of 1981. Although this occurred particularly in distribution and in public transport by road, all parts of the service sector had shown net employment decline by then, except medical services and some finance services.

At end–1981, the pipeline still contained forward reductions planned by government and corporate bodies. Some were multiplier effects of industrial recession, others the more direct result of government policy changes and cash limits in the nationalised sector. British Airways was planning to cut 10,000 jobs over three to five years,[27] British Rail 38,500 over 1981–5;[28] the Royal Navy planned, before the 1982 invasion of the Falkland Islands, to cut 25,000 civilian jobs from the closure of dockyards.[29] All the major car makers were planning job reductions, including a loss of 29,000 in Ford over 1981–5.[30] ICL, Britain's largest computer firm, was planning to cut its workforce by 5,200[31] and ICI was reducing its white-collar employment[32] and its activities in petrochemicals and plastics[33] by heavy rationalisation. The geographical distribution of some of these forward losses was not directly known. As a basic point of method it may be however that the study of decline is more efficiently considered at the level of major employers, rather than under the headings of industry groups. We are able in the next chapter to study the nature and spatial impact of corporate decision-making within many individual industries over the period 1976–81.

Notes

1. Employment in Scotland in companies wholly related to the North Sea oil industry increased from 13,500 at mid–1974 to 47,900 in the fourth quarter of 1980. The Scottish Office, *Scottish Economic Bulletin*, no. 23 (Summer, 1981), p. 22.
2. Annual change in real take-home pay shown by rates of growth in the Index of Average Earnings and the Tax and Price Index. *Financial Times*, 18 June 1981.
3. *Employment Gazette*, vol. 90, no. 2 (1982), Table 1.6. Figures quoted are expressed as four quarter moving averages.
4. *Employment Gazette*, vol. 90, no. 4 (1982), Table 2.19. Figures quoted are expressed as three month moving averages.
5. C. Waud, *Redundancy and Unfair Dismissal* (Associated Newspapers, London, 1981), p. 17.
6. P. Tidsall, 'It Depends What You Mean by Redundant', *The Times*, 16 July 1980.
7. F. Noble, 'Redundancy Statistics', *Employment Gazette*, vol. 89, no. 6 (1981), pp. 260–2.
8. A.R. Townsend, 'Recession and the Regions in Great Britain, 1976–80: Analyses of Redundancy Data', *Environment and Planning A* (1982 forthcoming).
9. *Financial Times*, 13 Jan. 1982.
10. D. Keeble, 'Industrial Decline, Regional Policy and the Urban-rural Manufacturing Shift in the United Kingdom', *Environment and Planning A*, vol. 12, no. 8 (1980), pp. 945–62.
11. *Financial Times*, 4 Dec. 1980.
12. *British Business*, 28 Aug. 1981, p.832.
13. P.J.S. Dunnett, *The Decline of the British Motor Industry* (Croom Helm, London, 1980), p. 157.
14. *Financial Times*, 11 Sept. 1979.
15. *Mechanical Engineering Industry EDC Short Term Trends*, (NEDC Books, London, 1978).
16. J. Hughes, *Britain in Crisis* (Spokesman, Nottingham, 1981), p. 26.
17. Ibid., p. 56.
18. Godley *et al.*, *Financial Times*, 19 April 1977.
19. Stone *et al.*, *Financial Times*, 29 June 1978.
20. *Financial Times*, 17 May 1979.
21. Hodge Recruitment Planning Limited, *Stocks Without Takers* (Employment trends survey no.1), (Hodge Recruitment Planning Limited, London, 1980).
22. Hughes, *Britain in Crisis*, pp. 42–3.
23. Manpower Research Group, University of Warwick, *Review of the Economy and Employment*, Spring 1981 (University of Warwick, Coventry, 1981).
24. *Employment Gazette*, vol. 90, no. 2 (1982), Table 1.3.
25. A. Gillespie and D. Owen, 'Unemployment Trends in the Current Recession', *Area*, vol. 13, no. 3 (1981), pp. 189–96.
26. *Mechanical Engineering Short-term Trends* (Engineering Employers' Federation, London, 1 March, 1982).
27. *Financial Times*, 8 August 1981.
28. *Financial Times*, 12 Feb. 1982.
29. *Financial Times*, 26 June 1981.
30. *Financial Times*, 9 April 1981.
31. *Financial Times*, 6 June 1981.
32. *Financial Times*, 31 July 1981.
33. *Financial Times*, 23 April 1982.

4 REDUNDANCIES AND CLOSURES IN THE BIG CORPORATIONS, 1976–1981

The reader may be surprised that Chapters 4 to 7 and Chapter 9 are partly based on a five-year collection of all reports of UK job losses in the *Financial Times*. There are sharp differences between the reporting of large job losses by the media and the world of academic writing; the reader may wonder which is the more accurate. Is it the picture of apparently sudden and irretrievable redundancies and closures presented as television headline news when large organisations announce extensive rationalisations of their plants (occasionally across the length and breadth of the country)? Or is it the longer-term, academic analysis of gradual change slowly but often relentlessly transforming an individual conurbation or set of sub-regions? How should we relate national statistical changes of the last chapter to the fate of individual Regions and communities in Part Two of this volume?

The emphasis, it is suggested, has changed in this recession; it has proved more necessary to interpose the role of the large industrial corporation between the national problems of production on the one hand and the task of understanding regional (or 'geographical') change on the other. This chapter therefore assesses the heightened degree of financial control now exerted over economic activity by leading national and international corporations. It compares their roles in redundancy and closures with traditional theory of the autonomous, more local firm. It identifies the top twenty UK employers and assesses, through reference to the financial press, those job losses which may be attributed to them *and their full network of subsidiary companies*.

The discovery of parent ownership of individual plants is more important for the study of their decline and possible final 'death' than for the study of initial patterns of location. Many of the large present-day industrial corporations post-date the original growth and location decisions of their constituent parts, which remain best understood in terms of successive past 'layers' of decision-making spread across the national map (as mentioned in Chapter 2). Their absorption into national entities is most readily understood in the case of the nationalised industries; for instance, British

Shipbuilders took over nearly all the traditional regional companies engaged in large-scale shipbuilding, repair and marine-engine building. Much less obvious is the cumulative process by which, through successive mergers and takeovers, private corporations either have assembled varied empires covering a large part of the activity of an individual industry, or have diversified into very different industries which have no dealings with each other. In both cases the company taken over may continue all its activities under its old name. Expansion of corporations may take a planned form, where new products or methods of production are established in new plants (for example by adding to their own large resources the financial inducements available in government 'assisted areas'). Or it may occur in an apparently random way, where a financial 'holding company' finds reasons to invest in a particular firm (as for instance when the international Lonrho Group bought holdings in the private steel industry of Sheffield). The pace of acquisition after 1950 was measured by Prais,[1] who estimates that the hundred largest manufacturing enterprises were responsible for 37 per cent of national manufacturing employment by 1968; Hart and Clarke[2] emphasise a further increase to 1975. The position is more extreme in some smaller Regions. Goddard[3] reports that the proportion of manufacturing jobs in the Northern Region controlled from headquarters ouside the Region increased from 52 per cent in 1963 to 78 per cent in 1973; Cross[4] records that by 1977, 64 per cent of manufacturing employment in Scotland was controlled from locations outside that country, including 36 per cent from foreign (non-UK) head ofices.

Approaches to the Geography of Employment Decline

If we approach employment decline through the national pattern of ownership of plants we are in fact laying aside a number of other approaches. These are, firstly, the economist's traditional approach through the individual firm, secondly the accounting framework of geographers' 'components of change' for individual areas, and thirdly the underlying view that employment decline has much to do with geographical conditions in the relevant surrounding area.

Much of the traditional analysis of business failure by economists concentrates on 'small' or 'small new' businesses, rather than on industries or multi-plant corporations. It centres on management failure, the high 'death-rate' of firms in their first few years, and what were thought to be fairly constant 'exit-rates'. Cross[5] as a geographer argues from a review of work on plant closures that too few studies exist to allow meaningful comparisons to be made. Traditional economic writing on the general theory of the firm relates implicitly to single-plant firms and their optimum size of plant in relation to long-run economies of scale. Even in these simple cases, the growth of firms is dependent on a complex mixture of factors. 'Most of them are unlikely to lead to consistent spatial variations in the rate of growth' (Gudgin[6]).

Redundancies and closures have in the past mainly been incidental objects of geographical studies. Even with the publication of several studies of the sub-regional 'components of manufacturing change' (see Table 2.3 above), incorporating job losses of various types, it was still clear to Fothergill and Gudgin[7] that there was 'no context in which to place the results for any one area'. At the end of the day this method was sometimes criticised as a rather elaborate accounting exercise, failing to get to the root causes of change or to identify the prime movers in the process of employment decline. Studies confined to a particular area could be related to an external context only by reference to the national statistical performance of relevant industries.

In a very general way we may assert that 'failure is not related to location' (Fredland and Morris[8]); Luttrell[9] established that failures of branch plants were attributable almost entirely to shortcomings of management and organisation, rather than to unwise choice of location. Massey and Meegan[10] maintain that while the environment of a plant may contribute to its closure it would be foolish to jump to conclusions over apparent spatial relationships and patterns. The age of a plant and its productivity may be more important than its external environment, and patterns of closure may show geographical regularity only for instance because of a concentration of plants established in the same historical period.

The inner city is however an area of debate where some research points to a more definite conclusion. Lever[11] shows how the below average post-war performance of inner city manufacturing can be explained neither by the industrial structure of the areas nor by movement to the suburbs, but by 'indigenous' processes: (1) internal operating costs – e.g. efficiency, wages, land/space costs, and the like; (2) external operating costs – e.g. transport and distribution; and (3) external costs such as uncertainty arising from town-planning policies. For the general mass of firms there do, on balance, seem to be critical difficulties in the particular environment of the inner city. However, the role of national forces in the employment run-down of the large inner city plant can also be very prominent, although varying in importance between cities. In Glasgow, the closure of British Railways' Cowlairs Workshops in 1963 contributed, with other large closures, to early concern about the inner city area of Springburn. In the Liverpool inner city area the Edge Lane works of Plessey, a national corporation in electrical engineering, reduced its workforce from 12,000 in 1970 to 4,000 in 1981.[12] Massey and Meegan[13] show how the cities of London, Birmingham, Manchester and Liverpool lost 27,000 jobs in the period 1966–72 in the government-inspired rationalisation of large plants in the electrical engineering and aerospace industries.

Redundancy and unemployment in individual labour market areas are the final subject of this study: it will be wise to assume, however, that they are only end-products of complex processes of change which may have their origins entirely outside the sub-region. Sayer[14] claims that much meticulous spatial analysis in industrial geography has been devoted to 'the way in which one set of chaotic conceptions, e.g. a sample of firms involved in diverse types of production, competitive situation and financial health, relates to another, e.g. particular geographical areas'. Massey[15] argues that the 'economy' of any given area comprises a great mixture of plants of different age and type. It will thus be a complex result of the combination of its succession of roles within the series of wider, national and international, 'spatial divisions of labour'. Likewise the reports which one might assemble from a good local newspaper of job losses in individual areas are at first sight 'chaotic' and refer to elements of past investment of very different origin, ownership and product. The reports contribute to the interpretation of local trends, but must be explained in relation to international, national or local control in the relevant production industries.

The preferred starting point must lie in changes in the nature, volume and manner of national production. Their relationship to employment change is not however straightforward. As Massey and Meegan[16] stress, the loss of jobs cannot be taken as a simple surrogate for even a slowdown in the rate of accumulation; there are many factors involved in the conception that goes by the name of employment decline; behind the aggregate numbers of jobs lost can lie different processes, causes and management strategies. Little is known so far about why job losses within an industry may hit some areas rather than others, but an approach is surely long overdue. Bearing in mind the growth of large corporations since the war, Holland[17] asserted by 1976 that the larger corporations of the UK together represented a 'meso-economic sector' which was powerful enough in its own momentum and behaviour to modify the role of the economy at large. It could be one of the factors systematically frustrating central governments' regional policies of the 1970s for the location of new investment. In reviewing the whole progress of industrial geography as of 1981, Wood[18] distinguishes Sayer's paper of 1980[19]: 'Instead of empirical generalisation, careful abstraction about the structures which govern industrial activity at particular locations should form the basis of explanation.'

Financial control, through multi-national companies, national holding companies, nationalised industries and other large corporations, is taken here as a central point around which to structure decisions which create job losses. This chapter attempts to provide such a national perspective for plant closures and contractions. By identifying large job losses by the names of the corporations concerned (rarely if ever mentioned in sub-regional studies) it can provide links between the different sub-regions affected by an individual financial group and its strategy. (If one of the common concerns about multi-national organisations is that their strategies fall outside the purview of the individual government, so too perhaps is there a practical problem that the strategies of multi-plant firms within the UK overlap the purview of individual industrial geographers working in different sub-regions.)

National Production Change and Corporate Strategies

Massey and Meegan have led the way in the UK in investigating and articulating the role of large corporations in employment decline. Subsequently to their study of large scale restructuring in electrical engineering and aerospace industries, 1966–72,[20] they recently applied a new set of concepts to a wider set of industries for the period 1968–73 in *The Anatomy of Job Loss*.[21] The Preface to this present volume acknowledges the great help of Massey and Meegan in loaning a copy of their script before publication. Since their concepts are of great interest they will be considered here before application to the very different recent period.

Massey and Meegan use the Census of Production as the starting point for their study, which is essentially concerned with precisely-defined industries rather than with corporations. They examine changes in output, employment and the capital stock of each industry. Moving between the Census of Production and secondary sources, they identify three forms of reorganisation as follows:

(1) *Intensification* involves improvements in productivity across a wide range of plants, without heavy new investment.

(2) *Investment and technical change* occur where employment decline is accompanied by heavy net capital investment; where there is significant growth in output, technical change is not associated with heavy job losses, but in other cases the new investment involves replacement and closure.

(3) '*Rationalisation*' involves complete or partial plant closures, the scrapping of capital equipment, and cutbacks in the labour force. These are the result of relative lack of profitability by comparison with other plants and possible alternative investments.

The writers stress that the various forms of reorganisation merge into and interact with each other, but that in principle they involve very different elements of possible variation in employment in different locations. In (2) there is an element of potentially mobile employment. Job losses under (3) may be much more 'lumpy' than under (1). All these changes are more likely in periods of recession; do they make the plants of large corporations more vulnerable than others in recession conditions? On the one hand it is held by the economist Prais,[22] or the geographer Watts,[23] that one virtue of large enterprises is that they are more likely than small firms to remain profitable during times of depression; the diversified company has more scope to operate cross-subsidisation. On the other hand, corporations may rationalise out of existence even plants which are individually profitable. The corporation (or especially the financial holding company) can switch support from less profitable to more profitable units much more easily than single-industry or single-plant firms.

Why is this field of research so novel? One reason for the lack of research on heavy 'rationalisation' through redundancies and closures in large corporations is that these actions are themselves an instrument of last resort, which had no widespread precedent before the financial and political climate which obtained in 1980. As Watts[24] points out, 'where there remains scope for changes within the existing plants rationalisation and closure, like spatial growth, is unlikely to occur'. Disinvestment is a decision which is unpopular to make. Katz[25] similarly observes that 'disinvestment decisions . . . are among the most difficult and emotionally loaded issues that must be faced'. There are indeed suggestions that many projects for de-manning had been in managers' minds for several years before the cyclically-influenced events of 1980 made them both the more necessary and the more politically tolerable in the industrial relations climate of the year. 'Rationalisation' is the form of change most likely in recession. For Massey and Meegan[26] 'rationalisation' including much simple closure is by 1981 a far more important source of job loss than 'technical change' and 'intensification'. Nonetheless the period 1976–81 as a whole included years of actual net employment growth (see Chapter 3) and is a rich laboratory for the application of different views of industrial strategies of change. The history of the British Steel Corporation in this period reflects all three strategies. 'Technical change' was involved as the opening of new plants, chiefly the Redcar Works (1979), increasingly precipitated the closure of smaller, high-cost inland plants (e.g. Corby 1979) to match demand forecasts which were revised downwards. A much more severe re-assessment of trading conditions and forward demand at end–1979 led to an extensive and systematic set of closures and manning reductions ('rationalisation'). The subsequent strategy is essentially to be characterised as 'intensification', through widespread economies and productivity improvements rather than through further large reductions of capacity (see below).

Corporate Disinvestment Strategies; Behavioural Regularity in their Locational Impact?

Did the reaction of different national corporations to the same sort of external circumstances produce any similarities in their rationalisation strategies? Was their behaviour in any way similar? The precise combination of adverse international factors (export competitiveness and import penetration) and domestic factors (high interest rates, de-stocking by customers, and energy prices etc.) varied in its impact on different corporations between 1976 and 1981. Corporations appear to have had varied experience of recession conditions and varied perceptions of the urgency of action. A common feature, however, was that virtually all major corporations, public and private, at some stage of our study period restructured their activities in the face of over-capacity and high costs. 'Intensification' was deemed insufficient. Therefore a selection of establishments for pruning or closure was made from the information and perceptions of a head office – normally, in the case of larger UK corporations, in London.

Any advance in understanding the choïce of plants for 'rationalisation' will be valuable, but research must recognise both the strategies listed above and the scope for behavioural interpretation. Watts[27] asserts that the degree of planning behind locational adjustments varies just as markedly as it does in spatial growth. It is not a question then of some automatically-determined outcome occurring on the ground as a precise result of financial and market pressures. It is partly a matter of a firm's independence, and partly of financial structures and labour processes which will vary according to economic and political circumstances of the day. It is however the scope for different selections of plant closures by a given corporation which gives this type of work its potential significance for public policy. Watts[28] writes that where the differences between plants are relatively small, the environmental setting of the various plants that are potential candidates for closure would need careful examination by an interventionist government. Cross[29] goes further and argues, in a separate context from the national debate about 'lame ducks', that perhaps in the interests of a regional economy certain plants should not be allowed to close (sic).

Past writers have put forward a limited range of propositions about the selection of plants for closure. These tend to focus around the age of investment. In a group of plants developed at different dates is it the older ones which will be more vulnerable to rationalisation or is it the younger, newer operations? Answers in the literature come together around the two extremes of the distributions, as if both older age and recent building produce vulnerability. It is usually assumed that the age of a factory tends to correlate with its having older plants which may become obsolescent in relation to technical and market demands. There is some international support for this in a recent study of investment and employment in manufacturing in US cities by Varaiya and

Wiseman.[30] More sophisticated notions, suggesting that the product or even the corporation has a definite 'life-cycle' are presented by, for instance James[31] and Levitt[32] respectively. Despite certain complexities, it seems that industrial investment does have a definite lifespan and that older plants broadly may be vulnerable.

New plants are likely to be vulnerable because they represent an untried interface between managers, workers, new production methods and the market. The precise relationships between establishment age and closure rates in the first ten years of a plant are in doubt. In Ireland O'Farrell[33] identifies no relationship between age of plants and the closure rate amongst new plants receiving government assistance. In contrast other studies (e.g. Collins[34]) conclude that new plants tend to experience a high mortality rate in their first five or six years, after which the rate settles down to become relatively constant. Henderson[35] was able to collate official data on the age of all plants (not just new openings) which closed in Scotland between 1966 and 1975. The main findings were that most closures occur in long established plants, since these are the most numerous, but that establishments are most vulnerable in their first five years of operation when their susceptibility to closure is significantly higher than at any other time.

This approach towards the extremes of the age distribution of plants may be related to the earlier work of Massey and Meegan[36] and Massey[37] in providing an *occupational* interpretation of the strategies of multi-plant organisation. This involved a 'de-skilling' process by which older plants in city areas of skilled labour were reduced in importance (or closed) relative to the expansion of newer plants employing semi-skilled labour, often in 'assisted areas'. Their detailed study was based on 25 firms undergoing rationalisation in the period 1966–72, principally in electrical engineering. There was variation between sectors and companies. Overall a net decline of 16 per cent in employment was accompanied by a switch in the proportion of jobs from inner city areas to 'assisted areas'. The authors projected their findings as *part of* fundamental structural change at the level of the national economy, involving contraction in the manufacturing base of the UK. The approach suggests that plants built in the same 'round of investment' in a given area would tend to have more in common with each other occupationally than with their respective industrial sectors in the Region. For instance, in a study of 400 employees of seven factories which had set up in North East England under regional policy, Townsend *et al.*[38] found that no less than 56 per cent of workers were classed as semi-skilled (see also the official 'ILAG' study[39]). The total employment of these plants has since been very variable. If this type of branch became recently *more vulnerable* in acute recession conditions, a key question is whether corporations rationalised such plants before others, a point which we must take up in the conclusions to this chapter and again in Chapter 9.

The Approach of the Individual Corporation to Redundancy and Closure

Redundancy is an extreme measure which carries its own costs. Employment loss itself does not necessarily occur in direct proportion to a fall in production and/or an increase in productivity. Brown[40] and his associates think that workforce reductions are greater where there is technical flexibility, and in larger establishments. Going further, they find that one reason for firms differing in the extent to which they shed labour in response to a fall in demand is that they may make other adjustments, chiefly through reducing overtime and increasing short-time working. The only clue for the causes of these differences in behaviour is that reductions in hours tend to be made less where the density of unionisation is greater. Once workforce reductions are attempted a whole series of measures may be considered, of which enforced redundancy may be only the last. The following generalisations are made by Brown:[41]

Method to Reduce Workforce	*Frequency of Use*
natural wastage	7 in 10 cases
voluntary redundancy	4 in 10 cases
enforced redundancy early retirement transfers within the organisation and shedding people over retirement age	3 in 10 cases
shedding casual and part-time workers	2 in 10 cases

This survey found that larger organisations, with their greater internal flexibility, were more likely to use voluntary redundancies, early retirement and internal transfers than the smaller. They attempted to handle managerial redundancy the most sensitively, chiefly out of self-interest, but also because the depressing effects of job-loss may be greatest on skilled workers and managers, whose previous rate of movement between jobs may have been low.

What about the effects of one organisation on another? Final closure releases assets of plant, machinery and skill which in normal times may be seen as positive assets for regional development. The disinvestment may generate resources of initiative and premises for local development of small firms, the more so if managers do not move to other areas within the 'internal labour market' of the corporation. In 1980–1 we witnessed the closure of whole sections and divisions of major corporations; the question must arise as to whether they influenced each other *psychologically*. Research at the Manchester Business School was reported in a letter to the *Financial Times*:

> Your columns have lately been full of news of plant closures and redundancy. I have the feeling that closure has become something of a fashion, judging by the reasons, or absence of reasons, contained in your reports. In many cases no doubt there may be no reasonable prospect, even on the most optimistic assumptions, of the plant or division concerned ever making a positive contribution to the group. It is right then that it should be closed. But the assumptions of one company's management are coloured by the assumptions of others, so that depression becomes the general view. Redundancy is not so unthinkable when everybody is doing it. . . .
>
> In spite of the apparent urgency, the full financial effects of closure and redundancy ought to be thoroughly examined and analysed before any decision is made. It should not be based just on the historic profits and losses shown by divisional accounting. Long-term forecasting and planning have become unfashionable to an extent not known for at least 20 years. The pendulum may now have swung too far against the long-term view. Excessive closure and redundancy could be one of the consequences.
>
> W. Whiting, 28 August 1980

This view is of great interest in adding an element of the

'diffusion of ideas' to the behaviour of larger corporations. It may contribute to the concept that there were 'waves' of redundancy in 1980–81, where previously job losses were largely effected by other means.

Public Knowledge of Individual, Larger Job Losses

This book presents outline results of a five-year survey by the writer of major UK job losses in the financial press. He was fortunate in having developed a system of assessing reports from the *Financial Times* (FT), from October 1976, well before the great increase in redundancies and closures in 1979–81. The FT and *The Times* then became the mainstay of media summaries such as weekly counting exercises of the *Sunday Times* and Independent Television News. Few newspaper readers were likely to have missed the largest job losses of this period, particularly in the steel and motor-car industries. However, it is difficult to assemble a full coverage of job losses in an area or a corporation over a period of time. Company reports gave periodic statements of the total workforce of some corporations. Beyond this, the main achievements lie with the radical fringe press. 'Counter Information Services', for example, 'is a collective of journalists who publish information not covered or collated by the established media'. They have published 'Anti-Reports' for example on the Ford Motor Company[42] or the Lucas Group.[43] Five different Community Development Projects together published an overall assessment of the impact of economic forces and individual corporations on their areas of study.[44] Most of the information is more systematically collected in government offices: these offices release information only in the aggregate forms already used in Chapter 3 so public information will gain from specific data for corporations and places.

The data used in the rest of this study represent a full coverage of all FT reports of job losses by individual employers (1 October 1976 to 1 October 1981). Their wide coverage results indirectly from the legal provision that prior notice of redundancy must be given to employees and their unions (if any). This prompts firms to 'set the record straight' by means of press notices. The coverage is imperfect. Firms may go to great lengths in relying on normal methods of natural wastage to keep their name out of the press. As justification of their eventual public decisions many companies report the previous loss of jobs through natural wastage; these reports too are part of our record. This total record consists of the sum of four categories which are used to distinguish the main types of job loss in tables: C (Closure), P (Partial closure), R (Redundancy), W (reported Wastage). The system was first used in an article on the period ending July 1980.[45] Advantages of its use are:

(1) FT reports are geographically specific; in manufacturing, nine out of ten reports of job losses are capable for instance of spatial referencing by county. Non-manufacturing job losses are included in the record and tables which follow.

(2) The reports cover 52 per cent of GB manufacturing job losses, as known from the statistical series ES955 (which was reported in the last chapter) both in the years 1977–79 and in 1980. The regional ES955 data must remain a more accurate *total* statement and are given in Chapters 5 to 7: there is regional variation in the FT coverage of notified redundancies, with over-representation in Regions with a 'large-plant' size structure. The risk of FT reports of redundancy being withdrawn without a further report to this effect has been investigated and is found to be small.[46]

(3) The FT source is invaluable because unlike all government sources it includes employers' names throughout; this provides, with the help of directories such as *Who Owns Whom*,[47] for the building up of information on the chronology of national corporations' disinvestment strategies; i.e., it is possible to relate a plant's job losses to its membership of a national or foreign corporation (if applicable).

(4) Final closures are always distinguishable in the reports from other redundancies, and this is important for the physical planning and economic prospects of individual sub-regions. This distinction is of great value as an indication of whether employment losses are permanent or transitory. Where contractions occurred without a closure there was little indication of any recovery occurring before 1982. In the case of large closures there was an increasing trickle of reports of the sale of the premises on the industrial property market, or the re-occupation of a government rented factory. The record as a whole goes a long way in indicating whether an area's industrial geography in 1981 was significantly different from that of 1976.

The available data are applied regionally in Part Two and Chapter

9, and to the strategies of leading corporations in the rest of this chapter.

Employment Losses in the Leading National Corporations

Geographers now recognise in practical research the large financial groups which dominate the evolution of national economic geography. Goddard,[48] for instance, has used *The Times 1000*[49] in locating the head offices of the UK's largest corporations; here we use it to appraise redundancies. The purpose of the directory is to provide comparative information on the size of each corporation (its capital employed), its volume of business (its turnover) and its rate of profits. The leading 1000 corporations are ranked each year in order of the size of their turnover. Data are also given on each corporation's number of employees, usually including overseas employees. Table 4.1 identifies the UK's twenty leading corporations ranked in terms of employment, including those in overseas or non-manufacturing activity, together with nationalised industries. (The activities of foreign multi-national corporations in the UK, and the employment of government itself, are not included at this stage.)

Job losses reported in each group are presented both by entries in Table 4.1 and through comments below on most of the corporations shown. We have related individual reports of job losses in the FT to the name of the parent corporation through use of the directory *Who Owns Whom*.[50] All companies registered in the UK which are subsidiaries of another, or of a nationalised industry, are alphabetically indexed against the name of the company which owns them. There are sometimes four or five links in the chain to find the ultimate 'parent ownership' of a company. All the subsidiaries of the leading 20 corporations of Table 4.1 were listed; all job losses of individual companies reported in the FT were then allocated to the 20 corporations, if appropriate. We thus have a means of relating the closure of say an obscure local textile firm, operating under its original name, to the disinvestment decisions of its rarely identified owner, which might be one of the large national corporations such as ICI or Courtaulds.

Table 4.1 covers just over three million jobs in 1979/80: our FT reports, 1976–81, enable us to locate just over 200,000 UK job losses for the same group of twenty corporations. Additional statements on aggregate job losses are reported below.

Table 4.1 Job Losses in the leading 20 Employers of the UK; cases reported October 1976–October 1981[a]

Corporations, including subsidiary companies	Employees 1979 80 (including overseas)[b]	Rank by employment[b]	Rank by turnover[b]	Jobs lost at known locations: No. of locations	Jobs lost at known locations: Jobs lost	Regions affected: No.	Regions affected: most[c]	Largest single case: Location	Largest single case: Jobs lost
General Post Office	411,000	1	—	0	The GB employment of the industry expanded by 3% mid-1976 to mid-1981				
National Coal Board	297,000	2	—	12	4,000	5	WA, YH, SC	Manvers Coke Works, S. Yorks.	700 R Feb. '78, C Feb. '80
British Rail	244,000	3	—	13	2,600	6	SE, NW	Ashford Works, Kent	950 C June, '81
Shell	n.a.	n.a.	2	3	1,200	3	SE, NW, SE	Shell Haven Refinery, Essex	550 P Dec. '78
BAT Industries (British American Tobacco)	185,000	4	3	4	800	2	SC, SE	Wiggins Teape Pulp Mill, Fort William Highland Region	450 P April '80
British Steel Corporation	181,000	5	—	40	67,200	8	WA, NO, EM	Shotton Steelworks, Clwyd	8,200 P July '79, R June '80, R March '81
BL (British Leyland)	176,000	6	10	28	38,500[d]	9	WM, NW, SE	Canley, Coventry	6,000 P Sept. '79
Electricity Council and Boards	158,800	7	—	41	4,900	6	SE, SW, WM	Marchwood Power Station, Hants.	n.a. P. Sept. '81
General Electric Co.	155,000[e]	8	12	15	6,300	8	NO, NW, EM	Hartlepool, Cleveland	2,700 R&W before Nov. '79
Imperial Chemical Industries	148,000	9	4	16	12,500	8	NW, NO, SE	Organics Division, Greater Manchester	1,650 W April '79
Lonrho	140,000	10	35	3	5,700	2	YH, NO	Hadfields Steelworks, Sheffield	4,700 R April '81, W before
Courtaulds	115,000	11	20	46	24,700	10	NW, NI, NO	Red Scar Works, Preston	2,600 C Nov. '79
British Petroleum	113,200	12	1	6	3,100	5	SE, WA, SC	Isle of Grain Refinery, Kent	1,700 C Aug. '81
Grand Metropolitan Hotels	108,600[e]	13	15	3	800	3	WM, SE, YH	Hawley's Bakeries, Birmingham, London & Rotherham, S. Yorks.	800 R Nov. '77
Guest, Keen & Nettlefolds	107,200	14	17	18	12,400	6	WM, WA, SC	GKN Sankey, Telford, Shropshire	2,000 R May '80, Jan. '81, Feb. '81
Imperial Group	101,800	15	6	16	5,700	8	SW, SE, EA	St. Anne's Board Mill, Bristol	1,800 C Sept. '80, R & W before
Consolidated Gold Fields	98,300	16	56	1	400	1	SW	Wheal Jane Tin Mine, Cornwall[f]	400 C May '79
Dunlop Holdings	95,000	17	26	7	6,100	5	WM, NW, SC	Fort Dunlop, Birmingham	2,500 R Jan. '79, Feb. '80, Dec. '80
Lucas Industries	87,500	18	52	4	4,500	3	WM, NW, YH	West Midlands	3,000 R in year-ending Jan. '81
Unilever	85,500	19	5	6	2,500	4	NW, SE, SC	Thames Board Mills, Purfleet, Essex	800 C Oct. '80

Note: a. Based on complete monitoring of the daily *Financial Times*: C (Closure); P (Partial closure); R (Redundancy); W (reported Wastage).
b. Based on *The Times 1000, 1980–81* (Times Books, London, 1980), pp. 6, 30–3.
c. The column indicates the three Regions with the greatest number of job losses in order: EA (East Anglia); EM (East Midlands); NI (Nothern Ireland); NO (Northern); NW (North West); SC (Scotland); SE (South East); SW (South West); WA (Wales); WM (West Midlands); YH (Yorkshire & Humberside).
d. Includes announcement of November 1981.
e. UK employment only.
f. Later re-opened by Rio-Tinto Zinc Corporation, with reduced labour force.

The table is led by three publicly-owned industries with surprisingly few job losses in our period of study. Despite some 'rationalisation', including the closure of rural sub-post offices, the GPO services – rank (1) as shown – of posts and telecommunications (now split into two organisations) showed no decline in employment in response to recession. The coal industry (2) was experiencing a lower rate of job loss than in the 1960s and early 1970s; there was a net decline in employment of ten per cent (30,000) between mid–1976 and end–1981, principally through productivity improvements and natural wastage ('intensification'). A threatened strike of February 1981 appeared to prevent a higher rate of pit closures, but the effects of recession contributed to a net loss of 12,000 workers in 1981.[51] This was not a good period for productivity improvements in railway operation (3); rail employment was reduced by nine per cent (20,000) over five years. However, it was in the 13 workshops of British Rail Engineering Ltd. that a closure (Ashford Works, Kent) and voluntary redundancies were announced in 1981, and that two closures and a major redundancy were *proposed* in 1982, Shildon Works (Co. Durham) and Horwich (Greater Manchester) for closure, with redundancy at Swindon (Wilts.).

Two publicly-owned manufacturing corporations, the British Steel Corporation (5) and BL (6) were already in severe difficulty at the beginning of the period. In 1976 the Steel Corporation employed 228,000 workpeople, whereas in September 1981 this total had been reduced to 109,000,[52] with the severest effects concentrated on Wales. Three phases of locational change may be identified:

(1) At the start of the period the closure of older and smaller works was a concomitant of 'technical change' through the planned expansion of modern large works, such as Teesside. Mounting losses in 1977 caused an acceleration in the negotiation of individual closures with unions, and notable closures followed at Hartlepool (Cleveland), Cardiff (South Glamorgan), Shelton (Staffordshire), Ebbw Vale (Gwent) and Bilston (West Midlands). However, in early 1978 the Corporation believed that it would 'be unable to proceed with any big closures before a general election'.[53]

(2) The general election of May 1979 brought stricter government financial discipline for the Corporation and a more explicit re-assessment of prospects. 'Rationalisation' plans announced in December 1979[54] involved a reduction of steel-

making capacity from 21.5m to 15m liquid tonnes per annum. The closure of steel-making at Shotton (Clwyd) and Corby (Northants.) was confirmed, but a new closure at Consett (Co. Durham) was accompanied by very heavy manning reductions at the large sites of Port Talbot (West Glamorgan) and Llanwern (Gwent). In all a reduction of 52,000 (from a level of 182,000) was both intended and virtually achieved, as the workforce stood at 132,000 by December 1980.[55]

(3) The newly appointed American Chairman, Mr McGregor, took a different path with his proposals of December 1980. Capacity was to be cut very little. A reduction of about 20,000 jobs was to be widely spread across many plants (and is therefore less fully represented in Table 4.1). It represents 'intensification' in the terminology which we have adopted in this chapter.

There were signs of financial improvement by the end of 1981, but the Corporation was intending to reduce employment to 90,000 by March 1982,[56] and possibly then by a further 20,000. The private steel industry contended, as part of their negotiations with the Corporation for joint rationalisation, that further reductions still were necessary. One result of these negotiations was that the Sheffield steel company of Hadfields effected 1,900 redundancies in 1981, thus reducing their labour force down to 700 compared with 5,400 in 1977.[57] This happens to be the largest single example of job losses in the international Lonrho group (entry 10 in Table 4.1).

BL reduced its workforce from 198,000 in 1977 to 97,000 at the end of 1981.[58] The reduction represents both improvements in productivity and cuts in capacity, and above all a smaller share of production for the British domestic car market. From being in a leading position in the early 1960s, the British car industry fell rapidly back throughout the decade in comparison with its foreign competitors. The crisis which struck BL in the 1974–5 recession may be seen as the result of the failure of the UK industry to keep up with international competition, particularly in the face of economies of scale achieved by EEC competitors. In the period 1976–81 exports stabilised at a comparatively low level; but BL's UK sales of cars fell back both in absolute terms and as a percentage of the domestic market, which stood at about 20 per cent in late 1979. There had already been one formal announcement of group job losses, with a programme of cutting 12,500 jobs in early 1978.[59] It is interesting to note that that year brought the announcement of the closure of more 'peripheral' factories in the group, for instance in London (Southall) and Merseyside (Speke). As from September 1979[60] a programme of 25,000 job losses and a co-ordinated programme of capacity reductions took effect; it involved large job reductions in the West Midlands itself, at Coventry and Castle Bromwich. Later a most modern plant at Solihull, also in the West Midlands, was announced for closure.[61] Meanwhile the bus and truck division, Leyland Vehicles, had been gradually reducing its workforce in Lancashire and Scotland. However, the delayed impact of recession brought the announcement of 4,100 redundancies in November 1981,[62] a 27 per cent reduction in employment compared with one of ten per cent in capacity. All in all over half the 38,500 group job losses shown in Table 4.1 were due to occur in the West Midlands Region (see Chapter 6).

The oil industry, petrochemicals and artificial fibres were among the strongest growth industries of the post-war period. They are mainly capital-intensive activities and we might expect the effects of recession on them to be contained behind a low profile through natural wastage of staff. Shell, Imperial Chemical Industries (ICI ranks 9) and British Petroleum (BP ranks 12) have leading positions as major employers in Table 4.1 because of the scale and growth of their industries. They all had regionally significant job losses, Shell and BP through the reduction of oil refining capacity itself on either side of the Thames Estuary, in Essex and Kent respectively. In addition to jobs lost at known locations, Shell cut UK staff by at least a further 1,500 through natural wastage and voluntary severance in refineries, offices and road tanker transport. BP and Shell both announced sharp cuts in their marine tanker fleets in 1981.[63] ICI had redundancies in plant closures at Kilroot, Northern Ireland and Ardeer, Scotland,[64] but its 12,500 job losses in Table 4.1 were to be achieved principally through natural wastage. After a large corporate financial loss in the first half of 1980, virtually all Divisions announced schemes of job reduction, including the merger of the Petrochemicals and Plastics Divisions. This led to a reduction in 1981 of 9,000 in ICI's UK jobs.[65] The Fibres Division was particularly badly affected, as it had made a loss every year since 1975, accentuated in 1980 by over-capacity throughout Europe, cheap imports from the USA and the recession.[66] An associated textile company closed mills throughout Lancashire.

The position in Courtaulds (rank 11) was extreme because the corporation specialises in the manufacture, among other products, of artificial fibres in modernised textile mills. As with ICI the greater part of its employment was in 'assisted areas' under regional policy, but the group had opened more new plants in them since 1966. In 1973 the group reported to a House of Commons Committee[67] that 66 per cent of its UK employment of 122,000 was in then 'assisted areas'. In these areas the group had received about £50m in government grants, 1966–72, including £12m at Skelmersdale (Lancashire), Spennymoor (Co. Durham), Carlisle and Workington (Cumbria): all four of these plants were among the 50 announced for closure before the end of 1980.[68] Similarly, large post-war plants were closed or reduced in scale in Northern Ireland, the second most heavily affected 'Region'. The worst affected Region was North West England, which had half the identifiable job losses, spread through all the former cotton districts as well as in Merseyside. Traditional locations of Courtaulds were also affected in North Wales, Coventry, Derby and Essex. Although there is occasional mention of new technical development to offset the losses, the picture presented by this corporation is that past investment, modernisation and diversification in the end failed to prevent wholesale rationalisation by a new generation of management. In all the employment level of 123,000 in 1975 was reduced to one of 80,000 by September 1980,[69] before further reductions were carried out.

Table 4.1 demonstrates the relative immunity from recession of three diversified corporations in the sectors of food, drink, tobacco and packaging. This is partly to do with the more stable consumer demand for food than for other goods in recession conditions. Two of them, BAT Industries and the Imperial Group, owe their ranks of 4 and 15 respectively to overseas activity in tobacco. The third, Unilever (rank 19), manufactures food products, animal oils, detergents etc. None of these groups had many job losses in the UK, but in each of them the largest single case of redundancy was in a subsidiary in the paper and packaging industry. The BAT subsidiary, Wiggins Teape, closed a pulp mill which was important for the Highland Region and which had been reportedly unprofitable since it was built with government assistance in 1966.[70] The Imperial Group's employment losses occurred in eight different Regions under the very different names of operating subsidiaries, including Smedley-HP Foods, Ross Foods, Buxted Chickens, Youngs Seafoods and Courage Breweries. The Group's job loss in Imperial Tobacco largely fell outside the period covered by Table 4.1 and included 1,700 employees in factory closures in Glasgow, Stirling and Bristol,[71] and 1,000 white collar staff in several locations.

Three engineering groups demonstrate somewhat more varied trends. The General Electric Co. (GEC, rank 8) is of great interest because it was the main focus of the mergers in electrical engineering studied by Massey and Meegan, 1966–72.[72] Ten years later it was in a comparatively stable state, sustained partly by a leading role in providing defence contracts. Among the 15 locations affected by job losses there was one closure and two large reported run-downs of employees, at Rugby, Warwickshire, and at the Hartlepool factory, Cleveland; this was affected, like competitors' factories, by a change in technology in orders for telephone systems by the GPO. Guest, Keen and Nettlefolds (GKN, rank 14), by contrast, depended heavily on supplying components to the vehicle industry and was unable to keep its workforce together after 1979. Its UK employment was reduced by 4,000 from 1978 to 1979 and by 23,000 in 1980 and 1981, leaving a UK workforce of 42,000.[73] A union spokesman stressed the firm's policy of increasing investment abroad at the expense of UK jobs. This reduction affected a very wide range of factories in Birmingham and the Black Country. The largest single set of job losses was at a large old-established works now included in Telford New Town; there were others at steel-making sites in Wales and at branch factories in Worcestershire, Devon, Dyfed, Powys, Strathclyde and Cleveland. Lucas Industries (rank 18) sustained large job losses, also in the Birmingham area, in the manufacture of electrical vehicle components. The Lucas declarations of job losses appear to have been bound up with negotiations over pay and productivity to an unusual extent. It is not clear what scale of job losses was involved in the group's aerospace business, but 12,000 were lost in its motor business in 1980 and the first four months of 1981.[74]

Conclusions of the Empirical Survey of Twenty Leading Employers

The reader will probably have been impressed by the power of the leading corporations as demonstrated in Table 4.1. All the twenty we have studied imposed some job losses on individual areas, with the apparent exception of the GPO. The sum total of job losses announced for known locations was 203,900. Of course, our method, which relies on the FT, may understate the rate of employment decline in those corporations which adopted a gradual or lower-profile style of reduction. If, however, one extends the study to include on the same basis the next thirty leading employers (with 50,000 to 85,000 employees), the general picture is similar. There are comparatively few job losses to report in the privately-owned groups in food manufacture, retailing and catering. In the nationalised sector there were increasing job losses in the National Bus group and British Airways, following a reduction of 20,000 jobs in British Shipbuilders' merchant yards. All manufacturing groups had redundancies, notably in electrical engineering (for example, the Plessey Group at Liverpool and Sunderland), and in textiles (Coats Patons).

Some of the main conclusions of the study of twenty corporations are as follows:

(1) Table 4.1 reflected the national changes in production described in Chapter 3. Job losses were heaviest in steel, textiles, vehicles and their supplying industries, and comparatively low in oil, foodstuffs and paper. There is a wider range of inter-company variation, as seen in this chapter, than variation between industries. Corporate diversification into the service sector appears to have reduced job losses and this is a salutary point. It is possible to give a very depressing picture of recession by concentrating on certain manufacturing corporations, such as Courtaulds, GKN and Lucas.

(2) Linkages between industries are mentioned only occasionally in reports of individual plant closures, but these may be important between the national corporations of Table 4.1. A reduction in orders from BL will affect GKN, Lucas Industries, Dunlop and British Steel, and in turn the coke production of the NCB. Changes in GPO ordering clearly affected work in GEC. A reduced demand for artificial fibres by Courtaulds may affect petrochemical output at individual oil refineries.

(3) Corporations do appear to vary in their styles of decision-making. The national 'master-plan', covering all plants, is more characteristic of the large public corporations with large (indivisible) plants (though the 'plan' is frequently overtaken by later events). Employment decline in some large private organisations is handled through plans made at divisional level (as in ICI or Lucas). In organisations with many small plants (as in Courtaulds or GKN) decentralised decisions were announced

almost weekly. Courtaulds stressed that it had 'no master closure list'.[75]

(4) The period of study is suitable for the approach of Table 4.1, of summing losses at known locations, because 'rationalisation' was prominent. In 1979–81 there is comparatively little mention of 'technical change' but examples can be found in most corporations. The table cannot fully bring out the volume of 'intensification' going on at many locations, partly under the very threat of 'rationalisation'.

(5) There are few corporations whose decisions affect only one Region. Even GKN, which has its headquarters in Smethwick, West Midlands and is one of the most regionally-oriented corporations, had job losses in six of the eleven UK Regions. The distribution of job losses between Regions in Table 4.1 may appear haphazard, although with some emphasis on the West Midlands and North West. If we arrange all of each corporation's job losses in date order from late 1976 to late 1981, we find that 13 of 16 groups *announced a loss of jobs in 'assisted areas' before any in the rest of the country*; two further groups, Consolidated Gold Fields and Lonrho had job losses only in these areas, and two announced their first losses in both types of area simultaneously. This finding is of importance for Chapters 8 and 9 and for the concluding remarks to this part of the volume.

This chapter has largely subordinated geographical variation to the role of national economic factors and corporate decision-making. What is the residual role of location factors themselves? There are clearly cases of closure where the loss of a local market is important for smaller independent suppliers and manufacturers. In many large corporations, however, the main linkages lie between plants of the same corporation in different parts of the UK or overseas. In this context it is suggested that it is *relative* location within the group of plants which is of importance. A plant in, say, Bolton may be better integrated in its respective groups of plants if its parent plant or the headquarters of the group lie in Manchester rather than in London. Distance played a systematic statistical role in the past expansion of many corporations by establishing 'moves' between UK sub-regions (Townsend and Gault[76]); we now have some evidence that the most remote plants have tended toward a higher closure rate in the period 1976–81. This would be consistent with repeated suggestions that small and outlying factories within an organisation were most vulnerable to closure, and with the view often advanced from Scotland and elsewhere (e.g. Cross[77]) that the regional concentration of control functions may over time favour the region which contains the company's headquarters. This view was propounded internationally by Thorngren[78] and Tornqvist.[79] Relative age and relative location may together partly determine the fate of different establishments within a corporation. Such variations may derive in their turn from the corporation's past strategies of development. Very possibly they have deliberately separated out different functions between plants in different labour market areas. Overall results must be tentative at this stage. Finding (5) above however is a clear one, that as a whole the leading national corporations contributed distinctly to a relative deterioration in 'assisted areas' in the first part of the period 1976–81. Later we shall find (Chapter 8) that this deterioration was greater than can be explained by factors of industrial structure, and Chapter 9 shows that it firmly involved post-war investments. The indications are, on balance, that national employers discriminated against factories in 'peripheral areas' (not least Merseyside) in the period 1976–79, and that this has some connection with the geography of the big corporations themselves.

Notes

1. S.J. Prais, *The Evolution of Giant Firms in Britain* (Cambridge University Press, Cambridge, 1976), p. 140.
2. P.E. Hart and R. Clarke, *Concentration in British Industry, 1935–75* (Cambridge University Press, Cambridge, 1980).
3. J.B. Goddard, 'Office Development and Urban and Regional Development in Britain' in P.W. Daniels (ed.), *Spatial Patterns of Office Growth and Location* (Wiley, Chichester, 1979), p. 43.
4. M. Cross, *New Firm Formation and Regional Development* (Gower, Farnborough, 1981), p. 89.
5. Ibid., p.111.
6. G. Gudgin, *Industrial Location Processes and Regional Employment Growth* (Saxon House, Farnborough, 1978), p. 153.
7. S. Fothergill and G. Gudgin, 'Regional Employment Change; a Sub-Regional Explanation', *Progress in Planning*, vol. 12, part 3 (1979), p. 168.
8. J.E. Fredland and C.E. Morris, 'Where New Small Businesses go Wrong', *Changing Times*, vol. 30, no. 1 (1976), pp. 21–3.
9. W.F. Luttrell, *Factory Location and Industrial Movement* (2 vols., Cambridge University Press, Cambridge, 1962), p. 4.
10. D.B. Massey and R.A. Meegan, *The Anatomy of Job Loss* (Methuen, London, 1982), pp. 123–9.
11. W.F. Lever, 'The Inner-City Employment Problem in Great Britain since

1952: A Shift-Share Approach' in J. Rees, G.J.D. Hewings and H.A. Stafford (eds.), *Industrial Location and Regional Systems* (Croom Helm, London, 1981), p. 193.

12. *Financial Times*, 14 Sept. 1981.

13. D.B. Massey and R.A. Meegan, 'Industrial Restructuring versus the Cities', *Urban Studies*, vol. 15, no. 3 (1978), p. 281.

14. R.A. Sayer, *Some Methodological Problems in Industrial Location Studies*. Paper presented to the Conference of the Industrial Activity and Area Development Study Group of the Institute of British Geographers, May 1980.

15. D.B. Massey, 'In What Sense a Regional Problem?', *Regional Studies*, vol. 13, no. 2 (1979), p. 235.

16. Massey and Meegan, *Anatomy of Job Loss*, pp. 17–30.

17. S. Holland, *The Socialist Challenge* (Macmillan, London, 1975).

18. P.A. Wood, 'Industrial Geography', *Progress in Human Geography*, vol. 5, no. 3 (1981), p. 415.

19. Sayer, *Methodological problems*.

20. Massey and Meegan, 'Industrial Restructuring versus the Cities', pp. 273–88.

21. Massey and Meegan, *Anatomy of Job Loss*, pp. 31–120. (Methuen, London, 1982).

22. Prais, *Giant Firms in Britain*, p. 99.

23. H.D. Watts, *The Large Industrial Enterprise* (Croom Helm, London, 1980), p. 99.

24. Ibid., p. 126.

25. R. Katz, *Management of the Total Enterprise* (Prentice-Hall, Englewood Cliffs, 1970), p. 242.

26. Massey and Meegan, *The Anatomy of Job Loss*, pp. 207–26.

27. Watts, *The Large Industrial Enterprise*, p. 115.

28. Ibid., pp. 278–9.

29. Cross, *New Firm Formation*, p. 129.

30. P. Varaiya and M. Wiseman, *Investment and Employment in Manufacturing in U.S. Cities, 1960–76*, Paper presented to the Western Economic Association, San Diego, California, June 1980.

31. B.G. James, 'The Theory of the Corporate Life Cycle', *Long Range Planning*, vol. 6, no. 2 (1973), pp. 68–74.

32. T. Levitt, 'Exploit the Product Life Cycle', *Harvard Business Review*, vol. 43, no. 6 (1965), pp. 81–94.

33. P. O'Farrell, 'An Analysis of Industrial Closures: the Irish Experience, 1960–73', *Regional Studies*, vol. 10, no. 4 (1976), pp. 433–48.

34. L. Collins, *Industrial Migration in Ontario* (Statistics Canada, Ottawa, 1972).

35. R.A. Henderson, 'An Analysis of Closures among Scottish Manufacturing Plants', *ESU Discussion, Paper 3* (Scottish Economic Planning Department, Edinburgh 1979).

36. Massey and Meegan, 'Industrial Restructuring versus the Cities', pp. 273–88.

37. Massey, 'In what Sense a Regional Problem?', p. 234.

38. A.R. Townsend, E. Smith and M.R.D. Johnson, 'Employees' experiences of new factories in North East England', *Environment and Planning A*, vol.10, no. 12 (1978), pp. 1345–62.

39. House of Commons Expenditure Committee, *Regional Development Incentives, Minutes of Evidence (from July 1973)* (HMSO, London, 1973).

40. W. Brown (ed.), *The Changing Contours of British Industrial Relations. A Survey of Manufacturing Industry* (Blackwell, Oxford, 1981), p. 116.

41. Ibid., pp. 116–7.
42. Counter Information Services, 'The Ford Motor Company', *Anti-Report No. 20* (Counter Information Services, London, n.d.).
43. Counter Information Services, 'Where is Lucas Going?', *Anti-Report No. 12* (Counter Information Services, London).
44. CDP Inter-Project Editorial Team, *The Costs of Industrial Change* (CDP Inter-Project Editorial Team, London, 1977).
45. A.R. Townsend, 'Geographical Perspectives on Major Job Losses in the UK', *Area*, vol. 13, no. 1 (1981), pp. 31–8.
46. There is clearly some risk of unreported reprieves. An earlier draft of Townsend (see note 45 above) containing 82 items was sent to all the regional offices of the Manpower Services Commission, who replied in all cases and were able to report that only three of the batches of job losses did not take place. 33 FT reports were sent to C.S. Crouch, research student, to 13 corporations and all agreed that the reports were correct.
47. *Who Owns Whom*, 1980–1 edn. (Dun and Bradstreet, London, 1980).
48. J.B. Goddard, 'Office Development and Urban and Regional Development', p. 53.
49. *The Times 1000*, 1980–1 (Times Books, London, 1980).
50. *Who Owns Whom*, 1980–1 edn.
51. *Financial Times*, 13 Jan. 1982.
52. *Financial Times*, 26 Sept. 1981.
53. *Financial Times*, 2 Jan. 1978.
54. *Financial Times*, 12 Dec. 1979.
55. *Financial Times*, 16 Dec. 1980.
56. *Financial Times*, 20 Nov. 1981.
57. *Financial Times*, 23 April 1981.
58. *Financial Times*, 15 March 1982.
59. *Financial Times*, 2 Feb. 1978.
60. *Financial Times*, 11 Sept. 1979.
61. *Financial Times*, 13 May 1981.
62. *Financial Times*, 21 Nov. 1981.
63. *Financial Times*, 18 June 1981.
64. *Financial Times*, 15 Oct. 1980.
65. *Financial Times*, 23 April 1982.
66. *Financial Times*, 10 Oct. 1980.
67. *House of Commons Expenditure Committee, Regional Development Incentives, Minutes of Evidence (from October 1972 to June 1973)* (HMSO, London, 1973), p. 305.
68. *Financial Times*, 4 Dec. 1980.
69. *Financial Times*, 24 Sept. 1980.
70. *Financial Times*, 15 April 1980.
71. *Financial Times*, 16 March 1982.
72. Massey and Meegan, 'Industrial Restructuring versus the Cities', pp.273–288.
73. *Financial Times*, 19 March, 1982.
74. *Financial Times*, 8 May 1981.
75. *Financial Times*, 29 May 1981.
76. A.R. Townsend and F.D. Gault, 'A National Model of Factory Movement and Resulting Employment', *Area*, vol. 4, no. 2 (1972), pp. 92–8.
77. Cross, *New Firm Formation*, p. 122.

78. B. Thorngren, '*How do Contact Systems Affect Regional Development?*', *Environment and Planning*, vol. 2 (1970), pp. 409–22.

79. G. Tornqvist, 'Contact Systems and Regional Development', *Lund Studies in Geography*, Series B (1970), No. 35.

Part Two

THE REGIONAL CONSEQUENCES

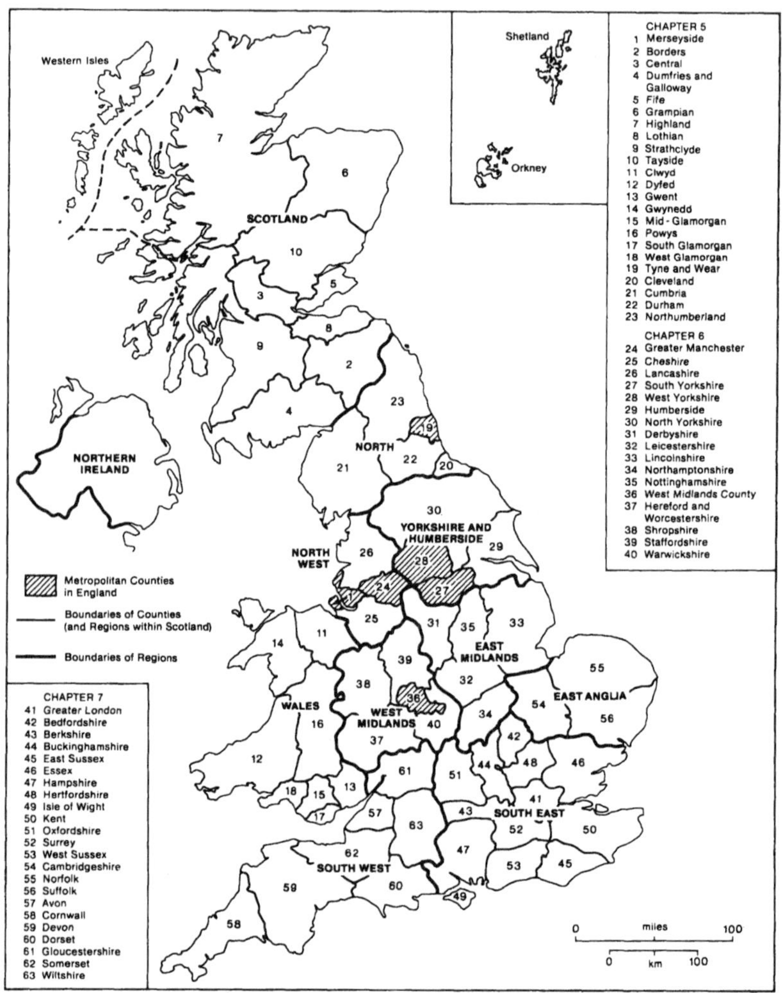

Figure 5.1: Reference Map, Regions and Counties of the United Kingdom, as from 1975

5 RECESSION IN THE POOREST REGIONS

Our aim in Part Two is to establish the impact of recession on different Regions. The eleven Regions of the United Kingdom, as depicted in Figure 5.1, may be grouped into three broad types for this purpose. For each group we shall try to identify the depth of impact of recession between 1976 and 1981. For each Region it is possible to distinguish its sensitivity to recession by comparison with 'expected' figures of redundancies. Deviations from predicted levels of job losses may in part be attributed to closures by major corporations or to recurrent difficulties in local industries, both frequently of permanent significance to regional problems. Space does not permit an exhaustive treatment, but Chapters 5 to 7 will mention all job losses over 1,000 known by firm in a five-year period. The tables represent two sorts of data:

(1) Statistics of 'redundancies occurring' in each separate Region of Great Britain are presented (as in Table 5.3 below) in the shape of 'actual' and 'expected' figures, the latter based on the industrial structure of each Region. (The statistics were introduced in Chapter 3; comparable data are not available for Northern Ireland.)

(2) A review of all *Financial Times* (FT) reports of job losses in each Region (as in Table 5.1 below) pinpoints with some certainty the largest contributors to employment decline in its component sub-regions. (The source was introduced in Chapter 4.)

The national framework of Part One should be kept in mind for the following questions. How far did the industrial pattern of recession, seen in the 'macro-economic' view of Chapter 3, account for the volume and nature of job losses in an individual Region? Does the control of important decisions by large corporations in the 'meso-economic' sector (Chapter 4) provide a better explanation? In the survey to be made in Chapters 5 to 7 we shall argue that the answer varies from Region to Region. Full comparison of the performance of different Regions is reserved to Chapter 8, where calculations on the growth of unemployment and redundancies are standardised and interpreted at a national level, and the impact of conurbation conditions is considered. Readers who are unfamiliar with the pre–1976 history of regional development in different parts of the UK are referred to existing standard works, such as House[1] or Manners, Keeble, Rodgers and Warren.[2]

This chapter is concerned with Northern Ireland, Scotland, Wales and the Northern Region of England; it also includes Merseyside. With that inclusion this group comprised the agreed 'hard core' problem areas of the UK from the mid–1930s to the mid–1970s. From 1966 to 1972, for instance, they were almost identical with the 'assisted areas' of regional policy: a definition which largely reflected the contemporary map of unemployment rates (see for instance McCrone[3] for further details). These in turn can be related to many other indices of social and economic well-being; Northern Ireland, Wales and the Northern Region (but not Scotland) had the lowest regional levels of per capita income in 1976 to 1980.[4] These Regions were accustomed to persistent deprivation; indeed, the constitutional problems of Northern Ireland, Scotland and Wales in the 1970s are inevitably associated collectively with their position as 'peripheral areas'. It will come as no surprise that in 1976–81 they experienced even higher levels of unemployment than before. Analysis of FT reports up to mid–1980[5] showed Clydeside (Scotland), Merseyside (North West) and Tyneside (Northern Region) to have a high rate of manufacturing job losses as from 1977, only overtaken at the end of that period by steel-making counties (mainly in Wales, Scotland and the North). Individual workers who had lost their jobs in traditional industries in the past, for instance in coal mining or ship building, then found themselves redundant (several times over in some cases) in newer 'replacement industries' in what we may call 'regional policy factories'.

We may, however, note some limits on the decline of these areas at least after 1979. Firstly, the four areas (including Merseyside) had 37 per cent of UK unemployment in 1978 (a proportion which was then increasing), but only 25 per cent of the total UK population and 23 per cent of all factory workers. Was it likely that a national recession, one led by manufacturing, would affect these areas proportionately and deal them a full 37 per cent of resulting job losses? Secondly, we have noted in Chapter 3 that the decline of employment in agriculture, coalmining and shipbuilding (which are concentrated to varying degrees in these areas) was not prominent in the recession conditions of 1980–1. In fact unemployment did not increase in these Regions at the same *rate* as in the rest of the UK in the years 1979–81. From this flow certain implications for policy, and others for the social impact of recession. The smaller *proportionate* increase in unemployment may have had some effect on the social adjustment to difficult conditions. The Scarman Report[6] on the London urban riots in Brixton of April 1981, in considering why rioting spread in July to some cities and not to others, was clear that there were equally deprived parts of the country where disorder did not occur. While Liverpool and several other English cities were badly affected, the other areas of this chapter, Northern Ireland, Scotland, Wales and the Northern Region, were virtually untouched.[7] The answer is complex. It is inescapable that they had never been prosperous enough since the war to recruit many overseas migrants; but perhaps also the unemployment conditions of 1980 were a less novel shock to their social system.

Job Losses Reported in 1976–81

A full survey of reports in the FT shows that in these areas, exceptionally, job losses were spread over most of the five years of our study. (This point must receive recurrent attention.) In Table 5.1 we present simply the 'largest cases'[8] of job losses reported in each part of 'the poorest Regions', by date of their first definite announcement. (Most of these losses involve 90 days notice of redundancy; thus job losses announced for example in October 1981 would not take place before January 1982.) We considered as eligible for inclusion losses in all sectors except construction and central and local government. This presentation tends to pick out decline in large plants and the industries which own them. However, other cases and aggregate redundancy data have been examined and inform the text.

The relevance of the preceding chapter is clear from a first inspection of the table. Of the 24 areas listed 17 sustained their biggest known job losses from the 20 leading corporations identified in the last chapter. BL (British Leyland) and the British Steel Corporation are dominant as publicly-owned enterprises. In three of the seven other areas the largest losses occurred in foreign-owned firms, a new feature not analysed in Chapter 4. Several of these are among the post-war factories appearing in the table.

Table 5.1: Job Losses in 'the Poorest Regions' of the UK: the Largest Cases Reported in each Sub-region, October 1976 to October 1981

Sub-region (see Fig. 5.1)	Organisation	Parent organisation	Jobs lost	Category[a] and month of report
Northern Ireland	Courtaulds (fibres)	—	3,300	Carrickfergus, P '78, '79, '80, C '81; Londonderry, R Nov. '79, C June '81; Larne, R Nov. '79, Feb. '80
1 Merseyside	BL (British Leyland)	—	4,600	Speke, P Feb. '78, R Nov. '78, C May '81
Scotland				
2 Borders	Turnbull Dyers	Cawdaw Industrial Holdings	100	Hawick, C Nov. '80
3 Central	BP Chemicals	British Petroleum	250	Grangemouth, R Sept. '81
4 Dumfries & Galloway	Spillers Bakeries	—	100	Dumfries, C April '78
5 Fife	Redpath Dorman Long	British Steel Corp.	300	Methil, R July '79
6 Grampian	Lawsons of Dyce	Unilever	400	Aberdeen, C May '79
7 Highland	Wiggins Teape (pulp)	BAT Industries	450	Fort William, P April '80
8 Lothian	Leyland Vehicles	BL (British Leyland)	2,100	Bathgate, R Jan. '80, Nov. '81; Edinburgh, C Jan. '80
9 Strathclyde	Talbot (UK)	Peugeot, France*	9,000	Linwood, R Nov. '79, R May '80, C Feb. '81
10 Tayside	NCR Manufacturing	NCR Corp., USA*	1,550	Dundee, R '76, '77, '78, '81
Wales				
11 Clwyd	British Steel Corp.	—	8,100	Shotton, P July '79, R June '80, R March '81
12 Dyfed	Duport Steel	—	1,600	Llanelli, R March '80, Sept. '80, C Feb. '81
13 Gwent	British Steel Corp.	—	8,500	Ebbw Vale, P '77, '78, '79, '80; Newport, R Aug. '79; Llanwern, R Jan. '78, Dec. '79
14 Gwynedd	Bernard Wardle	—	400	Caernarfon, R '79, C Feb. '80
15 Mid-Glamorgan	Hoover	The Hoover Co., USA*	2,200	Merthyr Tydfil, R '78, '79, '81
16 Powys	BRD (transmissions)	GNK (GKN)	800	Newtown, C Feb. '81, W before
17 South Glamorgan	British Steel Corp.	—	3,300	Cardiff (East Moors), C May '78
18 West Glamorgan	British Steel Corp.	—	10,100	Port Talbot, R May '79, Dec. '79, Jan. '81; Swansea, R March '78, May '80, Dec. '80
Northern England				
19 Tyne and Wear	British Shipbuilders	—	3,800	Rivers Tyne & Wear, R '78, '79, '80
20 Cleveland	British Steel Corp.	—	11,300	Hartlepool, C Dec. '77; Teesside, R '77, '78, '79, '81
21 Cumbria	British Steel Corp.	—	3,400	Workington, R May '80, Nov. '80, P Feb. '81, P May '81
22 Durham	British Steel Corp.	—	4,600	Consett, C Dec. '79, R & W before
23 Northumberland	Lonrho Textiles	Lonrho	300	Cramlington, P May '78, Oct. '79

Note: a. C (Closure); P (Partial closure); R (Redundancy); W (reported Wastage).
* Foreign-owned firms.

Source: *Financial Times* reports.

These are an important systematic feature, representing the largest cases under Northern Ireland, Merseyside, the Central and Highland Regions of Scotland, Lothian, Strathclyde, Tayside, Gwynedd, Mid-Glamorgan and Northumberland. Most of the closures in shipbuilding and steel are in nineteenth century areas of production.

Northern Ireland

Job losses in Northern Ireland's newer industries were more prominent in this period of study than those of older establishments, which include the main Belfast shipyard, Harland and Wolff (government owned). They contributed to a reversal in Northern Ireland's employment prospects between the 1960s and 1970s, and to pessimistic forecasts for the 1980s. Financial inducements for external manufacturing investment in the 1960s had attracted plants in light engineering and artificial fibres. The province achieved over one-third of UK capacity in artificial fibres, and by the early 1970s Courtaulds was Northern Ireland's largest industrial employer:[9] later the severe problems of the artificial fibres industry (see previous chapter) made the corporation the largest source of job losses (Table 5.1). The concentration of fibre plants owned by different corporations had arisen more by chance, in the process of replacing lost employment in the declining linen industry, than by design or through trading linkages.[10] Other job losses in fibres included the withdrawal of the Dutch firm AKZO from Antrim (2,000 jobs), of ICI from their Carrickfergus plant (1,700 jobs), and redundancies in the American firm Du Pont. Two other firms were known to have lost a thousand or more jobs: Grundig (West German), which closed its Belfast plant in the face of Far Eastern competition,[11] and Harland and Wolff. Teaching and civil service posts had been the main source of increased employment while manufacturing as a whole declined from 1959 to 1979.[12] This was of considerable welfare and political importance, yet by the same token the economy is extremely vulnerable to cuts in public expenditure.[13] The loss of several thousand public service jobs[14] contributed to an overall decline of 44,400 in total employment, mid–1979 to mid–1981.[15] From 1976 to end–1981 unemployment in the province increased from 11.0 per cent (60,900) to 18.9 per cent (108,700). It was feared that any upturn in the British or Irish economy might pass the province by, with the increased proficiency of the Republic's Industrial Development Agency on the one hand and the political troubles (reported to have cost 24,000 jobs, 1970–80[16]) continuing to deter new outside investors on the other. Continuing high unemployment here could be of great moment:

> Whilst full employment or excess demand for labour would not solve Northern Ireland's political and cultural conflicts it can scarcely be doubted that it would ameliorate them and perhaps go some way to undermining feelings of alienation and antipathy towards the whole society. It might even do more in so far as the willingness to engage in or condone violence is facilitated by the lack of employment and the sense of social rejection which it encourages.
>
> Gibson and Spencer, 1981[17]

There were few favourable economic developments in 1981, and 1982 began with a sharp contraction in production at the new De Lorean car plant, and further pessimism over the future of Harland and Wolff and smaller local firms. In Belfast, which had 15.3 per cent unemployment at end-year, plans went ahead for a government 'Enterprise Zone'.

Merseyside

Merseyside's reputation for heavy unemployment was warranted in this period and it is therefore discussed here separately from the rest of North West England (Chapter 6). It is a bigger labour market than Northern Ireland, with roughly the same experience of unemployment rates, 10.8 per cent (or 77,500) at mid-1976 and 18.7 per cent (or 134,100) at end-1981. Here too, the recession may be seen as an accentuation of deep-seated structural and demographic features, although in this case the impact of large branch closures was very strongly felt before 1980. If one ever had misgivings about large branch plants in regional development, Merseyside justified them by 1980. Branch plants were important here by the 1970s. Firstly, the historical dependence of the area on the docks, transport and commerce had led to little local manufacturing, except for instance in processing of imports for food. Secondly, the

Table 5.2: Job Losses in Merseyside Metropolitan County; the Largest Cases Reported in the *Financial Times*, October 1976 to October 1981

Organisation	Jobs Lost	Category[a] and month of report
BL (British Leyland)	4,600	Speke, P Feb. '78, R Nov. '78, C May '81
Mersey Docks and Harbour Co.	3,800	R & W since '76
Liverpool City Council	3,000	W & R Feb. '81
Plessey (telecommunications)	2,900	Speke & Kirkby, C June '78; Liverpool, W & R since July '78
Dunlop (tyres & golf balls)	2,600	Speke, P Jan. '79, R Jan. '80
Courtaulds (clothing, nylon)	2,500	Aintree, P March '78, P Sept. '79, C Feb. '81
Cammell Laird (British Shipbuilders)	1,900	Birkenhead, R March '78. Nov. '78, Aug. '79
Pilkingtons Glass	1,700	St. Helens, R Jan. '79, Feb. '81, April '81
Tate & Lyle (sugar)	1,600	Liverpool, C Jan. '81

Note: a. C (Closure); P (Partial closure); R (Redundancy); W (reported Wastage).

post-war surplus of labour was partly met by the attraction of large British and foreign plants under an apparently successful use of regional policy, which was going strong in the period 1966 to 1975. During that period Lloyd and Mason report the arrival of 74 plants from outside the North West, of which 46 were branch plants and 22 subsequently closed.[18] Both the Liverpool Inner Area Study[19] and Lloyd[20] stress that many of these plants settled in urban fringe areas of Liverpool such as Speke, Kirkby and Aintree.

Large plants of British corporations (several in urban fringe areas) dominate the manufacturing losses of Table 5.2 (1976–81). Before 1976 one strong thrust of regional policy had brought the motor car industry to Merseyside: the closure of BL's car and car body plant and of Dunlop's tyre production at Speke was a signal reversal of this policy. Plessey and Tate and Lyle had both been major employers in the 'inner city' of Liverpool: the adverse decisions of these national firms were significant setbacks for an area with few small factories. In most conurbations, the growth of service employment has been a cushion which could absorb workers displaced by manufacturing closures: here, job losses in Mersey

Docks reflect the profound effect of containerisation in the 1970s and the closure of much capacity, and Liverpool City's reductions of its own white-collar staff contributed to the decline of office jobs.

Overall statistics of decline are clearer than the precise reasons. Lane[21] shows that Merseyside's share of official redundancies in the UK expanded from 5.0 per cent in 1975 to 8.5 per cent in 1978, *before contracting in 1980*. Our own data show the area as one of the few with more job losses between October 1976 and December 1979 than in the ensuing 21 months. There has been some tendency for a national corporation to close its Merseyside plant before others elsewhere (though the area's leading employers, Ford, Pilkingtons and Unilever, were not very prominent for job losses). A few redundancy decisions here were associated with previous strike action, but the significance of the area's poor industrial relations image can easily be exaggerated. Part of it comes from the presence of industries which are nationally prone to industrial disputes (docks, motor vehicles and shipbuilding) and part from the presence of large plants. (A Department of Employment report[22] which adjusted for the first factor still found Merseyside the most strike-prone area of GB in 1968–73.) From July 1981 the image was worsened by urban riots, at a time when the area already had all three existing innovations in urban policy – an Inner City Partnership scheme, an Urban Development Corporation and an Enterprise Zone (at Speke). The fate of overspill areas beyond the County boundary will be apparent in Chapter 9; the County itself lost nine per cent of its population between 1971 and 1981.[23]

An Overall View of Scotland, Wales and the Northern Region

For full Regions of Great Britain it is possible to introduce another standard feature. Table 5.3 aims essentially to provide a simple summary of trends in the period 1976 to 1981. For the start of the period, 1976, some perspective is provided by listing the three largest industries together with total numbers unemployed. We then show official figures of the number of regional redundancies occurring during the period, firstly in the four calendar years 1976 to 1979, then in the individual years 1980 and 1981. The figures in brackets add some depth as they are 'expected' figures derived from national (GB) totals for the equivalent periods. For this purpose it is assumed that each Region receives redundancies from each

Table 5.3: Profile of Recession 1976–81, in Three Peripheral Areas of the UK; Data in Thousands

	Scotland		Wales		Northern Region	
Leading industries 1976[a]	1. Mechanical engineering 2. Food & drink 3. Agriculture, forestry & fishing		1. Metals 2. Mining etc. 3. Electrical engineering		1. Mechanical engineering 2. Chemicals etc. 3. Mining etc.	
Unemployment average, 1976	154.4		78.1		101.3	
Redundancies occurring[b] ('expected' figures in brackets)						
1976–9	109.4	(67.7)	51.0	(30.9)	69.0	(45.3)
1980	57.2	(45.3)	45.2	(27.3)	33.3	(29.9)
1981	58.8		36.4		40.1	
Unemployment average, 1981[c]	307.2		157.5		203.4	
Increase in unemployment, 1976–81	152.8		79.4		102.1	
Decrease in employment, 1976–81[d]	144.0		81.0		125.0	

Note: a. Census of Employment; leading industries by employment, Order Totals I–XIX.
b. Series ES955 of Manpower Services Commission.
c. For percentage rates, see Table 8.2.
d. Mid-year data; 1981 are provisional from *Employment Gazette*, vol. 90, no. 1 (1982), Table 1.5.

industry in proportion to its share of national employment in the industry at the start of the period (see also Chapter 8 for fuller documentation and comparisons). It will be seen that redundancies occurring exceeded the 'expected' figures in all the cases which are shown here. We saw in Chapter 3 that the relationship of redundancies to unemployment is normally complex; the overall picture provided by the table to 1981 must be treated with care. However, there is a close numerical relationship between the increase in unemployment and the estimated decreases of employment to 1981. These three parts of GB suffered such bad conditions that their total employees in employment declined by seven per cent in Scotland, eight per cent in Wales and ten per cent in the Northern Region by mid-1981.

Scotland

'The student of the Scottish economy is immediately presented with inconsistencies' (Warren, 1972[24]). This was still true ten years later, after the rise and fall of Scottish nationalism. On the one hand, Scotland's performance fell below expectations from 1976 to 1979; on the other hand, and somewhat remarkably by historical standards, in 1980 and 1981 employment fell only at the GB national rate. 'The indications are that the Scottish economy, while experiencing its share of the national recession, has not so far been disproportionately affected' (Scottish Economic Bulletin, Summer 1981[25]). Favourable factors included growth of employment in North Sea oil, and the volume of employment in electronics and the service sector (the last held up surprisingly well). Unfavourable factors included the spread of difficulties to large parts of the mechanical engineering industry, in addition to the troubles of textiles, shipbuilding and metals. Mechanical engineering is Scotland's leading industry (Table 5.3). It was also the leading source of redundancies in each year 1976 to 1979, contributing heavily to the 109.4 thousand redundancies occurring, well above the 67.7 thousand to be expected from the national distribution of job losses between industries. Even including North Sea oil, Scottish industrial production failed to grow at all between 1975 and 1979,[26] and by the end of 1980 it had fallen by ten per cent, chiefly in metal manufacturing, engineering and textiles. In previous decades regional policy and other factors had brought 280 overseas-owned manufacturing units into Scotland, representing 17 per cent of the country's factory employment at mid–1980.[27] It is imperative to ask whether foreign corporations behaved any differently from British ones in the recession.

The spatial distribution of features of manufacturing employment change is unusually well documented for Scotland.[28] From mid–1976 to mid–1980, manufacturing employment declined by an average of ten per cent (eight per cent from mid–1979 to mid–1980). Net job loss was widespread. It involved all administrative Regions, listed in Table 5.1, except the Borders and the Islands. It was fairly high in the Grampian and Highland Regions (nine per

Table 5.4: Job Losses in the Strathclyde Region of Scotland; the Largest Cases Reported in the *Financial Times*, October 1976 to October 1981

Organisation	Jobs Lost	Category[a] and month of report
Talbot UK (Peugeot)*	9,000	Linwood, R Nov. '79, R May '80, C Feb. '81
British Steel Corp.	6,500	Glasgow, C Oct. '77; Glengarnock, C Nov. '78; North Lanarkshire, R '77, '78, '79, '80
Singer (UK)* (sewing-machines)	4,800	Clydebank, C Nov. '79, R & W before
British Shipbuilders	3,300	Glasgow, P Aug. '79; Greenock, R Nov. '78, P Aug. '79
Birmingham Sound Reproducers	2,700	East Kilbride, P Nov. '79, C June '80
Massey-Ferguson* (harvesters)	1,500	Kilmarnock, C Nov. '78
Coats, Patons (thread, etc.)	1,350	Paisley, R Nov. '80, Nov. '81; Irvine, C Nov. '78
Burroughs Corporation* (computers)	1,200	Cumbernauld, R Nov. '80, Jan. '81, June '81
BL (British Leyland)	1,100	Hillington, C June '79; Glasgow, R Jan. '80, Nov. '81
Hoover* (washing-machines)	1,000	Hamilton and Carfin, C Sept. '78; Cambuslang, R March '81, Nov. '81

Note: a. C (Closure); P (Partial closure); R (Redundancy); W (reported Wastage).

* Foreign-owned firms.

cent), reflecting a downturn in oil-related manufacturing such as rig building. The net loss was proportionately smallest in Edinburgh and surrounding Regions (Lothian, Central and Fife). These figures pre-date redundancies at BL (Vehicles) in Lothian and British Aluminium at Invergordon in the Highland Region in early 1982.

Most striking was a 15 per cent decline in the large Region of Strathclyde which included losses of 18 per cent in engineering. Large job losses in this Region are separately listed in Table 5.4. Here is evidence of intense difficulty in the metal industries, both those of publicly-owned British corporations and those of no less than five foreign-owned corporations. Only one of the firms listed (Coats, Patons) lies outside the metals sector. The same firm is the only one with a Scottish headquarters; of course, if we extended the list to smaller cases it would include several traditional engineering groups and other factories still in local ownership, in which an 'appreciable weakness' was seen in the last economic study of the area.[29] Clearly, however, foreign investment in Strathclyde has not protected it from recession. In particular, foreign acquisition of the Linwood motor-car factory failed to save it. The closure of this plant contributed directly to Strathclyde's end–1981 unemployment rate of 16.9 per cent (186,100). Unfortunately, this Region had only 2,500 of the total 47,900 jobs in Scotland in companies wholly related to the North Sea oil industry,[30] and was probably less protected than Edinburgh by service employment.

The outlook seemed bleak for much of the Scottish population as 'high unemployment is likely to be with us for a considerable period of time whichever policies are pursued and regardless of their success' (The Fraser of Allander Institute, October 1981[31]).

Wales

The Welsh economy is less than half the size of Scotland's but is much more dependent on its two leading employers, the National Coal Board and the British Steel Corporation. This raises acutely the question of the nature and possible co-ordination of decision-making in the publicly-owned sector of the economy. 'After 1957/8, for instance, regional policy was left to "pick up the pieces" of the NCB's policy of contraction in the "development area"' (Morgan[32]). From 1965 to 1975 mining employment in Wales dropped from 94,000 to 42,000[33] (it declined by only a further 7,000 to end–1981). It was then the turn of the metal manufacturing industries to experience a similar drop, from 80,000 in mid–1976 to 39,000[34] at end–1981 (57,000 to 25,000 in BSC).[35] Remarkably much of this last was not even decided until late–1979 (cf. Chapter 4). Till then the overall Welsh Index of Industrial Production had almost kept up with that of the UK, 1975–9.[36] Then occurred 'the biggest restructuring of an industry in the country in the time taken'.[37] A final decision to close the Shotton Steel Works in Clwyd, North Wales (Table 5.1), gave this formerly fairly prosperous County the highest unemployment rate in Wales (17.9 per cent at end–1981). Most accounts agree that Gwent and West Glamorgan in South Wales were lucky to keep both their large modernised steelworks, at Llanwern and Port Talbot respectively, when their joint employment was cut by 11,300, successfully from the point of view of productivity.[38] In 1980, therefore, Wales sustained much more than its share of BSC job losses, and the total of redundancies occurring in all sectors (45,200, Table 5.3) approached twice the 'expected' level based upon its industrial structure.

Was the Steel Corporation the sole origin of job losses? The private steel industry suffered serious blows when Duport Steel abandoned an old plant in West Glamorgan (1,000 jobs in 1978) and a modern plant in Dyfed (1,600 jobs at Llanelli in 1981, Table 5.1), following reductions by GKN at Cardiff (over 1,000) and Wrexham. The private aluminium industry reduced its capacity in West Glamorgan. In other sectors, Courtaulds cut over 2,000 jobs in old and new works in Clwyd, and there were more closures in English and American branch factories in 1980–1, both in the South Wales valleys and in rural counties; an example in the GKN group is seen in Powys, 1981. In 1977, 16 per cent of manufacturing jobs were in plants owned by non-UK corporations.[39] The most important of these, Ford, continued development at Bridgend, but the second foreign employer, Hoover, reversed its expansion plans at Merthyr Tydfil (Table 5.1).

Regional policy was clearly overwhelmed in a wide range of areas. The government did upgrade the levels of assistance available in the worst-hit areas,[40] establish an Enterprise Zone in Swansea and accelerate the building of factories by its Welsh Development Agency. But they rejected[41] unanimous proposals of the Commons Select Committee on Welsh Affairs that new policies of saving existing jobs were essential to meet the crisis conditions of 1980.[42] They did, however, bow to miners' demands for the shelving of closures in the coal industry, where the Coal Board had seen the need for eventually closing 20 of the 35 remaining South Wales collieries.[43] The very high rate of redundancy in Wales fell off in the second half of 1981 (Table 5.3), and Welsh industrial production increased by one per cent in 1981 over 1980; but it was clearly a difficult if not impossible task to rebuild the Welsh economy to its former level of activity.

The Northern Region of England

This Region sustained the highest rates of unemployment in mainland Britain throughout our five years of study. It is not therefore surprising that it had the greatest proportion of long-term unemployed (Chapter 10) and the smallest proportion of men aged over 59 at work in any Region. In some ways the area may be seen to combine some of the worst features of both Scotland and Wales – the difficulties of engineering and shipbuilding, 1976–9, and sharp de-manning in the Steel Corporation in 1980–1. As in Scotland, gross domestic product and personal disposable incomes in the Region had grown in the early 1970s at a faster rate than the national average. 'In 1976, however, there was a turning point'[44] and from then on, as in Scotland, total regional output was almost static and the Regional share of national manufacturing investment declined. Redundancies were greater than 'expected' (see Table 5.3); they were headed by mechanical engineering in 1976, 1977 and 1978, and by shipbuilding in 1979. On Tyneside several important old firms engaged in major rationalisations each involving over 1,000 workpeople; these included Parsons (turbine generators), Vickers (heavy engineering and armaments) and the nationalised firms in merchant shipbuilding, marine engine building and ship-repairs. This period also demonstrated the vulnerability of the typical industries, in clothing and electrical engineering, brought to the area under post-war regional policy; Montague Burton closed several tailoring factories in Sunderland and Gateshead; Plessey closed a large telecommunications factory in Sunderland, and GEC reduced employment heavily at Hartlepool (Cleveland), which also saw the abandonment of the Region's last effort in building oil rigs. In County Durham and Cumbria the largest closures were those of Courtaulds (Spennymoor 1979; Carlisle and Workington 1980) until British Steel's closure programme took full effect.

Iron and steel was the leading source of job losses in 1980 and 1981, as might be predicted from national data (although the volume of losses was smaller than in Wales). The closure of the works at Consett, Co. Durham, rightly caught the interest of the media because of the isolation of the town (its problems were accentuated by the closure of a modern ball-bearing factory shortly afterwards). Less obviously, almost as many jobs were lost in a series of partial closures at Workington (Cumbria). The Cleveland works suffered over 11,000 job losses from a great variety of decisions (Table 5.1). In Cleveland capital investment had been a notable feature of both the steel industry and ICI, and had given the area an image of economic growth since the war. From 1979[45] it became clear that a lower rate of product development in ICI would be accompanied by more definite efforts to reduce the size of the workforce, including new measures of automation and managerial redundancy. This complex of factors was sufficient to give the County the highest unemployment rate of mainland Britain (18.7 per cent) at end-1981.

In April 1982 British Rail *proposed* the closure of Shildon Works, Co. Durham, with 2,200 staff. One by one then both the historic landmarks of the Region's technological evolution and the growth sectors of post-war planning fell prey to the reduction of employment. The Region's most rapid 'growth-point', Washington New Town, lost over 2,000 jobs in one year of recession conditions alone.[46] The Region's latest plan, the Northern Region Strategy,[47] lay statistically in ruins and rejected by the Conservative government.[48] Many efforts were still being made to stimulate small business and community enterprise, but the principal determinants of future unemployment figures were seen to lie in rates of migration, economic participation and registration for benefit; an unemployment figure of 275,000 (19 per cent)[49] was suggested for 1991 by the County Councils of the Region.

Conclusion

The profile of recession in these five areas is profoundly depressing from the point of view of people's employment. National recession aggravated already deep-seated difficulties in all cases, but added to them the withdrawal of post-war, externally controlled plants. At the end of 1981 there were still in these poorest Regions significant labour-market areas with less than the national (UK) average rate of unemployment – Aberdeen, Perth, Edinburgh, Carlisle and Barrow-in-Furness.[50] By and large, however, the structural difficulties of these five major areas of the UK were clearly asserted in this period. Beyond this, Table 5.3 showed that Scotland, Wales and the Northern Region had performed worse than structural conditions alone would lead one to predict. The balance of forces, as shown by leading job losses, varied between areas. Post-war 'branch factories' were of predominant importance in job loss in

Merseyside and Northern Ireland, the old nationalised industries in Wales and the North. Shipbuilding affected four of the areas (Northern Ireland, Merseyside, Scotland and the North), but perhaps less than was feared at one time. The problems of heavy engineering after the 1974–5 recession were present in two Regions (Scotland and the North). More rapid rationalisation of steel plants seriously affected Wales, the North and Scotland (in that order). All areas suffered from the withdrawal of investment by large corporations; the following were all involved in job losses in *two or more* of the five areas: BICC, BL, BP, British Shipbuilders, British Steel, Courtaulds, Dunlop, GEC, GKN, Hoover, ICI, Metal Box, Monsanto, the National Coal Board and Unilever. The role of foreign corporations was marked in the case of Strathclyde. The place of post-war investments in the recession is a subject deserving further analysis in Chapter 9.

In spatial policy all five areas received some recognition in the shape of Enterprise Zones, in Belfast, Liverpool (Speke), Clydebank (including the Singer Works site), Swansea, Newcastle/Gateshead and Hartlepool. Newcastle/Gateshead and Liverpool had Inner City 'partnership status'. The collective political force of our five areas was however greatly reduced from the days of the mid-1970s debates on devolution for Wales and Scotland, though possession by these countries of their own Secretaries of State and Development Agencies was of some significance. The inner city riots of Liverpool (July 1980) and continuing tensions in Ulster were both political stimuli to action and disincentives to investment. In some ways the most forgotten area of difficulty was the Northern Region. As the poorest Region of England it was left with no plan and no Minister with special interest in it; the scale and irreversibility of employment change were the occasion of stunned political silence.

Notes

1. J.W. House (ed.), *The UK Space, Resources, Environment and the Future*, 2nd edn. (Weidenfeld & Nicholson, London, 1977).
2. G. Manners, D. Keeble, B. Rodgers and K. Warren, *Regional Development in Britain* (Wiley, London, 1972).
3. G. McCrone, *Regional Policy in Britain*, 1st edn. (Allen & Unwin, London, 1969), p. 127.
4. Central Statistical Office, *Regional Trends* (HMSO, London, 1982), p. 150.
5. A.R. Townsend, 'Geographical Perspectives on Major Job Losses in the

UK, 1977–80', *Area*, vol. 13, no. 1 (1981), pp. 31–38.

6. Report of an Inquiry by the Rt. Hon. The Lord Scarman, *The Brixton Disorders, 10–12 April, 1981*, Cmd. 8427 (HMSO, London, 1981), p. 16.

7. P. Taylor and R. Johnston, 'Britons shall be Ruled', *Geographical Magazine*, vol. 53, no. 14 (1981), p. 898.

8. Selection of the largest case in a given area requires consistency. Major and minor job losses are in some reports grouped together, while in other cases they are not; the difference may be due simply to the nature of production or the style and politics of decision-making. We have summed the different reports in the same organisation in the five years period of study. Similarly, job losses in adjoining plants of the same organisation, or at plants in adjoining labour market areas, may have effectively the same impact as the single large case in one building. Therefore, in the preparation of Table 5.1, these different cases were also summed before identification of the largest case as an entry.

9. *Financial Times*, 9 June 1980.

10. P. McDonagh, *Industrial Development Policy and Employment Prospects for Northern Ireland*, paper presented to the Annual Residential Conference of the Regional Studies Association, Manchester, 8–9 July 1980.

11. *Financial Times*, 20 Aug. 1980.

12. N.J. Gibson and J.E. Spencer, 'Unemployment and Wages in Northern Ireland', *The Political Quarterly*, vol. 52, no. 1 (1981), p. 102.

13. Ibid., p. 107.

14. *Financial Times*, 7 Jan. 1981.

15. *Financial Times*, 17 March 1982.

16. R. Rowthorn, 'Northern Ireland; an Economy in Crisis', *Cambridge Journal of Economics*, vol. 5, no. 1 (1981), pp. 1–31.

17. Gibson and Spencer, 'Unemployment and Wages in Northern Ireland', p. 113.

18. P.E. Lloyd and C.M. Mason, 'Industrial Movement in North West England: 1966–1975', *Environment and Planning A*, vol. 11, no. 12 (1979), p. 1374.

19. Department of the Environment, *Change or Decay, Final Report of the Liverpool Inner Area Study* (HMSO, London, 1977), pp. 100–4.

20. P.E. Lloyd, 'The Components of Change for Merseyside Inner Area', *Urban Studies*, vol. 16, no. 1 (1979), pp. 45–60.

21. A. Lane, *What future for Merseyside?*, paper presented to the Annual Residential Conference of the Regional Studies Association, 8–9 July 1980.

22. 'Distribution and Concentration of Industrial Stoppages in Great Britain', *Department of Employment Gazette*, vol. 84, no. 11 (1976), p. 1221.

23. *Census 1981 Preliminary Report* (HMSO, London, 1981).

24. K. Warren, 'Scotland', in Manners, Keeble, Rodgers and Warren, *Regional Development in Britain*, p. 390.

25. The Scottish Office, *Scottish Economic Bulletin* No. 23 (HMSO, Edinburgh, 1981), p. 3.

26. Ibid., p. 33.

27. Ibid., p. 6.

28. Ibid., p. 21.

29. West Central Scotland Plan, *Supplementary Report 1, The Regional Economy* (West Central Scotland Plan, Glasgow, 1974), p. 317.

30. Scottish Office, *Scottish Economic Bulletin*, no. 23, p. 22.

31. The Fraser of Allander Institute, *Quarterly Economic Commentary*, vol. 7, no. 2 (University of Strathclyde, October, 1981), pp. 25–6.

32. K. Morgan, *State Regional Interventions and Industrial Reconstruction in Post-war Britain: the Case of Wales*, a paper presented to the Conference of Socialist Economists, May 1980.

33. *Department of Employment Gazette*, vol. 84, no. 8 (1976), pp. 839–50.
34. *Employment Gazette*, vol. 90, no. 4 (1982), Table 1.5.
35. *Financial Times*, 6 July 1981.
36. Welsh Office, *Welsh Economic Trends*, no. 7 (HMSO, Cardiff, 1980), p. 47.
37. P. Allen, Steel Products Group Director, British Steel Corporation, *Financial Times*, 6 April 1981.
38. *Financial Times*, 6 April 1981.
39. Welsh Office, *Welsh Economic Trends*, no. 7, p. 53.
40. Townsend, 'Geographical Perspectives on Major Job Losses in the UK, 1977–80', p. 36.
41. *Financial Times*, 1 Dec. 1980.
42. *Financial Times*, 28 July 1980.
43. *Financial Times*, 28 July 1980.
44. North of England County Councils Association, *Third State of the Region Report*, 1981, p. 12.
45. *Financial Times*, 18 May 1979.
46. Sources as for Table 9.2 below.
47. Northern Region Strategy Team, *Strategic Plan for the Northern Region*, 7 vols. (1977).
48. A.R. Townsend, 'The North – Where Now?', *Planner News* (November 1979), p. 12.
49. North of England County Councils Association, *Third State of the Region Report, 1981*, pp. 17–18.
50. Labour market areas of principal towns as presented in *Employment Gazette*, vol. 90, no. 1 (1982), Table 2.4. Aberdeen and Barrow-in-Furness owe their position to investment in oil development and naval shipbuilding respectively. Perth, Edinburgh and Carlisle are predominantly service centres.

6 RECESSION IN THE 'MANUFACTURING HEARTLAND'

Four Regions were more dependent than any others on manufacturing before the recession, and therefore felt its impact the most sharply in 1980. These Regions were the North West, Yorkshire and Humberside, the East Midlands and the West Midlands, each with more than a third of its workers in manufacturing in 1978.[1] After excluding Merseyside (already considered, but part of the North West), all of them sustained unemployment levels at or below the national average from 1976 to 1979. They then experienced (from mid–1979 to mid–1980) more rapid rates of increase in unemployment than any other Regions. In 1981 the East Midlands none the less remained below the national average, but the West Midlands had higher unemployment rates than Scotland – an unprecedented situation since records began, but one directly connected with its extremely high dependence on manufacturing industry.

The grouping of these four Regions in this chapter is based on their collective experience of recession, but has little precedent in the literature. Previous regional analyses commonly divided the UK into two, the 'assisted areas' and the rest. There was reason for this in terms of their different unemployment levels and regional policy status. More recently, Taylor and Thwaites presented work on *Technological Change and the Segmented Economy*,[2] in which they see 'Development Areas' receiving new technology through their corporate sector from 'non-assisted areas', and transmitting it to smaller firms only through weak intra-regional trading relationships. In the 'non-assisted areas' there are much stronger trading relationships and subcontracting between corporations and small firms, and the corporate sector is more open to the import of foreign new technology. This model reminds us, in this chapter and Chapter 7, that recession in large plants may be transmitted to smaller firms in the same Region through trading linkages, a familiar situation in the West Midlands motor components industry. Taylor and Thwaites, however, are clear that areas *between* the South East and the Development Areas combine some of the characteristics of the two extremes. Here we go further. Our four Regions are presented together because of common characteristics. They enjoyed more continuous diversification and technical change than the poorest Regions before and after the depression of the 1930s, particularly in developing lighter and more varied forms of mechanical engineering. For much of the post-war period their main centres were short of labour; they attracted Commonwealth immigrants to their working population[3] and exported 'mobile industry' to areas of higher unemployment (this applied to Greater Manchester and West Yorkshire as well as the Midlands[4]).

However, with hindsight we can see a broad 'southward spread' of difficulties into this overall area. 'North-East Lancashire' and 'South Lancashire' were made Development Areas from the late 1940s; other coal-mining areas of our four Regions and some agricultural towns received branch-plant investment from adjoining cities and conurbations. Small areas of Yorkshire and Humberside and the East Midlands qualified as 'assisted areas' from 1958. As a result of the Hunt Report (1969)[5] which recognised that the whole of the North West and Yorkshire and Humberside were suffering from slow economic growth and a poor environment, these two Regions were given the status of assisted 'Intermediate Areas' from 1972 to 1982. (So too were some adjoining coalfield areas of the East Midlands, though Stoke-on-Trent and North Warwickshire, the areas considered in the West Midlands, were not). The 1974–5 recession caused much concern over employment in a range of industries in these Regions, notably Yorkshire woollens and West Midlands motor cars. The West Midlands increasingly sought different treatment from the South East under the industrial location controls of regional policy.[6]

The four Regions together contained nearly half of Britain's manufacturing employment in the late 1970s. It is hardly surprising that the severe national recession in manufacturing made heavy inroads into their industrial base, especially in view of some characteristics identified in Table 6.1. Textiles were still, despite much rationalisation and industrial diversification, the leading industry of three of the Regions, the North West, Yorkshire and the East Midlands (which were the focus of important research on closures in the industry, 1967–72, by Healey[7]). Mechanical engineering, an industry in great national difficulties, stood among the 'leading three industries' in all four, and vehicle production was important in two (the West Midlands and the North West). Yet

Table 6.1 Profile of Recession, 1976–81, in Four Regions of England; Data in thousands

	North West (incl. Merseyside)		Yorkshire & Humberside		East Midlands		West Midlands	
Leading industries, 1976[a]	1. = Textiles 1. = Vehicles 3. Mechanical engineering		1. Textiles 2. Metals 3. Mechanical engineering		1. Textiles 2. Mechanical engineering 3. Mining etc.		1. Vehicles 2. Miscellaneous metal goods 3. Mechanical engineering	
Unemployment average, 1976	197.0		114.9		73.6		133.1	
Redundancies occurring[b] ('expected' figure in brackets)								
1976–9	138.6	(89.9)	60.8	(69.5)	28.6	(56.6)	50.9	(78.8)
1980	92.6	(67.6)	50.9	(54.6)	41.0	(40.7)	69.4	(71.5)
1981	91.7		63.1		33.7		59.6	
Unemployment average, 1981[c]	390.1		254.2		164.8		313.1	
Increase in unemployment, 1976–81	183.1		139.3		91.2		180.0	
Decrease in employment, 1976–81[d]	212.7		146.5		54.8		208.1	

Note: a. Census of Employment, leading industries by employment, Order Totals I–XIX.
b. Series ES955 of Manpower Services Commission.
c. For percentage rates, see Table 8.2.
d. Mid-year data; 1981 are provisional from *Employment Gazette*, vol. 90, no. 1 (1982), Table 1.5.

from 1976 to 1979 reported redundancies, except in the North West, were actually lower than 'expected' from the industrial structure of employment in each Region, and in many areas heavy redundancies were unknown. A sudden change occurred in 1980. The rate of redundancies increased more than fourfold in the East and West Midlands (see Table 6.1): Greater Manchester, West Yorkshire and Lancashire were among the seven counties of Britain with the highest rates of increase in unemployment.[8] In actual fact the experience of redundancy in the East and West Midlands and in Yorkshire and Humberside was closely in line with their 'expected' figures for 1980 (data in brackets, Table 6.1); that is to say that the national industrial structure of employment decline, described in Chapter 3, provides a broadly sufficient explanation of the incidence of job losses in these Regions. It is certainly true that by 1981 all the four Regions' traditional complexes of manufacturing activity had experienced serious reductions in activity, whether their basic ownership pattern was concentrated in corporations or small firms. Examples which will arise in our text below include the East Midlands' hosiery industry, Sheffield steel, North Staffordshire pottery, and West Yorkshire and Kidderminster carpets. By 1982 the industrialists of three of the Regions had found common cause in making joint representation over the Budget. In the first combined statement of its kind, the Chairmen of the Confederation of British Industries' North West, Yorkshire and Humberside and West Midlands Regions referred to their joint share of officially recorded redundancies, and the critical dependence of the three Regions on manufacturing.[9]

North West England (see also Merseyside, Chapter 5)

North West England did even worse throughout this period (1976–81) than its industrial structure would lead us to expect. This continued the established pattern of the 1970s:

> The North West is shown to have had a structural predisposition toward decline at the beginning of the decade . . . but, in the event, it is poor performance that emerges as the major cause of the region's decline from 1971 to 1977.
>
> Lloyd and Reeve, 1982[10]

The North West has the second largest regional economy of Britain, with nearly all branches of manufacturing industry represented in its maturely diversified structure. However, the small scale of its iron and steel industry offset the weight of textiles and clothing (seven per cent of 1976 employment) to give (in Table 6.1) 'expected' figures of redundancies which were no worse, as a proportion of employees in employment, than for the other Regions considered in this chapter. The differences lay in performance, which was systematically worse in nearly all sectors. For instance, 1980 redundancies in textiles were well above the 'expected' total of 14,300 (which itself derives from the detailed industrial structure biased towards cotton and artificial fibres). In that year recorded redundancies in virtually all 17 non-manufacturing categories exceeded expectations. Provisional estimates for mid-1981 showed an 8.1 per cent decline in total employment since mid-1976, compared with a national reduction of 6.0 per cent.[11] The difference was widely spread in its industrial origins, but it included a reduction of 26.9 per cent (53,100 jobs) in textiles, leather and clothing, and could not be accountable chiefly to changes in Merseyside (Chapter 5).

Textiles and clothing dominate the analysis at the corporate level (Table 6.2). Led by Courtaulds, Tootal, Carrington-Viyella and Vantona large corporations had bought out, rationalised and re-equipped most of the traditional cotton mills of Greater Manchester and Lancashire, and the rationalisation was now intensified. Courtaulds closed both a modern mill at Skelmersdale New Town and the large old Red Scar Works at Preston as part of 5,600 job losses in Lancashire (Table 6.2), exceeding Leyland Vehicles' commercial vehicle job losses of about 3,300 in the Leyland area. There were also extensive job losses in vehicles factories in Cheshire, with the bankruptcy of Fodens, Sandbach (2,500 jobs), and heavy reductions at the Vauxhall car plant at Ellesmere Port (3,000). The same area lost a further 1,600 jobs from the closure of the Bowater paper mill and 1,100 from the closure of the Burmah oil refinery (see also Chapter 9). Despite its image and association with some modern scientific industry and offices, Cheshire had an unemployment level above the national average by 1981.

Greater Manchester's experience of employment decline (Table 6.3) retraces its path of diversification since its early nineteenth-century initiation of world-scale cotton manufacture. 'From its

Table 6.2 Job Losses in the 'Manufacturing Heartland'; the Largest Cases Reported in each County, October 1976 to October 1981

County (see Figure 5.1)	Organisation	Parent organisation	Jobs lost	Category[a] and month of report
North West				
24 Greater Manchester	Tootal (textiles & clothing)	—	2,600	Bolton, Stockport etc., R & C '78, '79, '80, '81
25 Cheshire	Vauxhall (motor cars)	General Motors, USA*	3,000	Ellesmere Port, R Jan. '81
26 Lancashire	Courtaulds	—	5,600	Skelmersdale, C Dec. '76 & Dec. '80; Preston, C Nov. '79; Blackburn, C May '80; Lancaster, C Sept. '80; Nelson, C Sept. '80
Yorkshire & Humberside				
27 South Yorkshire	Hadfields Steelworks	Lonrho Group	4,700	Sheffield, R April '81, W before
28 West Yorkshire	Thorn Electrical Industries (TV sets)	—	2,200	Bradford, C March '78
29 Humberside	British Steel Corporation	—	2,600	Scunthorpe, R April '78, P Dec. '80
30 North Yorkshire	Maensons (clothes)	Waring & Gillow	300	Malton & Scarborough, C '80

East Midlands				
31 Derbyshire	Stanton & Staveley Group	British Steel Corporation	1,400	Stanton (near Ilkeston), R '79; Staveley (near Chesterfield), R '80 & '81
32 Leicestershire	GEC-Marconi (radar etc.)	GEC	600	Leicester, R Sept. '81
33 Lincolnshire	Aveling Barford (construction equipment)	BL (British Leyland)	1,100	Gainsborough, C June '79; Grantham, R June '79
34 Northamptonshire	British Steel Corporation	—	7,700	Corby, R Dec. '77, P Feb. '79, R Sept. '80
35 Nottinghamshire	TI Raleigh Industries	Tube Investments	2,600	Nottingham, R Oct. '79, Sept. '80, Jan. '81, Sept. '81; Worksop, C March '81
West Midlands (Region)				
36 West Midlands	BL (British Leyland)	—	22,000	Coventry, Cas. Bromwich, P Sept. '79; Solihull C May '81, etc.
37 Hereford & Worcs.	Wiggin Alloys	Inco Group, Canada*	750	Hereford, W before July '81
38 Shropshire	GKN Sankey (vehicle parts)	GKN	2,000	Telford, R May '80, Oct. '80, Feb. '81
39 Staffordshire	Josiah Wedgwood (pottery)	—	2,000	Stoke-on-Trent, C, R & W, '79, '80, '81
40 Warwickshire	GEC Machines	The General Electric Co.	1,000	Rugby, W & R since '76

Note: a. C (Closure); P (Partial closure); R (Redundancy); W (reported Wastage).
* Foreign-owned firms.

Source: *Financial Times* reports.

Table 6.3: Job Losses in Greater Manchester Metropolitan County; the Largest Cases Reported in the *Financial Times*, October 1976 to October 1981

Organisation	Jobs lost at known locations (approx)	Category[a] and month of report
Tootal (textiles & clothing)	2,600	Bolton, Stockport, Manchester, Salford, R & C '78, '79, '80, '81
ICI (dyestuffs etc.)	2,300	Oldham, C Jan. '77; Blackley, W March '79; Golborne, C March '80
Courtaulds (textiles & clothing)	2,200	Bolton, Rochdale, Oldham, Tameside, Stockport, Manchester, Wigan, R & C Feb., May, Aug. & Sept. '80
J. Myers (mail order)	1,900	Eccles & Stockport, C Aug. '80
Montague Burton (clothiers)	1,500	Oldham, C Aug. '78; Walkden, R May '79, C June '80
Stone-Platt (textile machinery)	1,350	Oldham, C Feb. '80; Bolton, P July '81
Carrington-Viyella (textiles & clothing)	1,300	Rochdale, Oldham, Stockport, Wigan, R & C, '77, '80, '81
Mather & Platt (mechanical engineers)	1,300	Manchester & Radcliffe, R Oct. '79, July '80, July '81
Heinz* (tinned foods)	1,150	Standish (nr. Wigan), C Jan. '79
ICL (computers)	1,000	Dukinfield, C Oct. '79
Greater Manchester Transport	1,000	R Oct. '80
British Rail proposed in April 1982 the closure of Horwich Works with 1,400 workers)		

Note: a. C (Closure); P (Partial closure); R (Redundancy); W (reported Wastage).

* Foreign-owned firms.

headquarters in Manchester, Tootal controls over 150 manufacturing centres and around 44,000 employees in all five continents';[12] yet it found it advantageous to cut employment in its home county apparently more than Courtaulds and Carrington-Viyella. The historic production of cotton led to associated production of dyestuffs, clothing, and textile machinery, reflected in Table 6.3 in recent job losses in the modern corporations of ICI, Montague Burton, Mather and Platt (who started in textile machinery) and Stone-Platt (whose more recent efforts at diversification out of textile machinery did not prevent bankruptcy in 1982). Perhaps greater concern was caused by the heavy rationalisation of more modern plants, including computer engineering by ICL at Dukinfield and later at their other factories in Greater Manchester (following the closure of plant at Winsford, Cheshire – 1,800 jobs), and of a number of large plants (some foreign-owned) in the Trafford Park Industrial Estate. The Estate was included in a government Enterprise Zone and the Manchester-Salford Inner City 'Partnership Area'. The Metropolitan County forecast for its area as a whole a decrease of perhaps 90,000 manufacturing jobs by 1991, following an estimated reduction of 41 per cent, from 641,000 to 375,000 between 1966 and 1981[13] – partly offset by a 24 per cent increase of service employment (Manchester is, after all, on several measures Britain's second city). But service employment was not thought to have increased after 1977, and by 1981 unemployment rose clearly above the national level:

> Change at a faster rate than at any other time in memory has been the main feature of the Greater Manchester economy in the past two years, with most of the developments proving decidedly unfavourable. Within that timescale, as one county official notes, trends that had been taking place over a long period such as the shift out of manufacturing, have been greatly accelerated with very serious consequences for employment. And where, until 1977 at least, much of the shake-out from industry was being accommodated by the steady growth of service jobs, this pattern too has been transformed.
>
> R. David, September 1981[14]

Yorkshire and Humberside

This Region was commonly thought to share relatively few interests and trends between its component parts. West Yorkshire and South Yorkshire, with their traditional specialisation respectively in woollen textiles and special steels, had little in common with each other, with the port interests of Humberside, or with the service centres and agricultural areas of North Yorkshire. Soon after its formation the Yorkshire and Humberside Economic Planning Council (1966)[15] noted that if there was a common thread in the Region's economic problems it lay in 'the comparatively slow rate of industrial growth'. Mining and textiles had been reducing labour at less than the national rate, and this contributed to lower unemployment rates than in North West England. Increasingly, from the late 1960s however, the government recognised (through decisions to upgrade 'assisted areas') that there were distinct economic problems in parts of Humberside and South Yorkshire, and industry reported growing problems in textiles and steel. On the other hand, unemployment in mid-1979 remained well below the national average in the large labour-market areas of Leeds, Sheffield, Huddersfield, Halifax and York.

The impact of recession in the Region was no smaller for being delayed, much of it until 1981. From Table 6.1 we would expect a severe impact on a Region specialising at large in textiles, metals and mechanical engineering. Between 1976 and 1980 inclusive, recorded redundancies occurring did not attain the levels (shown in brackets) 'expected' from its structure, but the Region was somewhat unusual in having appreciably more redundancies in 1981 than in 1980. This was due to the occurrence of over 10,000 redundancies in steel in four months, including those shown on Table 6.2 in British Steel, Scunthorpe and in the Lonrho Group, Sheffield. The Steel Corporation had gradually engaged in rationalisation and intensification in the Sheffield/Rotherham area (with the loss of over 1,600 jobs), but was also accused of instigating through subsidised price competition the heavy reductions in the Lonrho Group (Hadfields),[16] and at a rolling mill of Johnson and Firth Brown (a loss of 1,250 jobs).[17] Appreciable unemployment as a new feature in Sheffield was documented by Walker, who also pointed to some of the surviving contrasts within the same county: 'If the prospects for recovery in the skilled industrial centre of South Yorkshire are bleak, those of the long-devastated areas of Dearne and Rotherham are utterly depressing.[18]

Textiles were the Region's main source of redundancies in each year 1976–80, except for the closure of Thorn's colour television factory in Bradford in 1978 (see Table 6.2). Many firms had engaged in productivity improvements and rationalisation but these proved insufficient to meet the impact of competition from the EEC in woollens, and from the USA in the sale of tufted carpets.

Although public companies are responsible for over half the industry's output none of these is of major size. Redundancies were widely spread between a variety of plants and towns in West Yorkshire; the worst was the withdrawal of Associated Weavers from carpet production at its Bradford factory, with the loss of 1,000 jobs. About the same number was lost from successive reductions by Montague Burton at its Leeds clothing factories. A detailed published record of all redundancy reports for West Yorkshire[19] confirms that most of the job losses occurred in batches of 200 or less. A similar record calculates 'job gains' from all press reports of positive changes. It shows, for example, that nearly 8,000 jobs disappeared in engineering over 18 months (September 1979 to May 1981), and only 1,000 'job gains' could be set against them. Taking reports for all industries together, the County Council calculated an approximate 'job replacement ratio'. This fell from 0.89 in 1977 to 0.16 in 1980, before rising to 0.37 in the first nine months of 1981.[20] All in all the Council's provisional estimates of net employment change showed a loss of 90,000 jobs (more than ten per cent) in the three years ending in June 1981. Assuming that most disinvestment in textiles was final, its assessment of prospects in much of the county was pessimistic, and reminiscent of the earlier Hunt Report:

> The County Council has long been concerned at the severity of the building obsolescence affecting much of West Yorkshire. Much of the property released by the recession has little value for industrial use either because of the characteristics of the building (for instance mainly multi-storey, low headroom, numerous pillars, low floor loadings) or vecause of its location (for instance difficult access, limited space for parking and loading) or both. In addition new property tends to be in short supply, particularly in the west of the County where steep slopes and the legacy of industrial development mean that undeveloped flat sites are rare and development costs high.
>
> West Yorkshire County Council, 1981[21]

Four District authorities subsequently banded together in the Yorkshire Textile Area Group for the purposes of site development and mill re-development in areas of textiles decline.[22]

Recent 'green-field' development on Humberside however was not immune from recession. Expansion in the chemicals sector was severely checked. For instance, Laporte at Stallingborough reduced employment by 1,000 and there were many redundancies in different sectors in Hull.[23] The climax was the closure of the fishing industry, with the decision of the port's Fishing Vessel Owners Association to go into liquidation in February 1980. The industry, which gave employment to as many as 8,600 in 1976, blamed the extension of territorial waters on a 200–mile limit and the imposition of international quotas for herring and mackerel.[24] The adjoining large county of North Yorkshire continued, in contrast, to record unemployment levels well below the national average, chiefly it would seem because it had relatively few manufacturing establishments, but also because of the growth of activity on its new Selby coalfield.

In Yorkshire and Humberside, therefore, as in the North West, recession was general to manufacturing areas. It afflicted industries dominated by large corporations and also the general mass of textiles, clothing, engineering and miscellaneous factories of the larger cities. While many towns and cities of the two Regions qualified as 'programme areas' under the Inner Urban Areas Act of 1978, most parts of both Regions, with exceptions, lost their 'assisted area' status as Intermediate Areas in August 1982.[25]

The East Midlands

The East Midlands entered the recession with a recognised history of relative success behind it (Gudgin, 1978).[26] The downturn in the economy was serious in textiles, clothing, footwear and engineering, but the Region did not fare quite as badly as others; its performance was sufficient to contain unemployment levels below the national average in all five constituent counties. Since the war it had been able to overcome the structural difficulty of its dependence on textiles, engineering and mining (still apparent in 1976, Table 6.1). Thus from 1959 to 1975 manufacturing employment expanded by 7.4 per cent and total employment by 10.5 per cent – better than in all Regions except East Anglia and the South West.[27] From 1976 to 1979 there were moderate levels of redundancies chiefly in textiles and mechanical engineering. However, the overall pattern of relative success continued in these years, with somewhat greater proportionate gains in total employment than in the national record.[28] Even when we take the position forward to 1981 there are continuing distinctive features. The expansion of Northampton as a New Town helped to give the Region an increase of 4.8 per cent, 1971–81;[29] again a 'better' record than all Regions except East Anglia and the South West. Population growth and its demands for service employment partly explain the relatively low decrease in employment until mid-1981 (Table 6.1; gains in jobs 1976–9 must be offset against losses 1979–81).

Employment decreased and unemployment increased in the two years 1979–81 by over 100,000, or nearly seven per cent of the working population. Textiles, leather and clothing, with 11 per cent of total employment, suffered an estimated loss of 15 per cent (25,000 jobs). As in West Yorkshire these difficulties were blamed on the failure of the EEC's 'multi-fibre agreement' to contain imports at reasonable and stable levels. Courtaulds Knitwear said that loopholes relating to imports from Mediterranean countries had largely offset the benefits of curbs on imports from the Far East.[30] Losses of jobs were widely spread among small and medium-sized firms in the Leicester and Nottingham hosiery industries and in Northampton footwear. Our 'expected' figure of redundancies in 1980 (Table 6.1) is accurate partly because it takes account of the precise industrial structure of the Region and its concentration of hosiery and footwear production. There were, however, successive redundancies totalling more than 1,100 at Courtaulds' artificial fibres plant near Derby. The Region experienced somewhat more than its share of job losses in iron and steel, with (Table 6.2) the ending of iron and steel production at Corby (Northamptonshire) and market problems for the Steel Corporation's pipe plants at Stanton and Staveley (Derbyshire). In Nottinghamshire heavy losses (over 2,000) were due from the closure of the Chilwell Royal Ordnance Depot, expected early in 1982, following larger reductions, of more than 2,500, in the workforce at various factories of TI-Raleigh, whose sales of bicycles deteriorated badly as from Christmas 1980.[31]

This Region was among those at end–1981 showing a marked slowing in the growth of unemployment; this was associated with a reduction in the flow of job losses in 1981, because textiles redundancies had occurred early within the recession as a whole. More widely, we may compare its experience of recession with some interpretation of its previous success. Gudgin[32] considers that the key factor was the cumulative growth over the post-war years of local firms. In this context we may note the following impression:

> In an area where more than 90 per cent of the companies employ fewer than 200 people, there is some surprise at the relatively low number of bankruptcies, but this is attributed to the ability of smaller companies to adapt quickly to market conditions.
>
> L. Barling, 1981[33]

A second view is that the settlement structure of the area is favourable to economic growth. Greater Manchester, the West Midlands County and other conurbations were thought to suffer some economic difficulties because of the costs to industry of working in a conurbation environment: the East Midlands were seen to gain through containing a greater preponderance of semi-rural and rural sub-regions, which as a national type had proved a generally favourable environment for manufacturing employment growth at least until the mid–1970s.[34,35] It was even recorded that there were systematic differences between East Midlands settlements by size, from the largest category to the smallest.[36] This does not seem to be true in a recession. In the largely rural county of Lincolnshire we find significant job losses in several small towns:

Gainsborough Grantham	Aveling-Barford (BL) (construction equipment)	800, C June '79 300, R June '79
Bourne	Christian-Salvesen (packaging)	300, C Dec. '80
Essendine	Fiat-Allis (UK) (earth-moving equipment)	600, R April '81 C Aug. '81
Stamford Boston Long Sutton	BXL Plastics (BP) Lockwood Foods (canning)	250, C Oct. '80 400, C Dec. '80 600, C June '81

Together with over 1,000 redundancies in the City of Lincoln's engineering industry, these job losses cancel out the whole of the county's net increase of 4,100 manufacturing jobs, 1971–7.[37] It would thus seem that this large rural county provided no advantage for regional performance (though we have already noted a different experience with North Yorkshire).

A third view of the East Midlands, more evident in the financial press,[38] is that its larger corporations, being in diverse sectors, are unlikely to fall into difficulties together. The leading companies of the Region are Rolls-Royce (19,000 employees) and Boots (12,000 in pharmaceuticals), followed by TI-Raleigh, Plessey (telecommunications), Brush (electrical engineering) and John Player (cigarettes).[39] None of these, except TI-Raleigh, had reported difficulties at factories within the Region (despite important redundancies declared by Plessey at Liverpool and Sunderland – Chapter 5 – and others by Rolls-Royce near Coventry etc. It is true that Rolls-Royce had serious financial difficulties in 1971 and expected significant job losses in the years after 1981).. The aerospace and pharmaceuticals industries were exceptions to the general nature of industrial recession in 1979–81, but the containment of East Midlands unemployment does seem to be partly attributable to corporate factors.

The West Midlands

'Only a few years ago it was almost inconceivable that, for example, Coventry could replace Tyneside as the unemployment black spot of England; now it is probable. How has this change come about?' (S. Taylor, 1981[40]). The reader will have appreciated from Chapter 3 the growing difficulties of domestic motor vehicle and engineering activity, and from Chapter 4 how these were expressed in the decisions of BL, GKN, Dunlop and Lucas Industries. Here we must assess their joint impact on one of the most specialised manufacturing Regions of the world and its dominant core, the West Midlands Metroplitan County. However, the other counties of the Region did not escape the 1980–1 recession by having mainly different industrial structures.

The West Midlands (County) has in the past generally been considered immune from structural change through its ability to diversify and redevelop within the metal production and using sector of industry. This gave it strong gains in income, industrial employment and total employment, participation rates and net inward migration in the 1950s. But by the period 1960–6 growth was less than would be expected from the area's industrial structure.[41] Wood also detected a decline in productivity compared with other Regions from 1958 onwards; by 1975, when unemployment exceeded the national level, he could write that the 'rising

Table 6.4: Job Losses in West Midlands Metropolitan County: the Largest Cases Reported in the *Financial Times* October 1976 to October 1981[b]

Organisation	Jobs lost at known locations (approx)	Category[a] and month of report
BL (British Leyland)	22,000	Coventry, Cas. Bromwich, P Sept. '79; Solihull, R Jan. '81, C May '81; Longbridge, R March '81, Oct. '81 etc.
GKN (vehicle components etc.)	6,300	Birmingham and Black Country, R & C, '78, '79, '80, '81
Lucas Industries (vehicle components etc.)	?	Birmingham etc., R '80, '81
Birmid Qualcast (castings, motor cylinders etc.)	4,800	Smethwick and Birmingham, R & C, '79, '80
Cadbury-Schweppes (chocolate, tea)	4,300	Birmingham, P Feb. '78, R June '80, W Sept. '80
Rubery Owen (vehicle components etc.)	2,600	Darlaston, R June '79, March '81, C July '81
Talbot (UK)*	2,200	Coventry, R Oct. '80, Nov. '80, Jan. '81
Dunlop (tyres)	2,000	Birmingham, R Dec. '80

Between 1,000 and 2,000 job losses were reported at British Steel Corporation (Bilston), Birmingham Sound Reproducers, Massey-Ferguson (Coventry), Alfred Herbert (Coventry), the Laird Group's Steel Works (West Bromwich), Goodyear Tyre and Rubber (UK) (Wolverhampton), Vono Bedding (Tipton) and Tube Investments (Brierley Hill and Halesowen).

Note: a. C (Closure); P (Partial closure); R (Redundancy); W (reported Wastage).

b. County Council data report the announcement of 12,700 redundancies in the six months, October 1981 to March 1982, including more than 3,000 in BL (British Leyland).

* Foreign-owned firms.

unemployment levels are symptomatic not merely of a temporary "cyclical" setback, but of a much deeper malaise in the regional economy'.[42] BL and Chrysler were given state support, and shed respectively 15,000 and 8,000 jobs by 1977.[43] The years to 1979, however, saw some respite, with a small net growth of employment and recorded redundancies below 'expected' levels (Table 6.1), but with an unprecedented small net loss of population to other Regions.[44]

The Region entered the recession in 1979 still with a greater proportion of its workers than any other in manufacturing (44 per cent) or in the metal producing and using sector (31 per cent). This pattern was enough to give the Region in 1980 the largest number of 'expected' redundancies, per head of all workers, of any Region, a total of 71,500 (Table 6.1). Performance was in fact no better and no worse than this; 15,300 redundancies in motor vehicles exceeded expectations, based simply on its share of national employment in the industry (one-third), but this was offset by other factors, such as the greater variety and sophistication of metal production compared with other Regions. Table 6.4 shows that more identifiable job losses in the Metropolitan County (1976–81) were in the large vehicle assembly plants of BL, with no less than *22,000* out of more than 50,000[45] jobs lost, and Talbot (formerly Chrysler), and in groups involved in the supply of components and tyres (with the exception of Cadbury-Schweppes). The impact on smaller firms and component suppliers was widely appreciated, and the implications for wage-bargaining and the balance of industrial relations were fundamental for trades union officials. The County as a whole suffered nearly a threefold increase in numbers unemployed, from 77,100 at mid-1979 to 221,600 (15.9 per cent) at end-1981, including 81,300 unemployed for more than a year and 28,100 of ethnic minority origin. Papers of the County Economic Development Committee indicated that 'levels of this sort show every sign of becoming permanent and even increasing as the recession deepens',[46] rising to possible levels of 245,000 to 315,000 by end–1983. The same Committee established in 1982 the West Midland Enterprise Board to promote the area abroad, invest in companies and provide suitable factory space;[47] research by Williams[48] had shown that 70 per cent of firms in the Birmingham Inner City Partnership Area had such cramped sites that there was no room for expansion.

There had been only a modest scale of dispersal since the war to the surrounding counties of Staffordshire, Warwickshire, Hereford and Worcestershire and Shropshire. Thus employment decline in these counties had largely separate origins, though GKN was responsible for the largest redundancies in Shropshire at its old-established works now within Telford New Town (Table 6.2). In Worcestershire, Kidderminster shared some of the difficulties of the West Yorkshire carpet industry. A most striking illustration of the effect of exchange-rate problems on an exporting industry occurred in the North Staffordshire potteries: over 2,000 jobs were lost in Josiah Wedgwood's various premises and over 1,000 each in the Royal Doulton Group and Johnson-Richards Tiles. The County's previous largest closure was at the Shelton (Stoke-on-Trent) steelworks, with 1,300 redundancies. Thus unemployment affected all the Region's main population centres; prospects were more uncertain than in the East Midlands, which began to have more in common with the South East (Chapter 7).

Conclusion

The area covered by this chapter is crucial to the future performance of the economy. Precise inter-regional comparisons must await the contrasts evident in Chapter 7 and the national calculations of Chapter 8. It is apparent however that the four Regions are not fully a homogeneous bloc and that their precise boundaries have little to say about labour-market conditions. Even in late 1981 a few of their principal towns (York, Harrogate, Loughborough and Stafford) recorded unemployment rates a third or more below the national average.

All four Regions however illustrate widespread problems from the loss of export competitiveness and the inroads of imports on indigenous industries, despite considerable differences in the ownership structure of industry. Taken as a whole they represent a critical 'hinge area' of the economy around which any recovery in conditions might revolve, and in which General Elections of the 1980s will be decided. The deployment of the 1979 Conservative government's Enterprise Zones allowed one for each of the four areas studied, in Manchester/Salford, the Wakefield District, Corby New Town and Dudley (West Midlands County). That government also neutralised the effects here of regional policy, on the one hand through withdrawing 'assisted area' status from most places which had it in 1979, and on the other through ending 'IDC' controls on the location of industry, the latter in response to a House of Commons debate on West Midlands problems at the end of 1981.[49]

Notes

1. Annual Census of Employment, June 1978; manufacturing employees as a percentage of all employees in employment stood at: North West, 37.7 per cent; Yorkshire and Humberside, 35.6 per cent; East Midlands, 39.1 per cent; West Midlands, 44.7 per cent; Great Britain, 32.0 per cent. *Employment Gazette*, vol. 89, no. 3 (1981), pp. 141–5.
2. M.J. Taylor and A.T. Thwaites, *Technological Change and the Segmented Economy*, paper presented to the Regional Science Association, University of Durham, September 1981.
3. B.E. Coates and E.M. Rawstrom, *Regional Variations in Britain* (Batsford, London, 1971), pp. 134–5.
4. A.R. Townsend, 'The Relationship of Inner City Problems to Regional Policy', *Regional Studies*, vol. 11, no. 4 (1977), pp. 225–51.
5. Report of a Committee under the Chairmanship of Sir Joseph Hunt, *The Intermediate Areas* (HMSO, London, 1969, Cmnd. 3998).
6. P.A. Wood, 'West Midlands Leads the Downward Trend', *Geographical Magazine*, vol. 49, no. 1 (1976), p. 8.
7. M.J. Healey, 'Plant Closures in Multi-Plant Enterprises – the Case of a Declining Industrial Sector', *Regional Studies*, vol. 16, no. 1 (1982), pp. 37–51.
8. A.R. Townsend, 'Planning for the 1980s; Unemployment', *Planning*, vol. 379 (1 Aug. 1980), pp. 6–7.
9. *Financial Times*, 3 March 1982.
10. P.E. Lloyd and D.E. Reeve, 'North West England, 1971–7, A Study in Industrial Decline and Economic Re-structuring', *North West Industry Research Unit*, Working Paper Series, No.11 (School of Geography, University of Manchester, 1981).
11. *Employment Gazette*, vol. 89, no. 10 (1981), Table 1.5.
12. *Financial Times*, advertisement, 30 Sept. 1981.
13. Statistics of Greater Manchester County Council, reported in *Financial Times*, 30 Sept. 1981.
14. R. David, 'Great Pressure on Industry', *Financial Times*, 30 Sept. 1981.
15. Yorkshire and Humberside Economic Planning Council, *A Review of Yorkshire and Humberside* (HMSO, London, 1966), p. 7.
16. *Financial Times*, 23 April 1981.
17. *Financial Times*, 19 Feb. 1981.
18. A. Walker, 'South Yorkshire: The Economic and Social Impact of Unemployment', *Political Quarterly*, vol. 52, no. 1 (1981), p. 82.
19. Report of the County Council's Economic Steering Group, *Economic Trends* (West Yorkshire Metropolitan County Council, Wakefield, 1981), no. 17, p. 11.
20. *Economic Trends* (West Yorkshire Metropolitan County Council, Wakefield, 1981), no. 18, p. 30.
21. Ibid., p. 32.
22. *Financial Times*, 22 Dec. 1981.
23. 'Humberside's Year of the Great Depression', *Hull Daily Mail*, 26 Aug. 1980.
24. *Financial Times*, 21 Feb. 1980.
25. A.R. Townsend, 'Unemployment Geography and the New Government's "Regional" Aid', *Area*, vol. 12, no. 1 (1980), pp. 9–18.
26. G Gudgin, *Industrial Location Processes and Regional Employment Growth* (Saxon House, Farnborough, 1978).
27. S. Fothergill and G. Gudgin, 'Regional Employment Change: a Sub-Regional Explanation', *Progress in Planning*, vol. 12, part 3 (1979), pp. 210–11.

28. *Employment Gazette*, vol. 89, no. 10 (1981), Table 1.5.
29. Office of Population Census and Surveys, *Census 1981 Preliminary Report* (HMSO, London, 1981).
30. *Financial Times*, 23 Jan. 1980.
31. *Financial Times*, 10 Jan. 1981.
32. Gudgin, *Industrial location processes*, p. 298.
33. L. Barling, 'Smaller Concerns Show Remarkable Resilience', *Financial Times*, 13 March 1981.
34. Fothergill and Gudgin, 'Regional Employment Change: a Sub-Regional Explanation', pp. 181–92.
35. D.E. Keeble, 'Industrial Decline, Regional Policy and the Urban-rural Manufacturing Shift in the United Kingdom', *Environment and Planning A*, vol. 12, no. 8 (1980), pp. 945–62.
36. S. Fothergill and G. Gudgin, 'The Components of Rural Growth and Urban Decline in the East Midlands: 1968–75', *Centre for Environmental Studies Working Note* 573 (London, 1979).
37. Annual Census of Employment; unpublished county data supplied by Department of Employment.
38. *Financial Times*, 23 Jan. 1980.
39. *Financial Times*, 13 March 1981.
40. S. Taylor, 'De-industrialisation and Unemployment in the West Midlands', *Political Quarterly*, vol. 52, no. 1 (1981), pp. 64–73.
41. P.A. Wood, *Industrial Britain, The West Midlands* (David & Charles, London, 1976), p. 58.
42. P.A. Wood, 'West Midlands Leads the Downward Trend', p. 2.
43. *Financial Times*, 24 Feb. 1977.
44. West Midlands Planning Authorities' Conference, *A Developing Strategy for the West Midlands, Updating and Rolling Forward of the Regional Strategy to 1991* (West Midlands Regional Study, Birmingham, 1979).
45. Figure summed from data presented in *Financial Times*, 31 Oct. 1979.
46. Paper by the Chairman, Councillor G. Edge, November 1981.
47. *Birmingham Post*, 9 Feb. 1982.
48. H.E. Williams, 'Operating Characteristics of Inner City Firms: Site and Premises', paper presented to Department of Environment Conference on *Industry in the Inner City*, December 1980.
49. Statement to the House of Commons by J. McGregor, Under Secretary for Industry, *Hansard*, 4 December 1981.

7 RECESSION IN THE NORMALLY PROSPEROUS SOUTH

'The economy of the South East is healthy by comparison with the rest of Great Britain, mediocre by comparison with the EEC' (South East Joint Planning Team, 1976[1]). On several measures the South East, with the smaller adjoining Regions of the South West and East Anglia, improved its relative performance during our period of study. From 1977 to 1979 these three Regions, the 'South', showed a much clearer reduction in unemployment levels than others. In 1980 the recession tended to be regarded from London as a provincial affair, and some surveys of unemployment even in 1981 (for instance that by *The Political Quarterly*[2]) deliberately omitted the South. As justification for this, white-collar London commuters, and people in more fortunate sub-regions elsewhere, were affected only late in the recession and in moderate degree.

But by 1981 unemployment had doubled in most places. The South East rate of unemployment in the quarter ending November 1981 (9.0 per cent) was worse than the average for any GB Region in any year 1976 to 1979. Recession exacerbated the contrasts in unemployment, more perhaps than in most other Regions. Outside London, major urban areas in the South such as Southend, Chatham and Plymouth had unemployment above the new high national average, and traditional pockets of weakness, again mainly on the coast, also ranked high statistically as unemployment blackspots. In certain places including New Towns serious setbacks were caused by manufacturing closures. Many local authorities, including the Greater London Council itself, responded by setting up new industrial promotion agencies, much like areas studied in the previous chapter in the 1974–5 recession.

The modern binding link between these three Regions lies in the post-war dispersal to them of population, industry, offices and research activities from London. This dispersal has yet to transform all the sub-regions most remote from London. Net population migration to Cornwall has both co-existed with and contributed to a real unemployment problem;[3] East Anglian planners identified continuing problems for attention in much of Norfolk.[4]

Table 7.1: Profile of Recession 1976–81, in the 'Normally Prosperous' Regions of England; data in thousands

	South East	East Anglia	South West
Leading industries 1976[a]	1. Electrical engineering	1. Agriculture etc.	1. Mechanical engineering
	2. Paper, printing, etc.	2. Food, drink and tobacco	2. Vehicles
	3. Mechanical engineering	3. Mechanical engineering	3. Food, drink and tobacco
Unemployment average, 1976	316.3	33.9	102.9
Redundancies occurring[b] ('expected' figures in brackets)			
1976–9	113.8 (182.8)	13.8 (19.7)	48.9 (43.6)
1980	66.9 (114.4)	7.6 (13.3)	26.6 (26.1)
1981	92.7	11.5	31.0
Unemployment average, 1981[c]	606.5	65.5	166.0
Increase in unemployment, 1976–81	290.1	31.6	63.1
Decrease in employment, 1976–81[d]	306.8	23.5	5.6

Note: a: Census of Employment; leading industries by employment, Order Totals I–XIX.
b: Series ES955 of Manpower Services Commission.
c: For percentage rates, see Table 8.2
d: Mid-year data; 1981 are estimates from *Employment Gazette*, vol. 90, no. 1 (1982) Table 1.5.

Nevertheless, overspill from London has so substantially blurred the formal boundary of the South East Region, both by official schemes such as at Swindon and Peterborough and by the spontaneous migration of people and industry, that the overall trends of all three Regions may best be taken together. On this basis the South shows an estimated gain of 1.1 per cent in population[5] and a 2.0 per cent loss in employment, from 1971 to 1981.[6] These data stand in very different light when we break down this ten-year period. Firstly, employment is seen to decline by 3.6 per cent from mid–1976 to mid–1981 (see also Table 7.1), or 5.1 per cent from mid–1979 to mid–1981. Secondly, a study of the period 1971–9 shows that

> There can be little doubt that population migration within Great Britain during the 1970s was affected by the change in economic circumstances which began at the end of 1973 . . . Figures for transfers suggest that the onset of economic recession marked not only a general reduction in population mobility but also a fundamental change in the pattern of population movements between the various regions of Britain. Population dispersal from South East England, a movement which previously had been increasing in scale, was checked and then began to decline.
>
> A. Ogilvy, 1982[7]

These features were associated with a worsening but still *relatively* healthy economy. Large-scale manufacturing closures were less significant in the economy of the South than elsewhere, partly because of the particular structure of industry by size of establishment, age and product, and partly because of the high ratio of service sector employment. Even so, in 1977 seven southern counties had a greater share of their workers in manufacturing than the national average.[8] The South had more than one-third of GB employment in both shipbuilding and motor vehicles, and nearly half in the aerospace industry.[9] The role of large establishments in these industries meant that one or other of them represented the leading manufacturing industry of no less than 16 of the 22 counties of the South.[10] The building of naval ships, military aircraft and much other defence equipment in the three Regions contributes, along with the location of defence establishments themselves, to their leading national position in regional defence expenditure per head (1974–8[11]). As seen in Chapter 3, the aerospace industry showed little decline in employment before 1981; it does not feature in Table 7.2, although 1981's proposed cuts in naval spending do appear. Motor vehicles show important losses in Bedfordshire and Oxfordshire, as do shipbuilding and repair in Hampshire, Kent and Cornwall. The third element of Table 7.2 is the heavy job losses in colour television factories in East Sussex, Suffolk and Devon; these were all part of what Keeble[12] saw as a remarkable dispersal of industry to coastal areas of higher unemployment, which particularly involved light electrical engineering. The modest size of the largest cases in several counties suggests, however, that recent orderly growth in parts of the South may not have been greatly disturbed.

Table 7.2: Job Losses in the 'Normally Prosperous' Regions of England; the Largest Cases Reported in each County, October 1976 to October 1981

County (see Fig. 5.1)	Organisation	Parent organisation	Jobs lost	Category[a] and month of report
South East England				
41 Greater London	Port of London Authority	—	6,000	R '78, '79, '80, '81
42 Bedfordshire	Vauxhall (vehicles)	General Motors, USA*	3,300	Luton & Dunstable, R&W Jan. '81, June '81
43 Berkshire	Dresser Wayne (pumps)	Dresser Industries, USA*	200	Bracknell, P March '80
44 Buckinghamshire	Scot Meat	Unigate	1,200	Milton Keynes, C Sept. '81
45 East Sussex	ITT (colour TV)	International Telephone & Telegraph*	1,100	Hastings, C July '79: Brighton, R June '81
46 Essex	Ilford (film etc.)	Ciba-Geigy, Switzerland*	2,500	Basildon & Brentwood, C June '80
47/9 Hampshire & IOW	Royal Naval Dockyard	HM Government	6,000	Portsmouth, P June '81
48 Hertfordshire	Plastics Division	ICI	1,100	Welwyn, W April '79; Stevenage, P Nov. '79
50 Kent	Royal Naval Dockyard	HM Government	7,000	Chatham, C June '81
51 Oxfordshire	BL (British Leyland)	—	1,800	MG Abingdon, C July '80; Oxford R Jan. '81, March '81
52 Surrey	Ronson Products (lighters)	Ronson Corporation, USA*	500	Leatherhead, R Aug. '81
53 West Sussex	Deltaflow (taps & mixers)	The Delta Metal Co.	300	Crawley, C Feb. '81
East Anglia				
54 Cambridgeshire	Perkins Engines	Massey Ferguson, Canada*	1,600	Peterborough, R '79, '80, '81
55 Norfolk	Crane Fruehauf (trailers)	Fruehauf Corp., USA*	500	N. Walsham & Dereham, R July '80
56 Suffolk	Philips Industries (colour TV)	Philips, Netherlands*	1,100	Lowestoft, C Oct. '80
South West England				
57 Avon	St. Anne's Board Mill	Imperial Group	1,800	Bristol, C Sept. '80, R&W before
58 Cornwall	Falmouth Ship repairers	British Shipbuilders	900	Falmouth, R May '79
59 Devon	Rank-Toshiba (colour TV)	Joint ownership with Toshiba, Japan*	1,600	Plymouth, R Oct '80
60 Dorset	Kenwood Manufacturing	Thorn Domestic Appliances	300	Weymouth, C Sept. '80
61 Gloucestershire	Babcock Industrial & Electrical Products	Babcock International Engineering	300	Gloucester, C July '81
62 Somerset	Clark, Son & Morland	—	300	Glastonbury, R Dec. '79, April '81
63 Wiltshire	Garrard (record changers)	Gradiente, Brazil*	3,800	Swindon, R&W '77, '78, '80, '81

Note: a C (Closure); P (Partial closure); R (Redundancy); W (reported Wastage).
* Foreign-owned firms. Garrard originated as a British-owned organisation before takeover occurred. Garrard announced in February 1982 the transfer of remaining production to Manaus.

Source: *Financial Times* reports.

Greater London

At the centre of the system, an absolute decline of manufacturing employment predictably continued in Greater London, but as 79 per cent of employees in employment in the area (1976)[13] were already working in other sectors, the recorded unemployment levels stayed well below the national average. Indeed there were complaints of labour shortage as late as 1979 by the London Chamber of Commerce and Industry.[14] The decline of manufacturing employment in the 1960s and early 1970s has been documented by a variety of writers including Keeble,[15] Dennis[16] and Gripaios.[17] Table 7.3 uses new estimates for Greater London to extend the pattern to 1981. The overall trend for 1971 to 1981 describes a decline in employment of 11.4 per cent, compared with one of 10.2 per cent in population. Both Keeble[18] and Dennis[19] noted an improvement in the performance of manufacturing after 1975. Keeble was referring to the South East as a whole; nevertheless, it does seem that manufacturers' statistical returns to the Department of Employment indicate a slowing-down in the rate of decline in the GLC after 1976. If the 1981 provisional figure of

Table 7.3: Greater London Employment Trends, 1971–81, thousands of Employees in Employment, mid-year

	1971	1976	1978	1981	Percent change 1976–81
GLC Manufacturing	1,049	794	769	661	–16.8
GLC Non-manufacturing including	2,890	2,915	2,911	2,828	– 3.0
Distributive trades	525	493	499	456	– 7.5
Financial, professional and miscellaneous services	1,323	1,440	1,455	1,456	+ 1.1
Public administration and defence	334	350	335	319	– 8.9
GLC Total	3,939	3,709	3,680	3,498	– 5.9
Rest of South East, Total	3,308	3,537	3,612	3,451	– 2.4
South East, Total	7,247	7,247	7,292	6,940	– 4.2

Source: 1971–8, Census of Employment; 1981, provisional estimates of employees in employment, June from *Employment Gazette*, vol. 90, no. 4 (1982), Table 1.5.

661,000 is correct, it connotes a rate of decline slightly lower than the national average in the years 1978 to 1981. The use of the financial press cannot clarify this point, because under-reporting is at its worst in this large labour market, with its dense population of small establishments. FT data suggest that some of the largest industrial closures were in West London, with the closure of BL (British Leyland) factories at Southall and Park Royal (3,300 jobs), the Firestone Tire and Rubber Co. at Brentford (1,500) and the United Biscuits factory at Osterley (1,500). The closure of the *London Evening News*, however, cost over 2,000 jobs, and major reductions in the Hackney toy factories of Lesney Products cost 1,000 jobs. The other manufacturing loss of more than 1,000 workers was at the Ford Motor Co., Dagenham (1,300 job losses announced in June 1980[20]); the company later decided on a national reduction of 40 per cent (29,000) in its workforce by 1985,[21] and it seemed likely this must seriously affect the Dagenham factory (which employed 28,000 in 1979).

Many of London's non-manufacturing activities are of national scale and were only slowly and indirectly affected by recession. A number of national manufacturing groups closed or scaled down their office activities in central London. These groups included British Shipbuilders, the British Steel Corporation, ICI, Shell, the Imperial Group, GKN, Unilever, Tube Investments, Blue Circle, W.H. Smith and International Harvester. Several banks reduced recruitment heavily, and the P & O shipping line shed over 1,200 office jobs. Although some of the reductions seem to be token quantities and may not represent a trend of decentralisation, it appeared that industrial and commercial firms were being driven out of central London by high costs, and were being replaced by financial services.[22] The continued employment growth of some financial services in 1976 to 1981 is plain in Table 7.3. This also demonstrates some 'success' for national governments of both parties, and the Conservative administration of the GLC (till 1981), in reducing their own employment in 'public administration and defence' (see Chapter 10). The net effect was to leave a surplus of office accommodation in central London (approx. 2.25m. sq.ft. in the City of London and fringes at mid-1981[23]), though suburban office rents continued to rise strongly, especially in west and south London.

GLC policy and representations to Whitehall had already anticipated many of these changes in the area's economy. In 1976 the Council began to withdraw from its formal overspill agreements with places in surrounding Regions. The Labour government had already substantially rewritten its policy on offices in 1977 before the Conservative government scrapped Office Development Permits in 1979, the Location of Offices Bureau in 1980 and Industrial Development Certificates in 1981. Positive efforts focused on the Docklands Strategic Plan, approved in 1976, the Inner Area 'partnership schemes' of 1978 in Lambeth, Hackney-Islington and the Docklands, the Urban Development Corporation for the Docklands 1980, and the Isle of Dogs Enterprise Zone, 1980. Other initiatives included the GLC's London Industrial Centre, its new employment-drive of 1981, the London Enterprise Agency, and various promotional projects launched by individual London Boroughs. The Port of London Authority represents the largest single source of job losses in the period covered by Table 7.2, and was still engaged at end–1981 on its programme for the closure of docks in London. The average Greater London unemployment rate of 8.6 per cent (at the end of 1981) concealed a great variety of conditions for different socio-economic groups and different areas. The fact that this average unemployment level was as usual slightly lower than the average for the rest of the South East may not be significant (because of the volume of commuting across the GLC boundary); however it is remarkable that between June 1979 and December 1981 the number of unemployed increased (though from a low level) by a factor of 2.5 in both Greater London and the rest of the South East.

The Rest of the South East

At the height of the recession, events in the South East proved that labour market areas with a very good record of post-war growth were not immune from sizeable redundancies and closures. For a while it seemed that the media had found miniature Consetts in places such as Abingdon and Ashford, which suffered respectively the closure of BL's MG factory and British Rail's workshops. On the other hand there was some failure to appreciate the labour market implications of recession in air transport, involving large planned reductions in British Airways' staff, and 1,700 redundancies when Laker Airways (Gatwick) went bankrupt.[24] In all the decline of employment opportunities was unprecedented, and at the end of 1981 there was an average of only one notified employment vacancy for every 17 registered unemployed people in the 49 'travel-to-work areas' outside the GLC area. Viewed in somewhat longer time perspective, Table 7.3 shows however that employment levels in the 'Rest of the South East' showed an estimated overall decline, 1976 to 1981, of only 2.4 per cent (8.9 per cent in manufacturing); employment levels were still growing appreciably here, at least until 1978. There were virtually no reports of the closure of offices in these counties, and manufacturing declined at only about half the GLC area or GB rate.

It is helpful at this point to consider the South East as a whole. The South East Joint Planning Team saw its industrial structure as very similar to that of wealthy European regions.[25] Table 7.1 showed 'expected' levels of redundancies in the South East (including London) which were somewhat lower than in other Regions (relative to the size of the working population). This derives from a number of familiar features of the regional economy – the strong presence of instrument and electronic engineering, the aerospace industry, and printing and publishing, and the marked absence of metal manufacture and textiles. But the record of 'redundancies occurring' stood lower still in 1980. As in previous analyses of other data, industrial structure fails to explain any of the differences in performance between the GLC area and the rest of the Region. For instance, if we apply 1980 national rates of employment losses for individual industries to the structure of (1) the GLC area and (2) the rest of the South East we find virtually no difference in their 'expected' rates of manufacturing job losses. As manufacturing represents a *greater* proportion of all jobs in the 'rest of the South East' than in the GLC area and job losses are as usual *lower* in non-manufacturing sectors, then we would actually expect a higher rate of job losses outside the GLC's area than within it. Clearly this is not what happened; expectations were over-ridden by a continued geographical difference in performance, dictated by the systematic tendency towards a more favourable statistical outcome as a function of distance from inner London. Thus the 'rest of the South East' did better than the GLC's area. In turn there may be differences within the 'rest of the South East'. The Outer Metropolitan Area (a former statistical area which immediately surrounds the GLC) was a national centre of manufacturing growth 1959–66, but appears to show accelerating employment decline since then, and a more rapid growth of unemployment than the GLC area in 1980.[26] By contrast, Dennis has calculated that the

Outer South East showed a significant net manufacturing employment expansion as late as the period January 1976 to January 1980.[27]

Keeble and Hauser[28] had shown that dispersal within the South East was related to a variety of factors including labour supply (as measured by unemployment rates). In other words, industrial development in the South East had partly tended to act as a natural correcting factor to local unemployment. However, the following 'travel-to-work areas' all had unemployment rates above the *national* average at mid-1979: Milton Keynes, Clacton, Southend, Chatham, Sheerness, Margate and Ramsgate. The list was the same at the end of 1981, with the addition of Folkestone, Hastings and the Isle of Wight. Table 7.2 will explain how recession accentuated the problems of some of these areas, for instance Milton Keynes; but there were definite forward problems particularly in Kent and at Portsmouth. Kent already had significant closures of paper-making plants, the Ashford railway workshops and the BP oil refinery on the Isle of Grain (1,700 BP redundancies were announced in mid-1981[29]) even before the announcement in June 1981 of severe cuts in the Navy.[30] A consequence of the proposed loss of 20 warships – as planned before the Falkland Islands invasion, 1982 – was an intended reduction of 15,000 to 20,000 in civilian jobs, mainly the closure by 1984 of the Chatham dockyard and base (probably 7,000 jobs), and severe curtailment of activity at Portsmouth (6,000 jobs). Other losses of more than 1,000 jobs included the Vosper ship-repair yard, Southampton, and London Brick in Bedfordshire. It is possible to draw together tentative conclusions from this very varied pattern as follows:

(1) The more lasting legacy of the recession in the 'Rest of the South East' may be the accentuation of the relative decline (noted by Keeble[31]) in older, specialised industries in larger towns, such as Oxford, Luton, Chatham, Ashford, Portsmouth and Southampton.

(2) The relatively even past performance of South East counties will be broken. Some, such as Kent and possibly Bedfordshire, may suffer appreciably, but in Berkshire, West Sussex and Surrey large losses were fewer in 1976–81.

(3) There may be a further re-emphasis on unemployment in coastal towns.

(4) Closures in New Towns and overspill towns were so prominent that they will receive further attention in Chapter 9.

These are exceptions to a relatively good performance. The rate of job loss in the 'rest of the South East', 1976–81, is second lowest only to that of the South West Region.

The South West

Composition and performance in the South West Region as a whole are structured relatively more towards growth, and less towards decline, than in any other Region. One remarkable feature is that in 1977/8 nearly 13 per cent of regional GDP derived from defence expenditure, the highest regional figure in the UK.[32] Here it is more difficult to assert with confidence that recession conditions of 1979–81 were of permanent rather than just cyclical significance. Total population in the 1981 Census[33] showed an increase of 6.0 per cent over 1971; this is higher than in any other Region except East Anglia (see below).

The relationship between population change and employment change in the Region is obscured by marked immigration of retired people,[34] sub-regional variations,[35] and seasonal employment fluctuation in tourism,[36] agriculture and food processing. Seasonal changes appear to inflate the recorded total of redundancies (Table 7.1) more significantly than elsewhere. There have been planning problems in the past in matching employment to population, with poor employment opportunities in a number of labour market areas of the Region. In the 1970s there was moderate decline of employment in some large regional employers – for instance in British Aerospace after completion of the *Concorde* programme. Yet the overall employment performance of the Region has differed from most others. Inward migration of firms contributed to net increases in manufacturing in Somerset, Devon and Cornwall between 1966 and 1976 (though providing, as shown by Spooner,[37] only a partial answer to the unemployment problems of the 'assisted areas' of the South West Peninsula). This meant, most unusually, that the manufacturing employment levels of the Region had virtually regained their 1966 levels by 1978–9.

Table 7.1 shows only a small net decrease in total employment for the years 1976 to 1981, because the impact of recession here (1979–81) cost initially only the previous growth of the three years 1976 to 1979. Likewise the net increase of unemployment, 1976–81, concealed an unusually well-marked recovery (1976–79) and a somewhat less precipitate increase than elsewhere (1979–81). In 1976, as in most previous years, the South West had a higher average rate of unemployment than the West Midlands, the East Midlands or Yorkshire and Humberside. The impact of recession meant that it was overtaken by the West Midlands and Yorkshire and Humberside in 1980 and 1981. As in the South East and East Anglia, the 'expected' number of redundancies for 1980 lay below the national average (per head of working population) due to a 'favourable' structure, though here the actual number was very slightly worse than 'expected'. The Region has relatively little manufacturing employment, and aerospace provides nearly one-tenth of the total manufacturing jobs.[38] Table 7.2 provides a satisfactory impression of the sectors where large job losses did occur, insofar that it mentions all losses of 1,000 or more in the Region. Neither the Imperial Group's closure of a cardboard-making plant, nor the 'inner city' rioting in the St Paul's District in April 1980, was taken as a significant pointer to Bristol's future, which was seen as well placed for future investment from outside.[39] Swindon suffered the failure of one of its largest modern growth industries when Garrard ran down its record player factory, and production was taken over by a Brazilian firm and finally transferred to Manaus:[40] registered unemployment in Swindon was still below the national average when 1,200 redundancies were proposed for its railway workshops in April 1982. A joint ownership arrangement with a Japanese firm failed to prevent heavy reductions in Rank's colour TV factory in Plymouth and the closure of its branch in Redruth, Cornwall. Along with reductions carried out in ship-repairing in Falmouth and in modern tin mines nearby, these confirmed the existence of structural unemployment in the Region's only Special Development Area in the period 1979 to 1981.

East Anglia

'East Anglia is still in a transitional stage of industrialisation in relation to other parts of the country' (Central Office of Information, 1976[41]). On the one hand, the scientific and service industries of Cambridge make it most unusual from our point of view, as it had one of the very lowest officially-recorded unemployment rates in the country (5.3 per cent at end-1981); the growth of overspill towns under the Town Development Act ensured for wide parts of Cambridgeshire and Suffolk some of the most rapid growth rates of population in the country in the period 1961 to 1981, with an accompanying influx of manufacturing plants, as recorded by Lemon.[42] On the other hand, it is often forgotten that several of its coastal areas actually qualified as 'assisted areas' at one point in the past, between 1958 and 1961.[43] That may have been due to a narrow reading of unemployment statistics by the then government; but the weakness of these areas was strongly brought out in 1981 unemployment figures. For instance, at end-1981 Great Yarmouth suffered a recorded rate of 14.0 per cent and Lowestoft 12.9 per cent. The years 1979 to 1981 were marked by repeated redundancies and closures in the food processing industry, in beet-sugar plants, and in food and vegetable canning and freezing, as well as in engineering. Three multinational corporations are responsible for entries in Table 7.2, but the Dutch plant of Philips in Lowestoft was to be purchased by a Japanese corporation in the same industry. East Anglian Expanded Towns varied considerably in their number of redundancy reports. They were the most numerous for Huntingdon, Cambridgeshire, but the most serious for King's Lynn, Norfolk:

> Two years ago it had seemed as if the wide range of enterprises, from roll-on, roll-off cargoes in the docks to engineering, food preparation and packaging, glassware, sugar refining and agricultural engineering in the hinterland, would immunise the area from the recession. As late as October 1979 the King's Lynn and West Norfolk Council went to South Shields in Tyne and Wear to look for skilled men . . . A few weeks later, the food processing industry, which had long suffered from overcapacity, contracted. Within a short time seven of the East Anglian factories canning vegetables and fruit were closed . . . Outside food processing, one of the first closures – and least expected – was at Dynatron, where 390 people used to make cabinets for music centres and other hi-fi equipment . . . Two out of three who lost their jobs last November are still without work.
>
> *Financial Times*, 18 September 1981

Conclusion

'If you want to find the really booming places of contemporary Britain, you should travel diagonally across southern England, from Exeter via Taunton and Bristol and Swindon to Oxford, Milton Keynes, Northampton, Bedford and Cambridge to Norwich' (P. Hall, 1981[44]). Another 'growth axis', which has been promoted as 'Britain's Sunrise Strip',[45] comprises the sub-regions astride the M4 from Heathrow Airport via Reading, Newbury, Swindon and Bristol to Newport (Gwent). The argument is that communications, the 'quality of life' and the post-war development of large research laboratories in this sector of the Home Counties are providing the basis, through skills and linkages available in the area, for rapid growth in electronics and computing. A county such as Berkshire is seen to have entered the British recession late and to be a leader in national 're-industrialisation'.

This chapter has shown that, while the South was by no means immune from recession conditions, and it was doubtful whether there were any 'booming places' in 1982, the worst patches were sufficiently scattered and peripheral that they need not totally frustrate a search for 'growth axes'. But the evidence for extensive new productive investment was somewhat lacking; in travelling along Hall's axis, for instance, you had better not stray as far as Corby or Peterborough, or extend your journey to Plymouth or Yarmouth; it would be unwise to project USA experience of 'rural' growth too firmly onto the map of the South. It is true however that where factory redundancies have occurred in larger towns they appear in the South to have been generally cushioned in their effects by the economic resilience of these service centres. In London, where manufacturing job losses again accelerated, the resilience of service sector employment had the same effect. In the rest of the South East manufacturing decline was below 'expected' or average rates, and there was a general absence of reported job losses in dispersed offices. The overall effect, then, was that processes at work in the early 1970s often continued in recognisable shape though they were set back by recession conditions.

The experience of these Regions and of London in the 1974–5 recession was at the time a surprisingly sharp departure from past experience: but their reaction to events in 1979 to 1981 was actually slightly more favourable. If from Table 7.1 we sum the numbers unemployed, we find that these three Regions had precisely 33.3

per cent of the national register of unemployment in 1976 and 30.7 per cent in 1981. The difference is so small and inconclusive that it remains relevant to ask in the next chapter whether recession is fundamentally national.

Notes

1. South East Joint Planning Team, *Strategy for the South East: 1976 Review* (HMSO, London, 1976), p. 2.
2. Special issue, 'Unemployment', *Political Quarterly*, vol. 52, no. 1 (1981).
3. 'Unemployment in West Cornwall – a Study by the Department of Employment', *Department of Employment Gazette*, vol. 87, no. 5 (1979), p. 437.
4. East Anglia Regional Strategy Team, *Strategic Choice for East Anglia* (HMSO, London, 1974).
5. Office of Population Census and Surveys, *Census 1981 Preliminary Report* (HMSO, London, 1981).
6. Annual Census of Employment, 1971, and estimates for June 1981, in *Employment Gazette*, vol. 90, no. 1 (1982), Table 1.5.
7. A.A. Ogilvy, 'Population Migration Between the Regions of Great Britain, 1971–9', *Regional Studies*, vol. 16, no. 1 (1982), pp. 63–73.
8. Unpublished data of Department of Employment, Annual Census of Employment, 1977.
9. *Employment Gazette*, vol. 89, no. 3 (1981), pp. 141–5.
10. Unpublished data of Department of Employment, Annual Census of Employment, 1977.
11. J. Short, 'Defence Spending in the U.K. Regions', *Regional Studies*, vol. 15, no. 2 (1981), pp. 101–10.
12. D. Keeble, *Industrial Location and Planning in the United Kingdom* (Methuen, London, 1976), pp. 258–60.
13. *Department of Employment Gazette*, vol. 85, no. 12 (1977), p. 1351.
14. *Financial Times*, 17 Sept. 1979.
15. D. Keeble, 'Industrial Decline in the Inner City and Conurbation', *Transactions of the Institute of British Geographers*, New Series vol. 3, no. 1 (1978), pp. 101–14.
16. R. Dennis, 'The Decline of Manufacturing Employment in Greater London, 1966–74', *Urban Studies*, vol. 15, no. 1 (1978), pp. 63–73.
17. P. Gripaios, 'Industrial Decline in London: an Examination of its Causes', *Urban Studies*, vol. 14, no. 2 (1977), pp. 181–90.
18. D. Keeble, 'De-industrialisation Means Unemployment', *Geographical Magazine*, vol. 53, no. 4 (1981), p. 459.
19. Unpublished communication.
20. *Financial Times*, 24 June 1980.
21. *Financial Times*, 9 April 1981.
22. *Financial Times*, 13 Feb. 1982.
23. *Financial Times*, 13 Feb. 1982.
24. *Financial Times*, 13 Feb. 1982.
25. South East Joint Planning Team, *Strategy for the South East: 1976 Review*, p. 10.
26. A. Gillespie and D. Owen, 'The Current Recession and the Process of Re-structuring in the British Space-economy', paper presented at the European Congress of the *Regional Science Association*, Barcelona (1981).

27. Unpublished communication.
28. D.E. Keeble and D.P. Hauser, 'Spatial Analysis of Manufacturing Growth in Outer South-east England, 1960–67: 2. Method and results', *Regional Studies*, vol. 6, no. 1 (1972), pp. 11–36.
29. *Financial Times*, 1 Aug. 1981.
30. *Financial Times*, 27 June 1981.
31. Keeble, *Industrial Location and Planning*, pp. 269–73.
32. Short, 'Defence Spending in the U.K. Regions', p. 103.
33. Office of Population Censuses and Surveys, *Census 1981 Preliminary Report*.
34. South West Economic Planning Council, *Retirement to the South West* (HMSO, London, 1975).
35. South West Economic Planning Council, *A Strategic Settlement Pattern for the South West* (HMSO, London, 1974).
36. South West Economic Planning Council, *Economic Survey of the Tourist Industry in the South West* (HMSO, London, 1976).
37. D.J. Spooner, 'Industrial Movement and the Rural Periphery: the Case of Devon and Cornwall', *Regional Studies*, vol. 6, no. 2 (1972), pp. 197–215.
38. *Employment Gazette*, vol. 89, no. 3 (1981), pp. 141–5.
39. *Financial Times*, 15 Sept. 1980.
40. *Financial Times*, 4 Feb. 1982.
41. Central Office of Information, *The English Regions; East Anglia* (HMSO, London, 1976), p. 16.
42. A. Lemon, 'Postwar Industrial Growth in East Anglian Small Towns: a Study of Migrant Firms, 1945–70', *Oxford University Geography Research Paper*, 12 (1975).
43. Keeble, *Industrial Location and Planning*, p. 227.
44. P. Hall, 'Issues for the Eighties', *The Planner*, vol. 67, no. 1 (1981), p. 4.
45. 'Britain's Sunrise Strip', *The Economist*, 30 Jan. 1982, pp. 78–9.

8 IS RECESSION NATIONAL? EXPLANATIONS OF THE DISTRIBUTION OF UNEMPLOYMENT

'Practically every family in the land has a direct or indirect experience of this horrifying tale of hardship. From Dover to Dundee, it is the same story. And it is going to get much worse' (Eric Varley, chief Opposition spokesman on employment, 1981).[1] The upsurge in unemployment in 1980 and 1981 impressed Labour politicians because it involved new areas of the country, many of them Conservative constituencies in the 1979 Parliament. Features of the types of workers affected were striking: unemployment spread further among skilled manual workers and was high among ethnic minority groups and school-leavers, to some extent irrespective of area of residence. With job losses so widespread (as we saw in Chapters 5 to 7) was geographical variation still important? Is the spatial or regional component important in the new pattern of unemployment? If it is, can it be largely explained by variation in the industrial incidence of recession?

Politically, national and urban issues had already displaced much of the importance of regional policy before the recession began in 1980. While Eric Varley was a minister for industry in the 1974–9 Labour governments, multiple problems were recognised in the 'inner cities', including those of London and Birmingham. Labour's national Industrial Strategy[2] saw fit to help industries in all Regions; it included heavy financial aid to BL (British Leyland), centred on the West Midlands. We have seen that economic difficulties did indeed spread in the 1970s to industries not previously associated with employment decline. Did they spread far enough, either by 1979 or in the course of 1980–1, for us to say that recession was predominantly national in its effects?

This chapter concludes Part Two with systematic national analyses, drawing together for instance the levels of job losses 'expected' for different Regions in earlier tables. We may readily note some sub-regional variations, particularly how oil exploitation reduced unemployment rates well below the UK average in Grampian, Orkney and Shetland. It is essential that we consider sub-regional variation right across the country. Were there systematic differences between different types of sub-region, for instance between conurbations and rural areas?

Chapters 5, 6 and 7 observed three broadly different experiences of recession over the years 1976–81. In the traditionally 'poorest Regions' a run of job losses continuing from 1974–5 prevented any real improvement after the national peak of unemployment in 1977. On the other hand, unemployment there did not double from 1979 to 1981 as it did in the nation at large; this *proportionately* lower increase may be associated with features such as a less marked impact on retail spending reported in 1981 by Turner.[3] In the 'manufacturing heartland' unemployment improved a little from 1977 to 1979 but showed severe proportionate worsening in 1980. In the 'normally prosperous South' the balance was significantly different, with a better improvement from 1977 to 1979 and a less marked average deterioration from 1979 to 1981.

The main findings of this chapter are that these patterns could be predicted from the industrial composition of redundancies. They represent a change in patterns of cyclical sensitivity from those established in the 1930s, and a departure from the systematic 'urban-rural shift' of 1971–6, as reported by Keeble.[4] The most prominent feature from 1979 to 1981 was the systematic loss of jobs in a wide range of industries in all manufacturing areas. This impact was accentuated by the high dependence of the West Midlands and the North West as a whole on manufacturing industry. Scotland as well as the 'normally prosperous' southern Regions were to some extent 'protected' from recession by the scale of their service employment.

The Traditional Identification of British Problem Regions

The analyses to follow later in this chapter use data on employment and redundancy to *interpret* through 'shift-share' methods the pattern of recession. Unemployment statistics remain the most relevant, sub-national *measurement* of the scale of recession. As they are derived from those registering as unemployed, they are normally taken to understate the 'true' level of unemployment (Garfield, 1980).[5] Groups which have been excluded from the quoted 'unemployment total' in recent years include students, 'temporarily stopped' workpeople, and people on the government's various 'job creation' measures (for example the Youth

Table 8.1: Regional Unemployment in Selected Years, 1929–1936

	Percentages of insured employees				
	1929	1932	1936		Peak month
London	5.6	13.5	7.2	15.0	Jan. '32
South-Eastern	5.6	14.3	7.3	16.5	Jan. '32
South-Western	8.1	17.1	9.4	19.3	Jan. '33
Midlands	9.3	20.1	9.2	22.3	July '31
North-Eastern	13.7	28.5	16.8	31.0	Aug. '32
North-Western	13.3	25.8	13.1	31.3	Sept. '31
Scotland	12.1	27.7	18.7	29.6	Jan. '33
Wales	19.3	36.5	29.4	39.9	Aug. '32
Northern Ireland	14.8	27.2	22.7	33.4	Dec. '30
United Kingdom	10.4	22.1	13.2	23.1	Jan. '31

Source: *Ministry of Labour Gazettes*; last column extracted by C.S. Crouch.

Opportunities Programme). Workers who are not eligible for unemployment benefit – notably a high proportion of female workers – may choose not to register at all.

Pre-war and post-war unemployment data are not comparable because the pre-war base figures represented a smaller part of a smaller working population. Few of the English Administrative Divisions shown in Table 8.1 are congruous with post-war Regions. They do, however, establish a broad pattern of spatial variation which was to persist through the post-war years of full employment. Small variations can be seen between 1929 and 1936 in the rank-order position of constituent areas of the UK. However, the overall pattern was clear; it was attributable to the impact of structural difficulties in coal-mining, shipbuilding, metal manufacture and textiles (McCrone, 1969).[6]

It was broadly those same industries which continued to cause weakness in the post-war economy of the worst-hit Regions as unemployment increased after 1958, although Northern Ireland took the place of Wales as the area of greatest difficulty. The period since 1966 may be sub-divided as follows:

(1) National unemployment increased gradually (see Figure 1.1 of this volume) till the 1971 recession caused a peak in 1972. The five most peripheral Regions – those most assisted by regional

policy in this its 'strongest period' enjoyed a relative improvement. In the 'manufacturing heartland' Yorkshire and Humberside and the North West declined in their relative position and the West Midlands lost its better than average position.

(2) More marked 'convergence' in unemployment rates followed in a renewed national deterioration from 1973 to 1976. Peripheral Regions and most of the more prosperous Regions converged towards the national average. The claims of London, Birmingham and inner city areas generally came to challenge the supremacy of regional variations for spatial policy; academically, Keeble (1977)[7] questioned whether British spatial policy should be regional or urban.

(3) The period 1977 to 1979 is recognised as one of regional 'divergence' by Keeble (1981);[8] this was perhaps a somewhat surprising departure from previous trends.

(4) From 1979 to 1981 there is a measure of 'convergence' as the more prosperous Regions have a sharper proportionate increase in unemployment than parts of the country where it is already high. The West Midlands, however, clearly moves into a worse than average position.

We have now seen our main period of study (phases 3 and 4 above) in a longer time perspective; it seems clear that the recognition of 'convergence' in poorer Regions deserves caution when this is caused simply and temporarily by a national deterioration. There has been a number of short-term fluctuations in the precise relative positions of Regions. On the other hand there do appear to be unidirectional changes, such as the deteriorating position of the North West and above all the West Midlands. Gillespie and Owen[9] point out that the concepts with which we view these events may need revision. Thus, the 1980–81 recession may be not only quantitatively but also qualitatively different from the type of cyclical reaction with which we are familiar. The type of model developed by Thirlwall,[10] Brechling[11] and Cheshire[12] assumes that a given region will always respond to successive cycles in the same manner. However, later work, as by Frost and Spence[13] or Hepple,[14] suggests that the sensitivity of an area's reactions to cyclical variation may be very unstable over time. It may come to show unfamiliar patterns, as in the UK since 1971.

A Revised Basis for Assessing Changes in Unemployment

The patterns of 'convergence' shown in the last two recessions certainly enable us to say that unemployment is more evenly distributed and is spatially more national. Measures of *proportionate* change in different places thus have their uses. But they tend to overstate the problem of places with lower levels of unemployment, and to understate the problems of less prosperous areas. Thus Townsend[15] presented Buckinghamshire as having one of the highest rates of increase in unemployment in the year ending June 1980; in Table 8.2 (below) East Anglia is shown in column (e) to have had a higher proportionate increase than Northern Ireland. Alternative methods of comparing different areas' changes of unemployment were clearly needed in this recession; and three are presented by Gillespie and Owen[16] and their use is debated by Crouch.[17] Following Crouch, the basis used in the rest of this chapter is to ask what proportion of any area's working population has been added to the unemployment register in a given period. Thus between 1979 and 1981 we would subtract East Anglia's 1979 average rate of unemployment of 4.3 per cent from the later 8.5 per cent (answer 4.2 per cent), and Northern Ireland's 10.4 per cent from 16.9 per cent (answer 6.5 per cent). The main difficulty of this method is to ensure the use of consistent and relevant base figures in percentage rate calculations. It can provide comparison with measures of the net losses of jobs from the workforce as a whole. For instance, in the year ending June 1981, total GB employment was estimated to have fallen by 5.8 per cent; unemployment showed a net addition of 4.2 per cent of the workforce.[18] A precise equation of the two series cannot be sought. The Department of Employment recognises that an important trend of the last few years has been that 'discouraged workers' have left the labour force, and also that many women (as usual) have not registered for unemployment.[19]

A presentation of the pattern of regional change on the bases which have been described can be made in Table 8.2, which shows changes since the last peak year of 1977 in column (a). Proportionate increases between column (b) and (c), expressing the severe deterioration of 1979–81, are shown in column (e), and the figures in brackets express these values in rank order (the 'worst affected' Region is shown as 1, etc.); column (f) is calculated according to the method which has just been described above. The

Table 8.2: Changes in Percentage Unemployment, 1977–81, by Region

Percentage unemployed, annual averages, seasonally-adjusted excluding school-leavers

Region	(a) 1977	(b) 1979	(c) 1981	(d) 1982 June	(e) (c minus b)/b b	(f) c minus b
South East	4.3	3.5	7.6	9.0	114% (3)	4.0 (10)
East Anglia	5.0	4.3	8.6	9.9	98% (5)	4.2 (9)
South West	6.4	5.4	9.3	10.6	72% (9)	3.9 (11)
West Midlands	5.3	5.1	12.8	14.7	147% (1)	7.6 (1)
East Midlands	4.7	4.4	9.5	10.7	116% (2)	5.1 (8)
Yorks. & Humberside	5.3	5.3	11.3	12.7	109% (4)	6.0 (6)
North West	6.8	6.6	13.0	14.9	94% (6)	6.4 (4)
North	7.6	8.0	14.1	15.6	74% (8)	6.1 (5)
Wales	7.4	7.3	13.8	15.2	86% (7)	6.5 (3)
Scotland	7.5	7.4	12.7	14.1	70% (10)	5.2 (7)
Northern Ireland	10.0	10.4	17.0	19.2	63% (11)	6.5 (2)
United Kingdom	5.7	5.4	10.6	12.2	94%	5.1

Source: *Employment Gazette*, Table 2.1 (monthly).

West Midlands is the worst affected Region in both measures. In column (e) the East Midlands, the South East and Yorkshire and Humberside come next, and as a whole the 'manufacturing heartland' does badly. In column (f) however, these three Regions enjoy a low ranking; here three Regions follow the West Midlands; Northern Ireland, Wales and the North West; three Regions of 'the South' do well. For the purposes of this chapter, in which we seek to explain the 1977–81 changes by reference to the industrial structure of employment change in the whole labour market, we will focus on the pattern of column (f). Why in the period 1977–79 did 'the poorest Regions', with Yorkshire and Humberside, fail to share significantly in a modest improvement in unemployment? Why then did the different rank order of the final column emerge and remain almost stable during 1981; why, in particular, did the adjoining mainland Regions of the West Midlands, the North West and Wales suffer most from the onset of recession in 1979–81?

The Sub-regional Hypothesis

We are now seeking to understand departures from the national pattern of employment change at the regional level. For this purpose, recently published analyses would lead us to look at the *internal composition* of Regions:

> The greatest regional declines have occurred in regions which are dominated by big congested conurbations (North West, West Midlands and South East) with growth only in regions which are largely rural (East Anglia, South West, Wales, and to some extent the North).
>
> Keeble, 1981[20]

This is an accurate description of manufacturing employment change in much of the 1970s. It also suggests the means of calculating the expected performance of individual Regions developed by Fothergill and Gudgin in their volume *Regional Employment Change: A Sub-Regional Explanation*.[21] They stress that there were greater spatial contrasts in economic development within most standard Regions than between the Regions themselves. They divided 62 sub-regions of the UK into eight types of areas, ranging from London and the conurbations on the one hand to 'semi-rural' and 'rural' areas on the other. They calculated average rates of change for each of the eight national types of sub-regions, and applied these standard rates to the component parts of each Region. The results are more successful in predicting Regional change than calculations based on the overall industrial structure of Regions. Their calculations relate to the period 1959–75, but Keeble (1980)[22] also found systematic differences between four types of sub-regions for the period 1971–76. These analyses are remarkably similar to the official commentary on the first results of the 1981 Census of Population for England and Wales: 'Between 1971 and 1981 each metropolitan county lost population whereas for each region which included a metropolitan county, the non-metropolitan remainder gained population; and those regions without a metropolitan county gained most rapidly of all.'[23]

There are, however, grounds for believing that migration trends slowed down during the 1970s, as was shown by a study of detailed quarterly records by Ogilvy,[24] and that employment trends changed substantially between different areas towards the end of the ten years – whether or not they influenced the distribution of population before the 1981 Census or were specific only to deep recession conditions. In all it seems that the conventional wisdom of the 1970s, reflected in the above quotations, in decennial Census results and the studies by Fothergill, Gudgin and Keeble, applies much better to the first half of the decade than the second. Their studies of employment were hindered by delays in the availability of official statistics. At the time of writing the latest full Census of Employment relates to mid-1978,[25] and in earlier chapters we have therefore used alternative indications of later trends. Quarterly estimates based on sample surveys (which are more thorough for 'production industries' than others) are available for Regions and for individual national industries for subsequent dates.[26] They await revision on the publication of the 1981 (October) Census of Employment. The national data were utilised in Table 3.1 above, and regional estimates were tabulated in Chapters 5, 6 and 7. It would be wrong at this stage to draw final conclusions about the comparative performance of different individual Regions. Owen and Gillespie demonstrate changes from quarter to quarter in the relative performance of different Regions.[27] We may however be able to use these data broadly to compare different types of Region.

Table 8.3 presents extracts of the official record of employees in employment, based on the provisional quarterly data subsequent to

Table 8.3: Change in Total Employees in Employment by Region; Data for June (Provisional Series from 1978)

	Percentage change per annum			
	1971–6	1976–9	1979–1981	
Standard Regions	Total	Total	Total	Manufacturin[g]
South East	0.0	+ 0.3	− 2.5	− 6.2
North West	− 0.2	+ 0.2	− 4.3	− 7.6
West Midlands	− 0.2	+ 0.4	− 5.3	− 9.4
Scotland	+ 0.7	+ 0.1	− 3.6	− 9.4
Yorks. & Humberside	+ 1.0	+ 0.4	− 4.3	− 9.0
South West	+ 1.2	+ 1.4	− 2.2	− 4.9
East Midlands	+ 1.2	+ 0.8	− 2.9	− 6.8
North	+ 0.8	+ 0.1	− 5.3	− 9.5
Wales	+ 0.7	+ 0.2	− 4.4	− 10.7
East Anglia	+ 2.1	+ 1.0	− 3.3	− 6.5
Great Britain	+ 0.4	+ 0.4	− 3.5	− 7.8

Source: *Employment Gazette*, Annual Censuses of Employment and Table 1.5 (quarterly).

1978. This and all remaining tables of this chapter present the standard Regions of GB in order of the *size* of their working population; thus the first five Regions of the table contain conurbations, and the others, bar the North, do not. This layout enables us fairly readily to support the 'sub-regional hypothesis' for 1971–6; the South East, the North West and the West Midlands clearly performed worse than other Regions, and the South West, the East Midlands and East Anglia did best. These last three Regions also did best during the period 1976–9; but in the period of heavy recession, 1979–81, they were joined by the largest Region, the South East. On the other hand, the 'small Regions' of the North and Wales performed poorly, along with the West Midlands, the North West and Yorkshire and Humberside.

The results are not precisely the same as in Table 8.2 (based on unemployment data), but they go a long way toward confirming that the sub-regional hypothesis, in its simple form, is not applicable in conditions of heavy recession. A similar and direct assessment of the employment trends of different *sub-regions* is not possible. There were at the time of writing no official estimates of employment since 1977 below the regional level. It is, however, possible to view their increases in unemployment over the key period from mid–1979 to mid–1981. In earlier periods there was no reported research which posed a simple connection between the geography of employment decline and the location of increases in unemployment. However, it seems likely that this situation too changed after 1979 because of the suddenness and scale of the reduction in jobs, of the order of one million (GB) in 1980. To a considerable extent the increases in unemployment recorded for particular sub-regions in the period 1979–81 must be indicative of (generally somewhat larger) immediate reductions of employment in those areas.

Figure 8.1 adopts the method developed in this chapter for measuring increases in unemployment, and applies them to sub-regions of GB. It will be noted that the distribution of change is skewed, so that a majority of units added less than 5.6 per cent of their workforce (the national average) to the unemployment register in the two-year period. We may list the areas which exceeded this national average:

'Poorest Regions': Western Isles 8.4%; Clwyd 8.2%*; Cleveland 7.9%*; Durham 7.9%*; Gwent 7.4%*; Mid-Glamorgan 6.6%; Dyfed 6.5%; Strathclyde 6.5%; Central Scotland 6.1%; West Glamorgan 5.9%*; Powys 5.7%.

Regions of the 'Manufacturing Heartland': Northants 8.0%*; Shropshire 7.9%; West Midlands 7.7%; Staffordshire 7.4%; Cheshire 7.3%; Greater Manchester 7.0%; Humberside 7.0%*; West Yorkshire 6.6%; South Yorkshire 6.6%*; Lancashire 6.5%; Hereford and Worcester 6.5%; Lincolnshire 5.8%.

'Normally Prosperous' Regions: Essex 5.8%.

(*) denotes areas with major steel-making closures.

The list includes all the counties lying on the map between the conurbations of the West Midlands, Greater Manchester and Merseyside. Chapters 5 to 7 have provided examples of proportionately heavy job losses in such *provincial* conurbations, and of a long-delayed impact of recession in many non-metropolitan counties: but there are also contrary patterns, for instance, in the case of several steel-making counties. The question is whether there is any general difference between urban and rural areas when we average performance throughout the UK. The areal units used above and in Figure 8.1 are counties in England and Wales together with Regions and Island Authority Areas in Scotland. To facilitate comparison with previous work these areas

Figure 8.1: Net Increases in Unemployment, Mid 1979–Mid 1981, as Percentages of Total Working Population

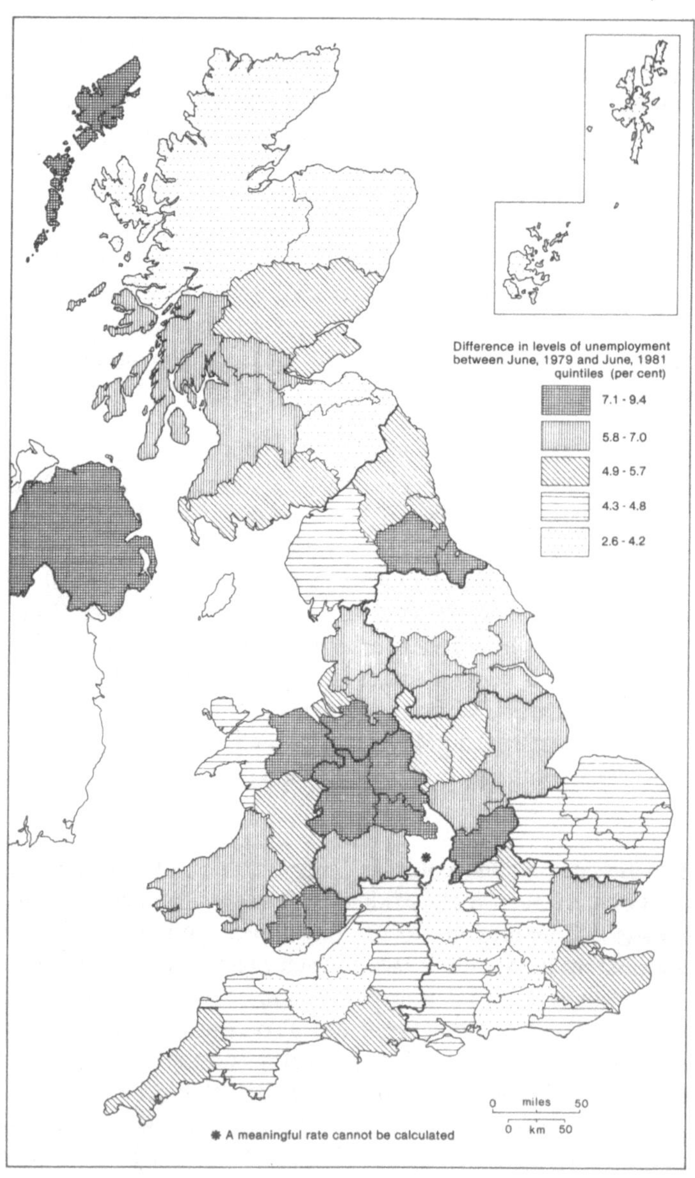

are grouped in the precise form adopted by Keeble in Table 8.4 (see Note a).

The doubling of national unemployment over this period was evenly spread between urban and rural areas generally. It is true that the 23 'rural counties' enjoyed a slightly better relative performance, but their total of 293,000 unemployed (June 1981) represented as high a percentage rate as in the less-urbanised counties. If we exclude steelmaking counties with major closures, the entry for the final column drops to 5.3 per cent for the rural counties and for the less-urbanised counties as well. This is insufficient to alter our conclusion that there is no urban-rural bias in unemployment trends during this formative period of recession.

What, however, is the bias? If we study the list (above) of counties with greater than average increases in unemployment, what do these areas have in common? The answer in fact is that they also had more than the national average (32 per cent in 1977) of their total employees in manufacturing employment, with the exceptions only of Shropshire, Lincolnshire, Dyfed and Powys. The relationship between these two measures is shown systematically in Figure 8.2. Of course the internal structure of manufacturing is itself of importance. An example is given by the seven counties in which aerospace is the largest industry. These enjoyed less than average increases in their net additions to unemployment in 1979–81; aerospace, as mentioned in Chapter 3, was one of only three industries to have a net increase of employees during 1980.

Table 8.4: Changes in Unemployment, 1979–81, by Type of Sub-region

	Per cent unemployed, June, including school-leavers			
Type of sub-region[a]	(a) 1979	(b) 1981	(c) (b minus a)/a	(d) b minus a
Conurbations	5.5	11.0	99%	5.5
More-urbanised counties	5.1	10.5	108%	5.5
Less-urbanised counties	5.8	11.5	98%	5.7
Rural counties	6.1	11.5	89%	5.4
United Kingdom	5.5	11.1	99%	5.6

Note: a. Sub-regions as defined in D.E. Keeble, 'Industrial decline, regional policy and the urban-rural manufacturing shift in the United Kingdom', *Environment and Planning A*, vol. 12, p. 962.

Source: *Employment Gazette* and unpublished base figures of Department of Employment, 1977.

Over much of the map of Britain it appears that the existing employment structure is the dominant force in differentiating the performance of sub-Regions in a period of decline. It supersedes in importance the environmental degree of rurality, stressed in past studies of manufacturing change. We extend this analysis to the conurbations in Table 8.5. We find here that the proportion of manufacturing employment has a more directly linear effect on the experience of unemployment, as is shown fairly clearly in Figure 8.2.

The table is concerned with 1.196 million workpeople, almost half the 2.578 million who were unemployed in June 1981. As a whole, this group of eight areas suffered changes which were almost exactly in line with national averages over the period. The largest area, Greater London, had the lowest unemployment throughout; heavy reductions in GLC manufacturing employment would have had relatively little overall impact on its unemployment because of the low proportion of workers in this sector. If we omit the GLC from the table, we find that average unemployment in conurbations

Table 8.5: Changes in Unemployment 1979–81; Conurbations

	Per cent unemployed, June, including school-leavers				
Conurbation	(a) 1979	(b) 1981	(c) (b minus d)/a	(d) b minus a	Per cent of 1977 employees in manufacturing
Greater London Council (GLC)	3.4	7.3	126%	3.6	21.2
Merseyside	11.3	16.9	47%	5.2	32.8
Tyne & Wear	9.6	15.0	57%	5.2	32.8
Strathclyde	9.8	16.1	67%	6.5	34.5
South Yorkshire	6.4	13.0	105%	6.6	37.4
West Yorkshire	5.1	11.7	130%	6.6	39.1
Gtr Manchester	5.5	12.6	133%	7.0	38.9
West Midlands	5.6	14.2	156%	7.7	48.7
Conurbations average	5.5	11.0	99%	5.5	32.4
United Kingdom	5.5	11.1	99%	5.6	31.9

Note: Published figures in col. (a) are based on mid-1976 denominators, all others on mid-1977.

Source: *Employment Gazette*, Table 2.4 (monthly).

Fig. 8.2: Net Increases in Unemployment, Mid-1979 to Mid-1981, as a Function of the Proportion of all Employees in Manufacturing Employment

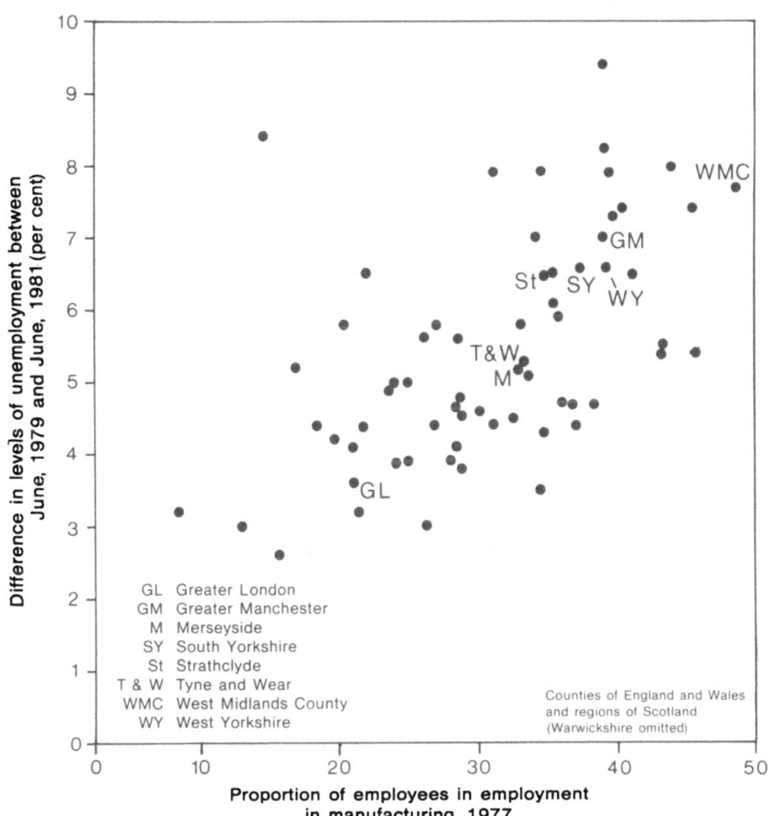

Source: Annual Census of Employment

rose from 7.0 per cent to 13.6 per cent of the workforce. The figures were moderated by less than average increases in this period in Merseyside, Tyne & Wear and Strathclyde, both because they were already suffering from the recessional cycle in 1979, and because they were less dependent on manufacturing than, say, the West Midlands. At the end of our period of study, in December 1981, Figure 8.3 shows Merseyside, Strathclyde and the West Midlands County among those areas with 15.9 per cent unemployment or more. They were accompanied by two steel-making counties, Cleveland and Clwyd, together with mid-Glamorgan and the more

Figure 8.3: Sub-regional Percentage Unemployment Rates in the United Kingdom, End 1981

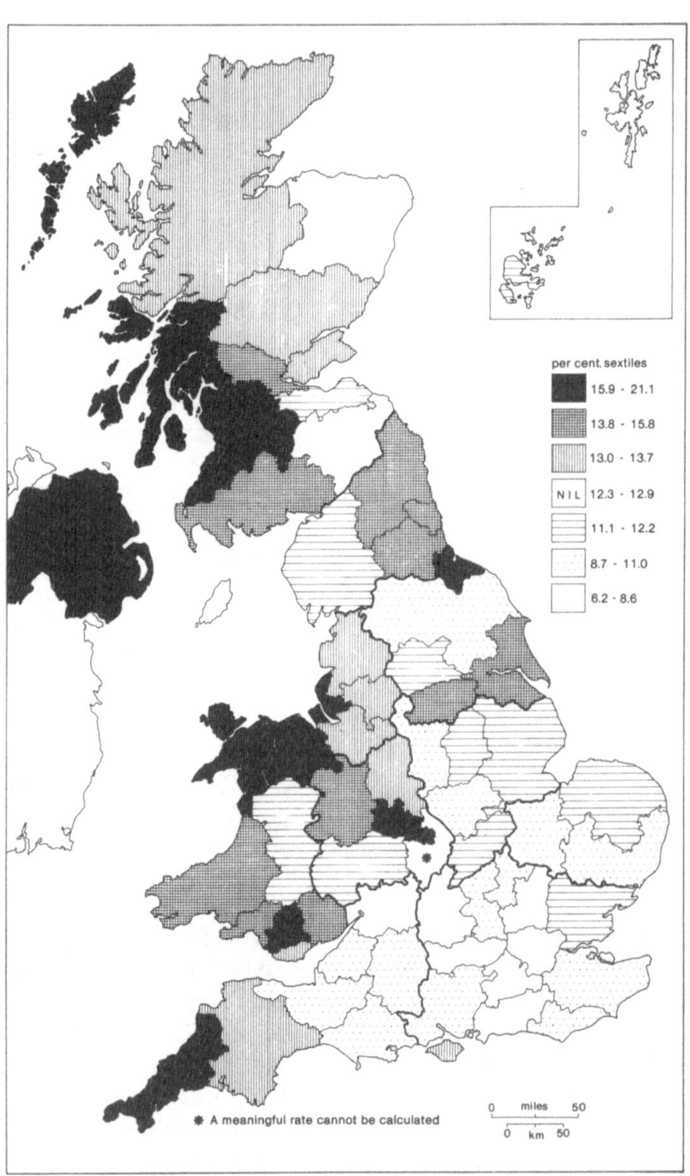

Source: *Employment Gazette*, vol. 90, No. 1 (1982).

classically 'peripheral' areas of Cornwall, Gwynedd and the Western Isles.

Conclusions must be provisional without firm data for net employment change, pending the availability of the 1981 Census of Employment for analysis in 1983. Patterns may clearly have changed after 1981 both structurally and geographically, perhaps as more effects of recession are diffused among different parts of the service sector, and as time allows for a more marked migrational response to relative unemployment levels in different places. However, the dominance of manufacturing in 1980–1 net job losses is well enough documented to sustain the main argument advanced here: that employment structure is more important than the difficulties of, say, a conurbation environment in determining the incidence of change in a strong period of decline. The recession is not a fully nationwide phenomenon, as the GLC area and most counties of the normally prosperous Regions sustained below average increases in the proportion of their workers who are unemployed. In explaining spatial variation we have discounted a systematic sub-regional explanation; we are led on to the analysis of industrial structure, for which fuller data exist for regional analysis in the next section.

The Industrial Structure Hypothesis

The regional impact of recession is likely to be more uniform if job losses are evenly distributed between different industries and sectors of the economy. Extensive work in the past has identified divergence in the employment trends of different Regions with the differential growth and decline of particular industries or groups of industries. This link was sometimes made in a simple descriptive way, by identifying the problems of, say, areas engaged in textile production or coal-mining with the overall national problems of those industries. A similar approach has been the basis of systematic calculations applying national rates of increase or decline in a set of industries to the employment structure of different Regions. In this way one may partly 'explain' their relative performances statistically and at least establish discrepancies for further investigation. Work in this field was refined in the 1960s by Brown[28] and others. It could interpret the past regular contrast between the West Midlands, with its then expanding metal-using industries, and certain peripheral Regions.

Such calculations nearly always leave a residual to be explained by particular factors in each Region. Because this 'indigenous' factor tended in later studies to grow at the expense of the significance of regional industrial composition, the 'structural' factor, some writers developed alternative explanations, chiefly the 'sub-regional hypothesis' (as above). The change followed the spread of industrial difficulties to more sectors, which we have repeatedly noted:

> By the 1970s and 1980s, this traditional structural influence explained only a small part of regional manufacturing shifts, largely because national de-industrialisation means that most manufacturing industries are recording similar rates of decline at the national level. Previous differences between growing and declining industries, and hence between growing and declining regions, have narrowed considerably if not disappeared.
>
> Keeble, 1981[29]

This view can embrace the 1971 and 1975 peaks of redundancies. Does it remain appropriate for the subsequent period of accelerating manufacturing employment decline? As we saw in Chapter 3, manufacturing job losses in the onset of recession in 1980 were indeed widely spread between the main industries. There were so many 'waves' of job losses in different industries that they tended towards a similar end-result. But when we looked in greater detail, for instance at the contrasting performance of motor vehicles and the 'aerospace industry' within the 'Vehicles Industry' as a whole, it became clear that this heavy period of decline showed industrial biases of possible regional significance.

An analysis has been conducted[30] to relate together these industrial and regional changes in the period 1976–80, including the 10 per cent drop in manufacturing employment in the year 1980 itself. The questions it asked were:

(1) Is recession 'national'? Some geographers may have seen a recession of this scale essentially as a national event, evenly distributed in its impact between industries and Regions, implying perhaps a *suspension* of previous spatially differentiated processes, including those of the sub-regional hypothesis. How large is the national component of change relative to the others?

(2) Is it structural? The reader who has followed 1980–1 media reports of job losses might detect a succession of national *waves* of redundancy, for instance in the iron and steel, motor vehicles, textiles, and pottery industries. Is there then a return to a more distinct 'structural' influence upon employment change in individual Regions than was identified in previous shift-share analyses by Fothergill and Gudgin[31] and by Keeble?[32]

(3) Is it 'regional'? Are there distinct spatial biases in the 'differential' component of change? If so, do the peripheral regions show the worst performance?

(4) Is the pattern consistent over time? Our main analysis can cover the calendar years 1976 to 1980. Did the heavy period of recession in 1980 involve a different pattern of job losses from that of the preceding years, 1976–79? How then is the acceleration of redundancy in 1980 best interpreted by regional analysts?

It would be wrong to pose these questions solely in terms of manufacturing analysis. We must also incorporate the smaller volume of job losses in other sectors, and therefore the differential effects of a manufacturing-led recession on the range of Regions, all with varying levels of dependence on it. We have already found in Table 8.2 that three adjoining Regions of Britain, the West Midlands, Wales and the North West, have shown the greatest worsening of percentage unemployment rates. In forecasts for the period 1980–85 the Manpower Research Group, University of Warwick[33] concluded that 'employment will decline most rapidly in Greater London, the West Midlands, the North West and Wales'. Do these two statements describe a basic new form of spatial shift? Does this shift arise from an identifiable composition of job losses in the recession?

The questions we have set can be approached through shift-share analyses in a consistent set of tables in the rest of this chapter. These tables apportion employment change in a Region into three 'components':

(1) National component (also known elsewhere as the 'regional share'): that employment change which would have occurred in a Region if employment in the Region had grown or declined at precisely the same rate as all employment in Great Britain as a whole.

(2) Structural component (also known as the 'proportionality

shift' or 'compositional component'): that employment change which would have occurred in a Region if each of the industries in that Region had changed its employment at the same rate as that industry nationally, *less* the national component. The structural component is thus a measure to show how favourable or unfavourable for maintaining employment levels was a Region's particular mix of industries in a given period. The sum of the national and structural components is equal to the 'expected' employment change, in fact to the figures which have already been given for each GB Region for 1976–9 and for 1980 in tables in Chapters 5 to 7.

(3) Differential component (also known as the 'regional' or 'competitive' component): the difference between the actual change in employment and the sum of the national and structural components, or in other words the difference between actual and expected employment change.

The application of shift-share analysis to a comparatively short period of heavy decline has little precedent. It does not appear, however, to lie beyond established practice, provided as usual that 'not too much can be expected to be revealed from its use' (Fothergill and Gudgin[34]) and that data deficiencies are recognised. The method is essentially a standardisation procedure, distinguishing 'national' and 'structural' components of change within expected figures of change for constituent units. Despite criticisms, most notably by Richardson,[35] the technique has been widely applied to questions of regional employment change, usually of 'growth' in the North American literature, as reviewed by Stevens and Moore.[36] It is, for instance, fairly widely accepted, as in Moore and Rhodes,[37] as a measure of the impact of regional policy on employment growth. The impact of national recession on the Regions is an event of even greater magnitude, exacting a loss of more jobs in a given time than were ever 'created' through regional policy.

Chapter 3 first introduced both the government's quarterly estimates of employees in employment, 'net job losses' (monthly, published in the Employment Gazette) and the unpublished ES955 series on 'redundancies occurring'. (The quarterly estimates deserve cautious consideration, but we use them here only in their most regularly published form, for GB manufacturing industries). These data were tested against each other for the calendar year of

1980. The total employment changes indicated in each source for Great Britain for each manufacturing industry were notionally allocated to Regions, pro rata with their 1978 share of all employees in that industry. Losses produced for each Region were then summed to give an 'expected' total of losses. This was then in turn divided by the 1978 manufacturing population in each Region. The resulting figures from the two sources agreed in showing the same Regions to have the worst expected proportionate performance (Wales, Yorkshire and Humberside and the West Midlands), and the same Regions to show the best expected proportionate performance (the South-East, the South-West and East Anglia). The calculations are shown in Table 8.7 below. Townsend[38] was able to take these results as evidence that use of the two sources together enables us to have some confidence in the validity of both. We will proceed to demonstrate the results of shift-share analyses:

(1) 'Redundancies occurring', ES955, 1976–79; total employment.
(2) 'Redundancies occurring', ES955, 1980; manufacturing and total employment.
(3) 'Net job losses' in manufacturing employment 1980.

Chapter 3 showed that the period 1976–79 was a 'plateau' of slightly falling unemployment accompanied by moderate redundancies. Will the shift-share analysis of redundancies help us to understand the regional 'divergence' in unemployment rates noted earlier in this chapter? If we refer to Table 8.6 we find that the 685,000 'redundancies occurring' in this period made up 3.1 per cent of the 1976 total of employees in employment (the proportion of manufacturing workers affected was higher). The 'structural shift' (the expected variation around the 'national shift') was comparatively small, being nowhere as much as 1.0 per cent of the total working population. Significantly, 'the South' was expected to show relative 'gains' from redundancies; all three constitutent Regions contained industries which had less need to reduce employment by these means. The total shift represents the sum of the shifts indicated in the three previous columns; we find that the 'differential shift' was of decisive importance in distinguishing the different Regions' performances.

The most pronounced feature of the period 1976–9 was then the importance of differential shifts. Under this heading, losses of 1.9

Table 8.6: Shift-Share Analysis of Redundancies Occurring in all Sectors, 1976–79, at Order Total level

	Redundancies occuring, 1976–79, as percentages of 1976 employees in employment			
Standard Regions	National shift	Structural shift	Differential shift	Total shift
South East	– 3.1	+ 0.6	+ 1.0	– 1.6
North West	– 3.1	– 0.3 (– 0.3)	– 1.9	– 5.3
West Midlands	– 3.1	– 0.5	+ 1.3	– 2.3
Scotland	– 3.1	– 0.2	– 2.0	– 5.3
Yorks & Humberside	– 3.1	– 0.4 (–0.3)	+ 0.4	– 3.1
South West	– 3.1	+ 0.2	– 0.4	– 3.2
East Midlands	– 3.1	– 0.7 (– 0.3)	+ 1.9	– 1.9
North	– 3.1	– 0.5	– 1.9	– 5.5
Wales	– 3.1	– 0.0	– 2.0	– 5.1
East Anglia	– 3.1	+ 0.2	+ 0.9	– 2.1
Great Britain	– 3.1	–	–	– 3.1

(Figures in brackets exclude textiles)

or 2.0 per cent of total 1976 employment contributed to total shifts of 5.1 to 5.5 per cent in four 'peripheral' Regions, the North West, Scotland, the North and Wales, where there was throughout only a weak, negative structural shift. The industries which showed the highest rates of redundancy in this period were shipbuilding, textiles, clothing and footwear, mechanical engineering and iron and steel (in that order). This partly explained the systematic differential performance of these 'peripheral' Regions. But another feature was the already high rate of closure among plants established in these areas under regional policies designed to redress previous industrial difficulty; these plants figure prominently in Chapters 5 and 9, and in earlier writing by Townsend[39] based on the *Financial Times*. They contributed to the high rate of job losses in the conurbations of Merseyside (North West Region), Tyne and Wear (Northern Region) and Clydeside (Scotland), which were the main centres of *increased* unemployment, mid–1976 to mid–1979, and of the regional 'divergence' we have already established in this period.

The pace of redundancy quickened in 1980 before falling off to some extent in mid–1981. Some variation in its industrial composition between 1980 and 1981 was seen in Table 3.1. We will give the calendar year of 1980 extended consideration, both for its 494,000 redundancies occurring and for an analysis of 'net job losses', which totalled 1,047,000. We will here include special analysis of manufacturing change. In this particular year, with new manufacturing investment at a low level, we may expect minimum 'interference' with the results from inter-regional relocation of new factories and the inhibiting effects of labour shortages. The debate in the literature about the industrial disaggregation of data is met by the availability and use of both data sets close to minimum list heading (MLH) level (in the 'net job losses' there were three manufacturing MLHs which show a 'positive' change in 1980; all the rest showed decreases).

We may begin to inspect these shift-share changes by reference to two comparative analyses of manufacturing, 1980: Table 8.7. For both types of data, the national component of change is dominant. This period of industrial recession was clearly and fundamentally a national phenomenon: regional variation in manufacturing is essentially a subordinate effect. In 'net job losses' (left-hand side of table) the average decline in employment of nearly 10.0 per cent covers variation in total shift between 6.6 per cent (South West) and 16.7 per cent (Wales). The range in 'redundancies occurring' is greater; the South East shows the most favourable outcome, Wales again the worst.

The *structural shift* is in both cases less important to the final outcome than the differential shift. Values for the North West, Scotland, the East Midlands and the North are remarkably low, although three of them are traditional problem Regions. This results from a number of factors – the improved position of shipbuilding in 1980; the relatively small size of their metal manufacturing industries; and the fact that motor vehicle manufacturing was not a large part of their industrial structures. In Yorkshire and Humberside a fairly large negative structural shift results from the combination of textiles and iron and steel among its main industries. By contrast most of the Welsh structural shift can be explained by employment decline in iron and steel, and that of the West Midlands by job losses in motor vehicles and metals. Shifts in aerospace and in a range of modern industries are responsible for the structural gains shown for the South West and the South East, respectively. In summary, these calculations themselves show that

Table 8.7: Shift-share Analyses of Manufacturing Employment Change, 1980, at Disaggregated Level; Percentages of 1978 Employees in Employment

Standard regions	Net loss of employees in employment Jan. 1980 – Jan. 1981 (77 industries[a])				Redundancies occurring, ES955 (95 recorded industries)			
	National shift	Structural shift	Differential shift	Total shift	National shift	Structural shift	Differential shift	Total shift
South East	−9.9	+0.9	+0.8	−8.2	−5.6	+1.1	+1.9	−2.7
North West	−9.9	−0.1	+0.6	−9.4	−5.6	−0.2	−1.6	−7.4
West Midlands	−9.9	−1.4	+0.1	−11.2	−5.6	−0.9	+0.2	−6.3
Scotland	−9.9	+0.1	−1.6	−11.4	−5.6	−0.2	−1.6	−7.5
Yorks & Humberside	−9.9	−1.9	+1.2	−10.6	−5.6	−1.0	+0.3	−6.2
South West	−9.9	+1.3	+2.0	−6.6	−5.6	+1.1	−0.0	−4.6
East Midlands	−9.9	−0.1	+0.8	−9.2	−5.6	−0.2	−0.2	−6.0
North	−9.9	−0.5	−1.8	−12.2	−5.6	−0.2	−0.6	−6.4
Wales	−9.9	−3.2	−3.6	−16.7	−5.6	−1.8	−4.1	−11.5
East Anglia	−9.9	+0.7	−0.3	−9.5	−5.6	−0.5	+2.0	−3.1
Great Britain	−9.9	—	—	−9.9	−5.6	—	—	−5.6

Note: a. As per Table 1.3 of *Employment Gazette* (larger MLHs).

the 'industrial composition' of employment decline in recession conditions of 1980 could be said

(1) to favour the South East, the South West and East Anglia ('the South');
(2) to provide the worst burden upon industrial employment in Wales, Yorkshire and Humberside and the West Midlands.

Net *differential shifts* are remarkably small for several Regions. Their breakdown often shows a number of compensating gains and losses; but metal manufacture, itself the largest absolute and proportionate source of job losses, has a powerful effect on regional differential shifts. This can usually be related to individual large closures which we have mentioned in Chapters 5 and 6. The engineering sector is responsible for the additional differential shifts in Wales and Scotland, where the effects of individual closures by corporations are evident, for instance in the redundancies at Singer (UK) Ltd., Clydebank. Positive differential shifts in the South East and East Anglia are very widely distributed between sectors. The differential shift column thus suggests a poorer manufacturing performance in the *peripheral* Regions, Wales, Scotland and the North.

The position decisively changes when at a broader level we incorporate non-manufacturing employment and recognise its still very varied relative importance in different Regions. The point has been made elsewhere by Gillespie and Owen[40] with reference to estimates of changes in employees in employment; but Table 8.8 refers to redundancies data. The inclusion of primary industries and services, with their lower rates of redundancy, depresses the national shift to a low apparent level of 2.2 per cent. Structural shifts, however, are relatively stronger than in Table 8.7 and are led by the West Midlands and Yorkshire and Humberside, not by 'peripheral' Regions with traditional problems of decline. Differential shifts are remarkably weak, but the greatest are in areas of past regional policy concern, Wales, the North West and Scotland.

If we were to standardise Tables 8.7 and 8.8, we would find that the inclusion of non-manufacturing sectors had had the most favourable effects on the South East, Scotland, the South West and East Anglia, and the most depressing effects on the total shift figures for the West Midlands, the North West and the East

Table 8.8: Shift-share Analysis of Redundancies Occurring in all Sectors, 1980, at Disaggregated Level; Percentages of 1978 Employees in Employment

	Redundancies occurring, ES955 (112 recorded industries)				Proportion of all employees in manu-facturing
Standard regions	National shift	Structural shift	Differential shift	Total shift	
South East	− 2.2	+ 0.6	+ 0.7	− 0.9	25.5
North West	− 2.2	− 0.4	− 0.9	− 3.5	37.7
West Midlands	− 2.2	− 1.0	+ 0.1	− 3.1	44.7
Scotland	− 2.2	+ 0.0	− 0.6	− 2.8	29.2
Yorks & Humber-side	− 2.2	− 0.6	+ 0.2	− 2.6	35.6
South West	− 2.2	+ 0.5	− 0.0	− 1.7	27.3
East Midlands	− 2.2	− 0.5	− 0.0	− 2.7	39.1
North	− 2.2	− 0.2	− 0.3	− 2.7	33.7
Wales	− 2.2	− 0.5	− 1.8	− 4.5	30.7
East Anglia	− 2.2	+ 0.3	+ 0.8	− 1.1	29.4
Great Britain	− 2.2	—	—	− 2.2	32.0

Midlands. Non-manufacturing redundancies are concentrated in distributive trades, construction, transport and miscellaneous services and it does not appear that the spread of these activities between Regions is of itself a significant cause of structural shifts, except for port-related activities in the North West. Of much more significance is the basic ratio of manufacturing to total employment indicated in the last column of the table; quite simply the four Regions just identified (the South East, Scotland, the South West and East Anglia) were those with less than 30 per cent of their employees in manufacturing in 1978, and the other three (the West Midlands, the North West and East Midlands) were those with more than 36 per cent in manufacturing.

The pattern of recession presented in Tables 8.7 and 8.8 is thus a complex one with several effects super-imposed upon one another.

The pattern of *differential shifts* is markedly traditional, with the North West, Scotland, the North and Wales showing worse than average deterioration, in manufacturing and total employment. *Structural shifts in manufacturing* are of a new kind and show their highest negative values in Wales, Yorkshire and the West Midlands in that order; but the inclusion of services in the analysis of *structural shifts in total employment* leaves the West Midlands the most vulnerable of all Regions of the country and strengthens further the relative positions of the South East, the South West and East Anglia.

The total shift column of Table 8.8 indicates that Wales, the North West and the West Midlands were the areas of heaviest proportionate job losses in 1980, and this corresponds with the analysis of percentage rates of unemployment in Table 8.2. Each of these areas appears to have reached this position by a different route:

(1) Wales was in the worst position through having had a disproportionately large share of British redundancies in steel, its main manufacturing industry, a differential effect in addition to a structural effect.

(2) The North West also suffered both differential and structural effects, but these were more varied; they resulted both from poor performance in individual manufacturing and service industries and from the Region's proportionate dependence on manufacturing.

(3) The West Midlands owed its above average deterioration to an unfavourable mixture of manufacturing industries suffering greater than average decline, and to its overall level of dependence on manufacturing, which was the highest in Great Britain.

If we look finally over redundancies in the calendar years 1976–80, we find that the steep increase in their incidence in 1980 brought with it:

(1) A marked worsening in the already poor structural position of the West Midlands.

(2) Somewhat surprisingly, the Scottish and Northern data represent a relative improvement in both their structural and differential shifts in 1980 compared with 1976–79.

(3) *Some* 'Regions without conurbations', the South West and

East Anglia, further improved their relative position, but so too did the South East where the values of structural and differential shifts were positive throughout.

Conclusions

The pattern emerging from the analysis is unlike that of previous recessions because of a sharp divergence between the South East and the West Midlands, which is partly due to manufacturing structure, but also to the smaller impact of recession on the service sector. In the rest of the country the order of performance changed, and Scotland suffered a less serious deterioration than before, indeed having lower unemployment rates than the West Midlands. This was a basically national recession. Yet it had a sufficiently new industrial composition to effect marked regional changes in the distribution of large amounts of additional unemployment. It extended the incidence of decline from 'peripheral' Regions further in to most other Regions, particularly the West Midlands and the North West. There were sub-regional variations according to the detailed incidence of difficulties for individual products and of corporations' decisions to rationalise plant, as was strongly evident in Chapters 5 to 7. The pattern of our results does not suggest, however, that the worst effects of rapid employment decline were consistently concentrated in conurbations (both Wales and the South East belie this).

Of course, 1981's redundancies were less severe in some of the industries affected most in the early recession in 1979 and 1980, notably in textiles and clothing; Yorkshire and Humberside suffered in 1981 many of the redundancies 'expected' in 1980. The 1980s may bring successive reactions to the recession in the pattern of non-manufacturing employment. For the longer term, however, this analysis has shown the possible type and scale of departures from past history. Recession is more widespread than in the pattern established in the 1930s and echoed since in minor cycles, and it is possible to see new regional trends affirmed as manufacturing employment is more widely affected by difficulties. Some of our results possibly represent an extreme case of cyclical sensitivity; but all the evidence is that the West Midlands is reacting worse at every stage of each successive recession (as observed by, for example, Wood[41]), while the Northern Region for example tends to suffer a proportionately smaller deterioration at the peak of a crisis (Northern Region Strategy Team[42]). The industrial analysis on which this chapter is based still reflects some bias in the pattern of redundancy towards geographers' regional specialisms in iron and steel, textiles and motor vehicles (if no longer to shipbuilding and coal) – the 'world of Stamp and Beaver'[43] which we noted in Chapter 1. As it happens therefore the more traditional approach of British Geography, which emphasises older industries and regional specialisms, is of great value in understanding the ongoing emphasis of decline. Clearly, many pre-war 'layers' of industrial investment across the map of Britain have been disappearing fast. But to a great extent we have found this to be a national recession; this means that parts of the post-war map of investment, in engineering, electronics and the like are also affected; we now turn our attention to a systematic review of post-war 'growth areas'.

Notes

1. *The Times*, 20 Sept. 1981.
2. G.C. Cameron, 'The National Industrial Strategy and Regional Policy', in D. Maclennan and J.B. Parr (eds.) *Regional Policy, Past Experience and New Directions* (Martin Robertson, Oxford, 1979), pp. 245–72.
3. G. Turner, 'Unemployment in a Nation of Shopkeepers; Let Them eat Cake – There's no Call for Bread yet'. *Daily Telegraph*, 13 Aug. 1981.
4. D. Keeble, 'Industrial Decline, Regional Policy, and the Urban-rural Manufacturing Shift in the United Kingdom', *Environment and Planning A*, vol. 12, no. 8 (1980), pp. 945–62.
5. W.R. Garfield, *The Measurement of Unemployment* (Blackwell, Oxford, 1980), pp. 68–94.
6. G. McCrone, *Regional Policy in Britain*, 1st edn. (Allen & Unwin, London, 1969), pp. 91–2.
7. D. Keeble, 'Spatial Policy in Britain: Regional or Urban?', *Area*, vol. 9, no. 1 (1977), pp. 3–8.
8. D. Keeble, 'De-industrialisation means Unemployment'. *Geographical Magazine*, vol. 53, no. 4 (1981), p. 459.
9. A.E. Gillespie and D.W. Owen, 'Unemployment Trends in the Current Recession', *Area*, vol. 13, no. 3 (1981), pp. 189–96.
10. A.P. Thirlwall, 'Regional Unemployment as Cyclical Phenomena', *Scottish Journal of Political Economy*, vol. 13, no. 2 (1966), pp. 209–19.
11. F. Brechling, 'Trends and Cycles in British Regional Unemployment', *Oxford Economic Papers*, vol. 19, no. 1 (1967), pp. 1–21.
12. P. Cheshire, 'Regional Unemployment Differences in Great Britain', *NIESR Regional Papers No. 2* (Cambridge, 1973).
13. M. Frost and N. Spence, 'Changes in Unemployment Rates in Great Britain 1963–1976', *Working Report 4, SSRC Research Project* (London School of Economics, 1978).
14. L.W. Hepple, 'Regional Dynamics in British Unemployment, and the

Impact of Structural Change', in N. Wrigley (ed.), *Statistical applications in the social sciences* (Pion, London, 1979), pp. 45–63.

15. A. Townsend, 'Planning for the 1980s; Unemployment', *Planning*, no. 379 (1980), pp. 6–7.

16. Gillespie and Owen, 'Unemployment Trends in the Current Recession', pp. 189–96.

17. C.S. Crouch, 'Comment; Trends in Unemployment', *Area*, vol. 14, no. 1 (1982), pp. 56–9.

18. *Employment Gazette*, vol. 90, no. 4 (1982), Tables 1.2 and 2.2.

19. *Employment Gazette*, vol. 89, no. 10 (1981), p. S6.

20. Keeble, 'De-industrialisation means Unemployment', pp. 460–1.

21. S. Fothergill and G. Gudgin, 'Regional Employment Change: a Sub-regional Explanation', *Progress in Planning*, vol. 12, part 3 (1979), pp. 155–219.

22. Keeble, 'Industrial Decline, Regional Policy, and the Urban-rural Manufacturing Shift in the UK', pp. 945–62.

23. Office of Population Censuses and Surveys, 'The First Results of the 1981 Census of England and Wales', *Population Trends*, 25 (1981).

24. A.A. Ogilvy, 'Population Migration Between the Regions of Great Britain, 1971–9', *Regional Studies*, vol. 16, no. 1 (1982), pp. 65–73.

25. *Employment Gazette*, vol. 89, no. 3 (1981), pp. 141–5.

26. *Employment Gazette*, Tables 1.2–1.5.

27. A.E. Gillespie and D.W. Owen, 'Comment; Trends in Unemployment', *Area*, vol. 14, no. 1 (1982), pp. 59–61.

28. A.J. Brown, *The Framework of Regional Economics in the United Kingdom* (Cambridge University Press, Cambridge, 1972).

29. D. Keeble, 'De-industrialisation Means Unemployment', p. 460.

30. A.R. Townsend, 'Recession and the Regions in Great Britain, 1976–80: Analyses of Redundancy Data', *Environment and Planning A*, vol. 14 (1982) forthcoming.

31. Fothergill and Gudgin, 'Regional Employment Change: a Sub-regional Explanation', p. 193.

32. Keeble, 'Industrial Decline, Regional Policy and the Urban-rural Manufacturing Shift in the United Kingdom', pp. 948–50.

33. Manpower Research Group, University of Warwick, *Review of the Economy and Employment* (University of Warwick, Coventry, 1981), p. 92.

34. S. Fothergill and G. Gudgin, 'In Defence of Shift-Share', *Urban Studies*, vol. 16, no. 3 (1979), p. 319.

35. H.W. Richardson, *Urban and Regional Economics* (Penguin, Harmondsworth, 1978).

36. B.H. Stevens and C.L. Moore, 'A Critical Review of the Literature on Shift-share as a Forecasting Technique', *Journal of Regional Science*, vol. 20, no. 5 (1980), pp. 419–38.

37. B.C. Moore and J. Rhodes, 'Evaluating the Effects of British Regional Economic Policy', *Economic Journal*, vol. 83, no. 7 (1973), pp. 87–110.

38. Townsend, 'Recession and the Regions in Great Britain, 1976–80: Analyses of Redundancy Data'.

39. A.R. Townsend, 'Geographical Perspectives on Major Job Losses in the UK, 1977–80', *Area*, vol. 13, no. 1 (1981), pp. 31–8.

40. Gillespie and Owen, 'Comment; Trends in Unemployment', p. 60.

41. P.A. Wood, 'West Midlands Leads the Downward Trend', *Geographical Magazine*, vol. 49, no. 1 (1976), pp. 2–12.

42. Northern Region Strategy Team, 'Causes of the Recent Improvement in the Rate of Unemployment in the Northern Region Relative to Great Britain', *Technical Report no. 11* (Northern Region Strategy Team, Newcastle-upon-Tyne,

1976).

43. L.D. Stamp and S.H. Beaver, *The British Isles, A Geographic and Economic Survey* (Longman, London, 1st edn. 1933, 6th edn. 1963).

Part Three

CONSEQUENCES FOR PAST AND PRESENT PUBLIC POLICIES

9 THE IMPACT ON GROWTH INDUSTRIES, NEW TOWNS, AND GOVERNMENT ASSISTED AREAS

Deep recession conditions may have many political repercussions affecting most arms of government. If we were to review the international sphere we would notice unsettling effects on many governments, on established trading relationships and on co-operation in the EEC. Nationally, many different departments of government would be wise to consider the effects of recession. What of the changing needs of education, training or police provision – or the financing of local government services? Examining the geography of recession, we have already referred extensively in Part Two to the central government's regional policy and 'inner city' policies. Now in Part Three we focus on issues such as these that affect individual labour market areas of the UK; both the new structure of unemployment and the relevant public policies. In Chapter 10 the attempts since 1976 to contain and reduce the public sector's own level of employment are mentioned. We review the distribution and prospects of unemployment in the 1980s before concluding with a review of the scope for and relevance of future spatial policies.

This chapter asks more fully what the impact of recession has been on the industries and employment which were located where they were under post-war spatial policies. At many stages since the Second World War, the government has directed or induced employers to invest in certain places rather than others – (1) the 'assisted areas', mainly in the 'poorest Regions',[1] and (2) the New Towns[2] and Expanded Towns (the latter are 'overspill' towns in the South East and some other Regions). The policy balance between these types of areas varied at different times, but at least policies for them all depended for any success on attracting investment, mainly in manufacturing industry. If we look now at the incidence of redundancy and closures in these areas we may observe a good sample of post-war new investment and may ask:

(1) Are the industries which expanded post-war more or less vulnerable than others to national recession?

(2) In particular, are their new branches more vulnerable to fail-

ure or closure than before 1976 (compared for instance with their 'parent' establishments)?

(3) Has the dependence of many New Towns and Expanded Towns on manufacturing proved critical in the circumstances of recession? To what extent was their viability and remaining growth put at risk?

(4) What is the result, in 'assisted areas', if some of the new industries have proved as vulnerable as the ones they replaced? Has regional policy been overwhelmed?

An Association between Industries' Post-war Expansion, Geographical Movement and Current Decline?

The recession has clearly picked out for closure some of the country's oldest-founded factories, for instance, Consett Steel Works which dates from the 1840s, or Singer UK of Clydebank (1881), recognised as the first large US factory investment in Britain. There is an overall association between the industries of heavy recent decline and their age, notably in the metal industries and textiles. In all, it has been estimated by the author that of all individual job losses reported in the *Financial Times* in the period 1976–80 nearly half occurred in economic activities which were traditional or indigenous to the areas in which they occurred, particularly in Wales, the West Midlands and Scotland. About a tenth occurred in cities with inner urban 'partnership areas' and in Glasgow. But the balance of job losses, nearly half, was in products developed mainly since the depression of the early 1930s, some in extremely 'young' factories.

Chapter 2 introduced the concept of Kondratieff that western economies have developed through long cycles of about 50 years. A group of the Conference of Socialist Economists wrote that:

> Each long boom has been closely associated with the growth of one or more particular industries . . . In the depressions that followed, it was these industries that generally suffered most markedly from decline and low profitability, whereas at the same time, the industries that would play a leading role in the next boom were already developing.
>
> CSE Microelectronics Groups, 1980[3]

A similar view is expressed by Dunford *et al.*,[4] who say 'The new world recession and the declining competitiveness of the national economy were leading to an accelerated rationalisation and restructuring of many industries that had played a leading role in the previous wave of expansion'. The industries which the CSE Group associate with a 1945–74 'long boom' are the assembly-line production of mechanical and electrical consumer durables, motor cars and petrochemicals. There is certainly evidence that *some of* the newer industries developed after the 1930s depression are now disproportionately vulnerable. The recession exposed domestic overinvestment in recent growth industries (e.g. artificial fibres or stereo equipment). It can be argued that the end of the 'long boom' itself is due to its new products meeting a ceiling of demand; for example the closure of several colour TV factories (Chapter 7) was associated with a decline in production in which new demand for sets was falling towards replacement level. It is often thought that the branches, as the last developed part of the corporations, are most marginal to their labour needs. They provide 'variable capital' in Marxist terminology, are dominated by semi-skilled work (Townsend *et al.*, 1978[5]), and are kept in use only while this is needed in the corporate division of labour (Massey, 1979[6]). They are also to some extent being replaced by cheaper labour in Third World countries.

We know in which industries geographical movement took place after 1945, and can compare their sectoral pattern with the national distribution of recent redundancies. The 'mobile industries' correlate up to a point with those in which overall national employment expanded, as explained by Keeble in 1976[7]; they often moved in search of labour. In movement to peripheral areas most of the factories successfully established in 1966–71 were in mechanical engineering, electrical engineering and textiles. Elsewhere, the pattern was more heavily dominated by mechanical and electrical engineering. A fine-grained analysis was conducted by Howard[8] for the last period of net growth of national manufacturing jobs, from 1953 to 1966, on which the first generation of New Towns, for example, depended when expanding their populations. For this period, the Board of Trade had a consistent definition of industrial 'moves'; a move occurred when new production was established in a different sub-region (within a UK set of 50) from that in which a 'parent' establishment could be identified. By 1966, 497,000 jobs had been established through industrial 'moves' in a period of UK net man-

Table 9.1: The National Impact on Previously Mobile and Less Mobile Industry, Expressed in Terms of Employment Change, thousands

Industries defined by groupings of 1958 Standard Industrial Classification[a]	Employment at end 1966 created in all 'moves'	Net employment change thousands		
	1952–65	1953–66	1966–Dec. 79	Dec. 79–Dec. 80
(1) Expanding industries, 1953–66, more dependent on 'moves':				
Electrical goods and scientific instruments	+ 110	+ 328	– 99	– 76
Motor vehicles and aircraft	+ 67	+ 148	– 73	– 64
Selected chemicals and man-made fibres	+ 42	+ 103	– 18	– 33
Glass, cement, abrasives etc,	+ 12	+ 37	– 46	– 20
Hosiery, carpets and 'other textiles'	+ 9	+ 21	– 38	– 22
(2) Expanding industries, 1953–66, less dependent on 'moves':				
Selected mechanical engineering	+ 75	+ 357	– 162	– 87
Paper, printing and publishing	+ 20	+ 150	– 78	– 33
Selected miscellaneous industries	+ 28	+ 115	– 5	– 45
Selected food, drink and tobacco industries	+ 31	+ 114	– 58	– 26
Selected metal goods	+ 22	+ 103	– 80	– 58
Metal manufacture excluding castings	+ 12	+ 55	– 151	– 70
(3) Contracting industries, 1953–66, with some 'moves':				
Total	+ 68	– 708	– 624	– 171
Manufacturing Total	+ 497	+ 822	– 1,431	– 704

Note: a. The Table uses a regrouping of industries (Minimum List Headings of the Standard Industrial Classification) such that each group is composed of industries which expanded their employment between 1953 and 1966, or of ones which contracted.

Source: R.S. Howard, *The movement of manufacturing industry in the United Kingdom* (HMSO, London, 1968), Table 9, p. 27.

ufacturing increase of about 822,000. Table 9.1 relates this past period of expansion to the net decline of manufacturing employment of 704,100 in the calendar year of 1980. The first column shows the distribution between sectors of the 497,000 jobs established through 'movement'; the remaining columns are concerned with three periods of change in total employment in manufacturing.

Our purpose here is to draw a broad contrast between expanding and contracting industries. From the first two columns we find, for instance, that in motor vehicles and aircraft production job gains from movement were equivalent to 45 per cent of net employment expansion (the highest ratio in the table). The average ratio for expanding industries, 1953–66, was 28 per cent; the groups of industries with a higher ratio are placed here in group (1), those with a lower ratio in group (2). There were also 'moves' in contracting industries (3) such as textiles, clothing and footwear, which established branches in peripheral areas in search of labour. Apart from these, there is a good correlation between expansion and movement in this period.

Seven of the 'expanding industries' (on a crude comparison) lost more jobs in 1980 than they gained from the industrial 'moves' which took place over the whole period 1952–65. Four of the five industries of group (1) enjoyed a cyclical recovery of employment from 1976 to 1979, but the group as a whole sustained a 9.2 per cent reduction of jobs in 1980. Group (2) sustained losses of 10.3 per cent, virtually the same as the national rate of 10.1 per cent for manufacturing. The industries of previous contraction, group (3), showed a rate of loss of 11.0 per cent. On this evidence it cannot be said that 'past growth industries' have as a whole sustained a worse than average loss of jobs in the recent difficult economic circumstances; they may seem to have done so if one looks at certain industries only, but the overall evidence is very slightly the other way. However, they have suffered the worst *proportionate downturn* in their employment trends, and it is remarkable enough that they performed virtually as badly as the rest of industry.

The 'moves' which we have recorded here provided jobs about equally for peripheral areas and for other Regions including their New Towns. What is clearly implied is that recession has put employment as much at risk on industrial estates in New Towns and 'assisted areas' as in older established industrial areas. Areas dependent on new branches of the motor industry have clearly been more vulnerable. To the extent, however, that 'growth areas' of the

1950s and 1960s relied on manufacturing employment for their economic development (as shown, for instance, by Luttrell[9]) then they share the general greater vulnerability, demonstrated in the last chapter, of all manufacturing areas. We will examine these general points in more detail with reference to the two types of policy.

The Withdrawal of New Town and Expanded Town Investments

By the end of 1978 Great Britain's 28 official New Towns had developed over 314,000 jobs in industry in over 3,900 premises.[10] There were, additionally, over 60,000 jobs in over 1,350 offices. In Expanded Towns factories completed by mid–1978 were occupied by over 1,600 firms under the Town Development Act (England and Wales), 1952. The first generation of New Towns, designated between 1946 and 1950 mainly for London, benefited from a period when a full half of UK industrial 'moves' were allowed destinations in the South East and East Anglia Regions. It was estimated that New Towns and Expanded Towns together attracted probably about 40 per cent of all London migrant plants established in the two Regions.[11] They thus provided much of the expansion space for Britain's powerhouse of post-war industrial growth. The second generation of fourteen British New Towns, designated between 1955 and 1971, had more of a regional planning role: to draw population and industry out of the South East (for instance to Northampton or Peterborough), to provide for housing overspill (of Birmingham, Liverpool or Glasgow), or to act as regional growth areas (e.g. Washington, Tyne & Wear). We will now examine the effect on them of recent national industrial decline.

New Towns were virtually the only areas for which reliable statistics of 1981 employment were available before 1983. The Town and Country Planning Association organise regular surveys of New Town employment and these provide the source of Table 9.2.[12] British New Towns as a whole expanded their industrial floor-space by 23 per cent in the period studied, but were not able to maintain factory employment in the face of national recession. In 15 months when national employment began to fall (first four columns of Table 9.2), the strong expansion of the later generation of New Towns (for example, Northampton) explains a net increase of jobs in the 24 Towns as a whole. The older Towns of the London Ring and Scotland were already experiencing a levelling-out or decline of

Table 9.2: Changes in Industrial Activity, 1978–81, 24 New Towns, GB

Grouping of New Towns	Total Industrial Development since Designation					
	Dec. 1978		March 1980		March 1981	
	Employment (thou)	Size sq m (mil)	Employment (thou)	Size sq m (mil)	Employment (thou)	Size sq m (mil)
London Ring	69.5	2.09	64.2	2.19	63.7	2.21
Scotland	48.3	1.77	45.6	1.86	37.4	1.91
Other assisted areas[a]	46.4	2.12	53.7	2.40	54.4	2.77
Other[b]	33.4	1.52	47.5	2.02	48.5	2.35
Total, 24 Towns[c]	197.6	7.50	211.0	8.47	202.0	9.25
Total, GB	7,122	n.a.	6,811	n.a.	6,061	n.a.

Note: a. Aycliffe, Central Lancashire, Cwmbran, Newtown, Peterlee, Runcorn, Skelmersdale, Warrington, Washington.
b. Corby (an assisted area since 1980), Milton Keynes, Northampton, Peterborough, Telford.
c. Excludes Crawley, Redditch, Stevenage, Welwyn Garden City, for which comparable data were not available.

Source: Town and Country Planning; vol. 47, nos. 2–3 (1974), p. 142; vol. 49, no. 10 (1980), pp. 372, 376; vol. 50, nos. 11–12 (1981), pp. 328–35.

Table 9.3: Job Losses in UK New Towns; the Largest Cases Reported in the *Financial Times*, October 1976–October 1981

New Town[a]	Organisation	Parent organisation	Jobs lost	Category[b] and month of report
Corby, Northants	Tubes Division[†]	British Steel Corporation	7,700	R Dec. '77, P Feb. '79, R Sept. '80
East Kilbride, Strathclyde	Birmingham Sound Reproducers	—	2,700	P Nov. '79, C June '80
Antrim, N. Ireland	British Enkalon (fibres)[†]	Akzo, Netherlands*	2,000	P Jan. '81, C July '81
Telford, Shropshire	GKN Sankey (vehicle parts)[†]	GKN	2,000	R May '80, Oct. '80, Feb. '81
Peterborough, Cambs	Perkins Engines[†]	Massey Ferguson, Canada*	1,600	R '79, '80, '81
Milton Keynes, Bucks	Scot Meat	Unigate	1,200	C Sept. '81
Cumbernauld, Strathclyde	Burroughs Machines (computers)	—	1,200	R Nov. '80, Jan. '81, June '81
Skelmersdale, Lancs	Courtaulds	—	1,200	C Dec. '76 & Dec. '80
Stevenage, Herts	Platignum (pens & plastics)	—	900	W '76 – '81
Irvine, Strathclyde	Monsanto[†] (fibres)	Monsanto, USA*	800	C Aug. '79
Irvine, Strathclyde	SKF (UK) (ball bearings)[†]	SKF, Sweden*	800	W Sept. '78, P Jan '79
Newtown, Powys	BRD (transmissions)[†]	Guest, Keen & Nettlefolds	800	C Feb. '81, W before
Basildon, Essex	Ilford (films etc.)	Ciba-Geigy, Switzerland*	800	C June '80
Welwyn Garden City, Herts	Plastics Division	ICI	750	W April '79
Hemel Hempstead, Herts	Duplicating Machine Division[†]	AM International, USA*	650	C July '80
Craigavon, N. Ireland	Goodyear (rubber)	Goodyear, USA*	500	R June '79, June '81
Washington, Tyne & Wear	Timex	—	400	R Aug. '80
Warrington, Cheshire	Coventry Climax (lift trucks)	BL (British Leyland)	350	R Sept. '81

Note: a. All New Towns except Central Lancashire, where planned new growth was very small.

total manufacturing employment. In one calendar year of recession (last four columns of Table 9.2) the employment trends of virtually all Towns worsened. They experienced an average decline of 4.3 per cent. This was, however, less than half the national average decline in manufacturing employment, and it was heavily concentrated in the Scottish Towns, led by Irvine. Four English Towns each lost between a quarter and a sixth of their industrial estate jobs: Telford, Corby, Hemel Hempstead and Washington.

Table 9.3 is similar in layout to tables in Part Two and refers to individual job losses greater than 300 both in New Towns and their vicinity (not merely those within the property or designated area of the New Town corporations). What is striking in Table 9.3 is the role of large British-owned corporations (e.g. ICI, BL, GKN and Courtaulds), and of eight foreign-owned multi-national corporations controlled from no less than five industrialised countries. There was often an element of chance as to which New Town attracted which particular multi-national corporation in the first place, and as to the way in which different corporations later chose to rationalise their post-war acquisitions and investments. The table does, however, show one repeated tendency, toward plant rationalisation in the vehicle industry. It provides examples of lost employment in distinctively post-war industries, including artificial fibres, plastics, computers and photographic film. Several of the entries relate to comparatively low-paid female employment, while others, taken on their own, are not necessarily serious employment losses relative to size of the respective Towns.

Conversely, the case of Irvine New Town, Strathclyde, with two entries in the table, illustrates how a number of industrial decisions may combine to produce a complete change of prospects. The area was chosen as a New Town in 1966 because of the precedent of successful attraction of industry, linked with the promotion of a Glasgow overspill housing scheme by the Burgh Council:

> In 1973, advance factories were being let before they could be built. Professor Ronald Nicholl, of Strathclyde University, advised the Scottish Council that the north-central Ayrshire region, which includes Irvine, would be the major growth point for Scottish industrial development in the next two decades. But this optimism has been completely overturned by the recession.
>
> *Financial Times*, 23 August 1980

As a result of closures and redundancies in the Town, job losses at the nearby large works of ICI Ardeer and closures at BSC, Glengarnock and Massey Ferguson in Kilmarnock, the unemployment rate had reached 23.2 per cent by end–1981. This was exceeded among the principal towns of mainland Britain[13] only by Consett (24.9 per cent), a steel closure area. This is admittedly one extreme. But consider the case of Stevenage, the first New Town to be designated by government (1946) and one of several located in the normally prosperous county of Hertfordshire:

> Two weeks ago a 'for disposal' sign went up outside ICI's factory in Stevenage New Town, the first to appear in front of a major plant since the town was built more than 30 years ago. Last Friday Bowater shut a massive corrugated board factory. Kodak will pull out soon . . . Compared with many other industrial centres these are not dramatic events. But they are historic in the short life of the new town . . . They illustrate graphically how the recession is eating into industries in the south as well as the north. But they also show how uncompetitive some manufacturers had become, even in New Towns, before the recession. Stevenage has also discovered, like other towns, the drawbacks of depending mainly on 'branch' factories. It is these which big groups close first.
>
> *Financial Times*, 4 March 1981

These comments demonstrate the ubiquity of manufacturing recession, but require some qualification. Most New Town Development Corporations were to be wound up in the early 1980s;[14] there is indeed little demographic and planning need for their further special contribution to regional house-building. A number of New Towns (mainly around London) had attracted office employment as a valuable form of diversification, in which there was little evidence of major reductions before 1982. Table 9.2 showed that more recent New Towns had been steadily expanding their volume of available factory space before and during the national recession. Their marketing skills in attracting industry should make the most of this asset if and when national factory investment recovers. Indeed New Towns do appear to have attracted a considerable share of available investment in the depths of recession, particularly through searching for opportunities in micro-electronics (for example in Scotland) or developing 'science parks' (as at Warrington). Nonetheless, Mil-

Table 9.4: Job Losses in GB's Major Official Expanded Towns; the Largest Cases Reported in the *Financial Times*, October 1976–October 1981

Town[a]	Organisation	Parent organisation	Jobs lost	Category[b] and month of report
Linwood, Strathclyde	Talbot (UK) (motor cars)	Peugeot, France*	9,000	R Nov. '79, R May '80, C Feb. '81
Swindon, Wiltshire	Garrard (record changers)	Gradiente, Brazil*	3,800	R & W '77, '78, '80, '81
Ellesmere Port, Cheshire	Vauxhall (motor cars)	General Motors, USA*	3,000	R Jan '81
Winsford, Cheshire	ICL (computers)	—	1,800	R Aug. '80, C Nov. '80
Ellesmere Port, Cheshire	Bowater (newsprint)	—	1,600[c]	C Aug. '80[c]
	Burmah Oil (refinery)†	—	1,100	C May '81
Ashford, Kent	British Rail Engineering (wagons)†	British Rail	950	C June '81
Swindon, Wiltshire	Pressed Steel-Fisher (car bodies)	BL (British Leyland)	650	R March '80
Winsford, Cheshire	Metal Box (cans)	—	500	C Sept. '80
King's Lynn, Norfolk	Dynatron (music centres)	Philips, Netherlands*	400	C Aug. '80
	Fitch Lovell (canning)	—	350	C July '81

Note: a. Towns with official overspill agreements under the Town Development Acts, and with 400,000 sq ft of factory space completed and/or under construction, and associated with public housing programmes at mid-1971.

b. C (Closure); P (Partial closure); R (Redundancy); W (reported Wastage).

c. Consolidated – Bathurst of Canada were due to employ 450 on reopening the plant in 1983 (FT July 11, 1981).

* Foreign-owned plants, Talbot UK and Garrard originated as British-owned organisations before foreign takeovers occurred. Gradiente announced in February 1982 the transfer of remaining production to Manaus, Brazil.

† Pre-war plants.

ton Keynes itself was showing reduced growth even before its first major closure (see Table 9.3). In the wake of recession the demand is only for small premises. It appears that it will take a long time (especially in Antrim, Telford, Irvine and Newtown) to absorb the impact of job losses shown in Table 9.3.

Table 9.4 repeats the same task for those former Expanded Towns which attracted significant amounts of industry (see Note a). The development of these Towns was usually more modest and ad hoc than that of formally planned New Towns (Scargill[15]), even before the Greater London Council itself began to withdraw support for the policy in the 1970s. Outside the South East the legislation was taken up for the purposes of industrial diversification (as at Swindon) or to provide housing at industrial growth points (as at Linwood and Ellesmere Port, for workers from Glasgow and Liverpool respectively). The final failure of the Linwood motor-car plant in 1981 and the sharp contraction of Vauxhall's workforce at Ellesmere Port were of wide significance for the history of regional policy in Britain. The Linwood plant was opened by the British Rootes Group in 1963 before successive takeovers by Chrysler (USA) and Peugeot (France); it was Scotland's only motor-car plant. The table is dominated by redundancy in the vehicles industry, but we again see the impact of rationalisation in factories for musical equipment, computers and petrochemicals, with the most serious combination of redundancies at Ellesmere Port. Many of the job losses in Expanded Towns, as in New Towns, were among group (1) of Table 9.1 above, i.e. 'expanding industries more dependent on "moves"', chiefly electrical goods and scientific instruments, motor vehicles and selected chemicals and man-made fibres. A further large proportion fall under group (2), particularly in expanding parts of mechanical engineering.

A further test of the impact of recession is provided by reference to the increase in unemployment in New Towns and Expanded Towns. Nearly all the London Expanded Towns are sufficiently isolated to form their own 'travel-to-work areas' with separately quoted unemployment rates. Under official methods of calculation many New Towns fall in wider travel-to-work areas, and it is not meaningful to quote separate unemployment rates for them. We can, however, isolate and sum the numbers registered as unemployed at the local Employment Offices covering each town, and consider increases over time. This method does not refer to proportions of the working population (as was preferred in Chapter 8), but

Table 9.5: Changes in Unemployment, 1979–81, New Towns and Expanded Towns

Grouping of Towns	Total registered unemployed, June (including school-leavers) at local employment offices			
	(a) 1979	(b) 1981	(c) b − a	(d) c ÷ a
GB New Towns				
London Ring	9,800	24,600	14,800	150%
Scotland	9,800	18,500	8,700	89%
Other assisted areas	16,200	31,600	15,400	95%
Other GB New Towns	17,100	43,400	26,300	154%
Total, GB New Towns	52,900	118,100	65,200	123%
Major Expanded Towns				
East Anglia	4,900	11,300	6,400	131%
Other London Expanded Towns	11,000	25,200	14,200	129%
E & W Midlands	4,400	12,100	7,700	175%
Assisted areas	11,700	24,700	13,000	111%
Total, major Expanded Towns (as defined in Table 9.4)	32,000	73,300	41,200	129%
Total, Great Britain, thousands	1,281.1	2,576.6	1,295.5	101%

Source: Mimeographed monthly statistics of Regional Manpower Intelligence Units, Manpower Services Commission.

is employed in Table 9.5. These post-war 'growth areas' experienced on average a greater *proportionate* increase in unemployment than the nation at large (1979–81) and than their respective Regions; they exceed the high rates of increase in the Midlands and South East. The highest New Town rates of increase were experienced in Corby (225 per cent) and Bracknell, Redditch and Northampton (190–200 per cent). As a whole unemployment in the 'London Ring' of New Towns rose faster than in the South East as a whole. This is consistent with findings of Gillespie and Owen that the Outer Metropolitan Area (the area surrounding Greater London) increased its male unemployment 50 per cent faster than Greater London itself in the year ending February 1981.[16] Areas around the West Midlands conurbation deteriorated as rapidly as the conurbation itself; this will partly explain the high entry in Table 9.5 for the East and West Midlands. The entry for 'assisted areas' under major Expanded Towns is affected by the regional factor of lower proportionate increases in unemployment in the North and Scotland as a whole; but the most rapid increase of all Towns considered was recorded by Winsford in Cheshire, where unemployment increased by 241 per cent.

So it is certainly *possible* that towns based on post-war industry can be very vulnerable to recession conditions. A widely spread group of areas, New Towns and Expanded Towns, which were by definition largely dependent for their growth on post-war 'mobile' industries, suffered *more* than other labour market areas from the onset of recession. This was marked if like Winsford (Cheshire) and King's Lynn (Norfolk) they are fairly isolated. We must, however, bear in mind certain underlying and qualifying factors. The very high unemployment rate at Telford (19.3 per cent at end-1981) was partly attributed to demographic factors and to the statistical behaviour of commuting areas. In many New Towns the youthful age structure of the population adds to the scale of unemployment among school-leavers, and in Telford the specific past timing of housing growth was critical in this respect.[17] Again, it is asserted that people often move to New Towns and 'Expanded Towns' chiefly to obtain houses, while commuting back to jobs in the conurbation; the loss of jobs in the conurbation (e.g. that of the West Midlands) leads to a disproportionate number of registrations for unemployment in the area of residence (e.g. Telford) if the labour market is difficult there too.

Beyond all this we have the great dependence of these 'growth areas' on manufacturing, when the real growth industries have in most Regions been service activities. Few of the areas we have been reviewing here have developed successfully as diversified service centres, against the competition from the pre-existing hierarchy of towns. Townsend[18] has shown that, outside conurbations, unemployment does tend to vary inversely with the service status of towns; we thus have a further reason for the generally worse than average performance of New Towns and Expanded Towns in this manufacturing-led recession, even though some may have performed better than the national average in manufacturing itself.

The Impact of Recession on 'Regional Policy Factories'

As we have seen, the 'growth areas' of New Towns and Expanded Towns had a part to play in focusing investment in 'assisted areas'. However, the re-birth of regional policy in the period 1958–63 was first aimed directly at areas of higher unemployment, at 'blackspots' created by past mining and industrial redundancy. In Chapter 5 we found many examples of renewed recession in the 'replacement industries' of the poorer Regions of the UK. It remains here to assess at large the withdrawal of activity from factories established as a result of regional policy (including those in parts of England which fell under Chapters 6 and 7), before looking at the difficult position for future spatial policies in Chapter 10.

There has in the past been a tendency towards unduly polarised views of regional policy: either that it was largely a failure, or, with mounting evidence by the mid-1970s, for example from Keeble,[19] that it was a strong force. In reality neither of the extreme views was likely to be the overall case. With full employment in the core regions of the economy it could show some success; with the gradual ending of full employment it was in any case likely to decline in importance in the 1970s:

> There is some evidence that employment was higher in the three main Development Area regions by at least 20,000 per annum (cumulative) during the period from 1966–71, and by some 11,000 per annum (cumulative) from 1971–6, than might have been expected on the basis of trends in the late 1950s.
>
> Marquand, 1980[20]

Marquand reports major changes in the spatial pattern of development since 1971. The volume of movement was lower, and the destinations were no longer closely associated with regional policy measures. This change in the 1970s can be linked with many of the factors we have discussed earlier: the faltering nature of industrial investment (especially after 1973); the reduced share of manufacturing in the economy; and the growth of unemployment in 'normally prosperous Regions'. These made it more difficult to refuse industrial development certificates in those areas (Chisholm;[21] Moore, Rhodes and Tyler[22]). As Massey and Meegan[23] point out, a reduced rate of movement to 'assisted areas' did not have to result from the net decline of manufacturing employment. However, in

Table 9.6: Total Spending on Regional Policy, 1975–82, in Great Britain, at Constant (1980) Survey Prices, £ Million

1965/6	1,132	1979/80	565
1976/7	1,102	1980/1	652
1977/8	672	1981/2	623(forecast)
1978/9	740		

Source: Government Expenditure Plans, 1981/2–1983/4, Command 8125, *SO*, March 1981.

the mid-1970s a number of policy factors further reduced the status of regional policy (Manners[24]): the national Industrial Strategy, described by Cameron,[25] and some job creation schemes were applied on a national basis; the acceptance of the Inner Urban Areas Act, 1978 more than offset the impact of the new Scottish and Welsh Development Agencies and any more helpful aspects of EEC membership.

What was new in the 1976–81 period was some absolute reverses, in the shape of reduced financial provision for regional policy and a much increased rate of redundancy and closure among previously established 'regional policy factories', as already suggested in the previous chapter. The first feature is shown in Table 9.6. The main financial cut was the ending of the Regional Employment Premium in 1977. Although it was a subsidy to the payroll of all manufacturing firms in 'assisted areas' there were few substantiated suggestions that its withdrawal led directly to job losses. The second major change saw reductions in Regional Development Grants and the areas eligible for them, announced by the incoming Conservative government in mid-1979 and summarised by Townsend.[26] A large proportion of the total sums paid in such Regional Development Grants goes into capital intensive investment by corporations such as ICI or the British Steel Corporation (sic). The data may not therefore give an accurate view of industrial activity at large in 'assisted areas', e.g. in 1977–82.

Activity on the government's own industrial estates provides a more precise view of trends in this period. These properties were run under a variety of names since their inception in 1936; Table 9.7 shows data for properties in present and former 'assisted areas' of England (together with some rural areas of the country specified by the Development Commission). The table covers less than half the 'regional policy factory' jobs in England. However, this is a sizeable

Table 9.7: Changes in Activity, English Industrial Estates

	Total employment,[a] at June			Changes
	(a) 1976	(b) 1979	(c) 1981	(d) 1979–81
North East England	73,900	72,200	61,100	- 15%
Cumbria	7,900	7,800	6,000	- 23%
North West (mainly Merseyside)	20,400	18,800	15,300	- 19%
Doncaster Office Area	500	1,600	2,000	+ 28%
South West England	2,500	3,700	2,900	- 23%
Total, England	105,000	104,100	87,200	- 16%

Note: a. Since 1979 the Corporation has been encouraged by the government to sell off its property. The 1981 employment data include the Corporation's assessment of employment in sold factories, based on the 1976 and 1979 method of recording employment, to allow comparison of figures.
Source: English Industrial Estates Corporation, Annual Report and Accounts, 1981; unpublished data supplied by EIEC.

spread of activities which clearly shared in both the stagnation of national manufacturing job levels, 1976–79, and in a marked decline in the two years ending at mid-1981. *The recorded reduction of employment of 16 per cent is exactly the overall national GB rate.* The Corporation recorded an 'unprecedented' number of factories being vacated ahead of expiry of leases in the financial year 1980/1, many of them in the larger sizes.[27] Overall, the number of factories and tenants continued to increase, but there was a fall in the total floor space occupied and a rise of 30 per cent in the level of vacant stock. As in the New Towns, therefore, the building of more premises was accompanied by a fall in employment, but here it happened faster. This decline in the number of workers per square metre is of great interest to planners if it proves permanent.

Post-war records show many closures in 'regional policy factories', but at a very gradual rate. More than 4,000 factory 'moves' between UK sub-regions were recorded for 1945–65: of these about 1,000 had closed by the end of 1966, and this is shown by Sant[28] to represent an overall closure rate of about 1.9 per cent per annum. There was modest cyclical variation, and some evidence of worse performance in 'peripheral areas' until 1960. Henderson's calculations[29] show that performance in these areas was about 50 per cent worse than the national average for 'mobile factories' in the period 1972–75. However, he was still talking about closure rates of the order of 4 per cent per annum, which is the figure he cites for all

Table 9.8: Provisional Estimates of Job Losses in 'Regional Policy Factories' 1976–91, Compared with Previous Openings, thousands

	Openings of manufacturing units from inter-regional 'moves'		FT reports of job losses allocated to same group of factories	
	1945–65[a]	1966–76[b]	Oct. '76 – Dec. '79	Jan. '80 – Oct. '81
Northern Ireland	39.8	12.5	2.7	8.3
Scotland	94.7	28.9	9.2	13.2
Wales	93.7	32.7	4.8	7.8
North	89.6	33.9	11.0	6.2
North West	104.8	20.9	16.0	13.4
South West	36.9	20.5	—	2.4
Total	459.5	161.9	43.6	51.0

Note: a. Units surviving and employment at end 1966. Board of Trade, *The movement of manufacturing industry in the United Kingdom, 1945–65*, HMSO (1968), Appendix B, 40.
b. Units surviving at the end of 1976 and employment in mid-1976, *Regional Statistics*, 1980, HMSO (1980), Table 10.7.

Scottish New Towns, 1966–75. Government research data on the movement, opening and closure of factories do not extend far into our present period of study; however our *Financial Times* (FT) records suggest a dramatic change in the previous stability of post-war factories in 'assisted areas', as it was documented by Sant, Clark[30] or Atkins.[31]

Provisional estimates have been made of the approximate number of jobs lost from 1976 to 1981 from factories attracted to 'assisted areas' since the war. They were compiled by allocating all FT reports of job losses to a number of categories, principally from the writer's own full-time research experience of three UK peripheral Regions. Extensive checking on the origin of factories was not possible, so the results in Table 9.8 are intended to indicate only orders of magnitude which are on the 'low side' of a possible range of figures, given inevitable under-reporting of less conspicuous job losses through natural wastage etc. They are compared in the table with the previous scale of job provision from factory movement to the main 'assisted areas' (although of course there was a modest level of expansions, not counted here, in 1976–81). Table 9.8 suggests that about one job in six in 'regional policy factories' had been lost in the recession by late 1981. There were variations in place and time; it does appear again, as in Chapter 8, that the North (including Tyne and Wear) and the North West (including Merseyside) suffered more than other areas before 1980. The highest rates of job losses in the five years 1976–81 were in the North West and Northern Ireland, where losses broadly eliminated the benefits of ten years' previous work. The lowest rate of losses occurred in Wales, though many smaller factories closed there in 1981, many dating back to the period 1945–51. The level of FT reporting appears to be higher than for most other types of factory, but it would be most unlikely to approach full completeness.

Table 9.7, supported by Table 9.8, leads to a definite suggestion that the rate of job loss in 'regional policy factories' was at least as high as in their parent industries and corporations. In the past Sant[32] shows that closure rates in branch factories generally were higher than in 'lock, stock and barrel' factory moves, although the position changed in 1966–71. There is also the view[33] that rationalisations in the early 1970s tended to involve the heavier reduction of the parent plant than the 'assisted area' branch. The 1976–81 reports provide important examples of closures in the London area being tied with keeping jobs in 'assisted areas'. Leyland National eventually decided to transfer production of their closed London bus factory to their newer Workington plant when their skilled workers at Lowestoft refused to have semi-skilled work there.[34] Hoover, after a period of public uncertainty, chose to close its Perivale, West London, plant and to concentrate production at two 'assisted area' plants in Merthyr Tydfil, Mid-Glamorgan and Cambuslang, Strathclyde;[35] Borg-Warner (manufacturers of automatic transmissions) closed its plant at Letchworth Garden City in order to concentrate production at Kenfig Hill, South Wales.[36] (Some of these cases stimulated opposition in London, but it is not known whether there was any government intervention on behalf of the Regions.)

Conclusions

It is clear, however, that the balance of reports shows a pronounced withdrawal of large plants and foreign corporations from the 'assisted areas' along with many almost routine smaller cases. The size of Talbot's UK withdrawal from Linwood to Coventry, of BL's from Speke, Merseyside, of Vauxhall's (so far partial) withdrawal from Ellesmere Port, and of Courtaulds closures in most assisted Regions and Northern Ireland, is likely to decide the balance of any future calculations based on jobs. We conclude this chapter by answering the questions with which it began:

(1) Manufacturing industries which expanded after the war were on average as likely to suffer employment decline in the conditions of the early 1980s as previous contracting industries. This in itself is a striking conclusion, but the size of plants in some of the industries, and the variations between, say, the aerospace industry and motor vehicles, have meant that some 'growth areas' of post-war investment have been very vulnerable to recession.

(2) The previous stability accorded to large branch plants now carries no confidence.

(3) New Towns and Expanded Towns have on average sustained less than the national rate of decline in factory employment from the recession. Nevertheless the effects for the existing populations are serious when combined with demographic and travel-to-work patterns, irrespective of the reduced population targets given to New Towns in 1977. The compilers of Master Plans would have done better to search for greater dependence on office employment and service activities at the outset.

(4) The assisted Regions are more dependent on their own resources than at any time since the 1930s, and it is difficult to forecast when their larger vacant premises will be re-occupied. As in London and the New Towns, bodies like the English Industrial Estates Corporation are concentrating on the provision of much smaller industrial premises, but it is difficult to see this method providing full employment.

Notes

1. J.D. McCallum 'The Development of British Regional Policy', in D. Maclennan and J.B. Parr (eds.), *Regional Policy, Past Experience and New Directions* (Martin Robertson, Oxford, 1979), pp. 3–42.
2. F. Schaffer, *The New Towns Story* (MacGibbon and Kee, London, 1970).
3. CSE Microelectronics Group, *Microelectronics, Capitalist Technology and the Working Class* (CSE Books, London, 1980), pp. 4–5.
4. M. Dunford, M. Geddes and D. Perrons, 'Regional Policy and the Crisis in the UK: a Long-run Perspective', *International Journal of Urban and Regional Research*, vol. 5, no. 3 (1981), p. 380.
5. A.R. Townsend, E. Smith and M.R.D. Johnson, 'Employees' Experience of New Factories in North East England; Survey Evidence on some Implications of British Regional Policy', *Environment and Planning A*, vol. 10, no. 12 (1978), p. 1349.

6. D. Massey, 'In What Sense a Regional Problem?', *Regional Studies*, vol. 13, no. 2 (1979), p. 237.

7. D. Keeble, *Industrial Location and Planning in the United Kingdom* (Methuen, London, 1976), pp. 139–42.

8. R.S. Howard, *The Movement of Manufacturing Industry in the United Kingdom* (HMSO, London, 1968), pp. 26–33.

9. W.F. Luttrell, 'The Growth of Industry', in H. Evans (ed.) *New Towns, the British Experience* (Charles Knight, London, 1972), pp. 80–7.

10. P. Blake (compiler), 'Britain's New Towns: Facts and Figures', *Town and Country Planning*, vol. 47, nos. 2–3 (1979), pp. 132–66.

11. South East Joint Planning Team, *Strategic Plan for the South East: Studies volume 1: Population and Employment* (HMSO, London, 1971), p. 133.

12. Table 9.2 covers 24 of the 28 official New Towns in Great Britain for which comparable data for industry were available for three dates in the period 1978 to 1981. The data relate only to industry developed since the date of designation and therefore exclude the extraneous influence of older activities in the area, such as the closure of steel-making at Corby New Town or changes in the previous industrial base of Northampton or Peterborough.

13. *Employment Gazette*, Vol. 90, no. 1 (1982), Table 2.4.

14. Statement of Mr Peter Shore, Secretary of State for the Environment to the House of Commons, 5 April 1977.

15. D.I. Scargill, 'The Expanded Town in England and Wales', in R.P. Beckinsale and J.M. Houston (eds.), *Urbanisation and its Problems. Essays presented to E.W. Gilbert* (Oxford University Press, Oxford, 1968), pp. 119–42.

16. A. Gillespie and D. Owen, *The Current Recession and the Process of Restructuring in the British Space-economy*, paper presented to the 21st European Congress of the Regional Science Association, Barcelona, 25–28 August 1981.

17. L. Barling, 'Uphill Task to Counter Recession', *Financial Times* supplement on Telford New Town, 4 Nov. 1981, p. 35.

18. A.R. Townsend, 'Unemployment Geography and the New Government's "Regional" Aid', *Area*, vol. 12, no. 1 (1981), p. 16.

19. D.E. Keeble, 'Spatial Policy in Britain: Regional or Urban', *Area*, vol. 9, no. 2 (1978), pp. 304–12.

20. J. Marquand, 'Measuring the Effects and Costs of Regional Incentives', *Government Economic Service Working Paper No. 32*, Department of Industry, London, 1980, p. 109.

21. M. Chisholm, 'Regional Policies in an Era of Slow Population Growth and Higher Unemployment', *Regional Studies*, vol. 10, no. 2 (1976), pp. 201–13.

22. B. Moore, J. Rhodes and P. Tyler, 'The Impact of Regional Policy in the 1970s', *CES Review*, Vol. 1 (1977), pp. 67–77.

23. D.B. Massey and R.A. Meegan, *The Anatomy of Job Loss* (Methuen, London, 1982), p. 199.

24. G. Manners, 'Reinterpreting the Regional Problem', *The Three Banks Review*, no. 111 (1976), pp. 33–5.

25. G.C. Cameron, 'The National Industrial Strategy and Regional Policy', in D. Maclennan and J.B. Parr (eds.), *Regional Policy, Experience and New Directions* (Martin Robertson, Oxford, 1979), pp. 297–322.

26. Townsend, 'Unemployment Geography and the New Government's "Regional" Aid'.

27. English Industrial Estates Corporation, *Annual Report and Accounts*, 1981, p. 4.

28. M. Sant, *Industrial Movement and Regional Development* (Pergamon, Oxford, 1975), pp. 102–9.

29. R.A. Henderson, 'An Analysis of Closures among Scottish Manufacturing

Plants' (*ESU Discussion Paper 3*, Scottish Economic Planning Department, Edinburgh, 1979), p. 22.

30. U.E.G. Clark, 'The Cyclical Sensitivity of Employment in Branch and Parent Plants', *Regional Studies*, vol. 10, no. 3 (1976), pp. 293–8.

31. D.H.W. Atkins, 'Employment Change in Branch and Parent Manufacturing Plants in the U.K.: 1966–71', *Trade and Industry*, vol. 12, 30 August (1973), pp. 437–9.

32. Sant, *Industrial Movement*, pp. 106–8.

33. D.B. Massey and R.A. Meegan, 'Industrial Restructuring versus the Cities', *Urban Studies*, vol. 15, no. 3 (1978), p. 281.

34. *Financial Times*, 2 April 1980.

35. *Financial Times*, 23 Oct. 1981.

36. *Financial Times*, 30 Jan. 1980.

10 REGIONAL POLICIES IN RECESSION?

The effects of a decade of regional policy were cancelled out by the sheer scale of the recession, as Chapter 9 has shown. The Conservative government of 1979 chose to reduce the scope and power of such policies. Spokesmen for individual Regions began to look like just another special interest group in politics. Subsidies for declining areas of whatever kind – assisted areas, inner cities, rural buses or rural factory developments – appeared discredited. But this was not all. These palliatives were only the explicit part of government's spatially variable expenditure. Other cuts in public expenditure fell unevenly from place to place, so that the 'fiscal crisis of the state' (O'Connor, 1973[1]) held many and different implications for different areas.

The Stabilisation of Public Sector Employment

For many provincial areas the growth of public sector spending had actually been the main source of employment growth: *merely to end this growth* in the period 1976–81 was itself a substantial change in the balance of employment opportunities; thus public expenditure cuts became a central feature of regional employment change. In the decade 1966 to 1976 GB manufacturing employment declined by 16 per cent (1,309 thousand); total employment in the main public sector services – education, medicine and public administration – increased by 32 per cent (1,127 thousand, including part-time staff). What is more, the South East had below average increases in such employment; the highest increases were experienced in Northern Ireland, followed by other 'peripheral Regions' which had lagged behind the average in the provision of services, by Regions of greater population growth (e.g. the East Midlands), and by Regions which received civil service offices transferred from the South East. As shown by Parry[2] the distribution of public employment between Regions was still uneven in 1977.

The national record shows a complete change of trend after the imposition of public expenditure cuts by the Labour government in

Table 10.1: Employment of the Three Leading Public Sectors, GB, thousands (figures in brackets exclude part-time females)

	Education	Medical services	Public administration	All other services[a]
1966, June	1,218	930	1,390	8,106
1976, June	1,834 (1,148)	1,250 (863)	1,581 (1,432)	8,279
1978, June	1,820	1,263	1.554	8,552
1981, June	1,760 (1,094)	1,343 (905)	1,526 (1,369)	8,387
1981, December	1,757	1,359	1,509	8,272

Note: a. Orders XXI–XXVI of the Standard Industrial Classification (1968), less MLH 872 (Educational Services) and 874 (Medical and dental services).
Source: *Employment Gazette*, Table 1.4 (quarterly).

1976 followed by the Conservatives from 1979. These aimed to reverse, and certainly checked, the well-established growth of employment in education and public administration, although the number of jobs in medical services was still growing (at a modest rate) at the end of 1981. Detailed changes during this period are best recorded in the Joint Manpower Watch[3] for the main types of local authority staff in England and Wales; data are usefully given as 'full-time equivalents'. In the year-ending June, 1977 there was a reduction of 0.8 per cent in local authority employment, followed by small increases in the succeeding two years, before reductions of 1.8 per cent in 1979–80 and 2.0 per cent in the year-ending June, 1981. These included redundancies for manual staff such as those of the school meals service, and it was expected there would be a loss of up to 50,000 teachers (with about 10,000 redundancies) by 1984.[4]

The civil service at end-1981 was the smallest for 14 years. The Conservative government had reduced the size of the service by 52,500 since taking office and aimed to reduce it by a further 50,000 (to 630,000) by 1984.[5] These changes carried direct implications for the Regions in the curtailment of existing programmes to disperse offices to provincial sites. Department of Employment estimates subsequent to the 1978 Census of Employment are insufficiently detailed and reliable at the regional level to assess spatial variation in the overall pattern of public sector employment change, but reduced recruitment must clearly be seen as a widespread element of national unemployment.

The 'New Unemployment': Composition and Structure

We have concentrated on the origins of unemployment at the levels of job losses in large corporations, of widespread redundancies in industry, and, in the last section, of reduced recruitment by agencies of the state itself. We have attempted where possible to relate these processes to geographical variation in the distribution of total unemployment, although we would deplore an excessively 'area-based' approach to questions of deprivation at large. Statistics remain intractable: as the official UK level of registered unemployment reached the figure of three million early in 1982 the Manpower Services Commission itself suggested that the 'real' level, including the unregistered and potential workers deterred by the recession from entering the labour market, amounted to four million.[6] Unfortunately, our further comments must be confined to the official registers (and changes in registration procedures in late 1982 were due to produce an unusually marked discontinuity in official statistics).

The new levels of unemployment may conceal marked changes and variations in its composition. The unemployment register, as we mentioned in Chapter 3, normally represents a fairly rapidly changing body of people as they join and leave it. Now there is far more 'long-term unemployment', a cumulative result of recession, concentrated in poorer socio-economic groups. Economic and demographic analyses of unemployment tend to treat the following almost as *separate* phenomena:

(1) The overall spatial distribution.
(2) The long-term unemployed (including older and/or unskilled workers).
(3) Youth unemployment, including school leavers.
(4) Registered female unemployment.
(5) The share of unemployment suffered by ethnic minorities.

Geographical work has naturally tended to concentrate on (1), the regional distribution at the aggregate level. Items (2), (3) and (5) above all increased their shares of total unemployment after the last national peak of 1977. But there was comparatively little thought about the intersection of items (1)–(5), and what there is (apart from 4) is almost entirely confined to the broad level of standard Regions (in the monthly *Employment Gazette*). The data are in fact thoroughly recorded in Employment and Careers Offices. Figures for the above items are not confidential, and unpublished extractions of data for all the GB statistical areas of the Manpower Services Commission[7] are used here to support the reading of Tables 10.2 and 10.3.

The social and political costs are particularly painful with 'long-term unemployment', however it is defined. It affects physical health including mortality (Gravelle, 1981[8]) and mental illness (Brenner, 1973[9]), and there is evidence that the psychological effects are serious after six months. Continuous unemployment for a year is a useful criterion which incidentally implies that people included are beyond the reach of seasonal influences. The table must be understood alongside a decline in the relative importance of short-term unemployment: between January 1976 and January

Table 10.2: Long-term Unemployment in Great Britain, 1976–82; Duration of Registered Unemployment, Males and Females

January data, Great Britain	6–12 months	Over 1 year	Total unemployed
1976, thousands	207.3	182.3	1251.8
1982, thousands	675.5	862.5	2957.3
	%	%	%
1976, per cent of total	16.6	14.6	100.0
1979, per cent of total	17.7	24.1	100.0
1981, per cent of total	19.9	18.8	100.0
1982, per cent of total	22.8	29.2	100.0
January 1982, per cent			
Scotland	22.3	30.3	100.0
Wales	21.5	31.8	100.0
North	21.7	34.1	100.0
North West	23.6	32.3	100.0
Yorks & Humberside	22.8	30.3	100.0
East Midlands	22.7	29.5	100.0
West Midlands	24.7	33.5	100.0
South East	23.2	23.3	100.0
South West	20.9	26.2	100.0
East Anglia	20.3	24.1	100.0

Source: *Employment Gazette*, Table 2.6 (quarterly).

1982 the proportion of people on the register who were employed for four weeks or less declined from 16.5 to 8.7 per cent, while those unemployed for six months or more rose from 31.0 per cent to 52.6 per cent, and the numbers unemployed for over one year increased nearly five-fold, shooting up rapidly in 1981 to reach the level of 863,000 at the beginning of 1982. Most economists believed the number would pass one million and stay at that level for at least three and possibly as many as ten years.

From Table 10.2 we can also take stock of the regional incidence of this long term unemployment at the end of our period of study. At January, 1982 it varied from 23.3 per cent of the total unemployed in South East England to 34.1 per cent in Northern England; the next highest Regions were a familiar group, the West Midlands, the North West and Wales. Unpublished data for all the 'travel-to-work areas' of GB at the same date naturally showed a wider range of variation, between ten per cent (the Shetland Islands) and 49 per cent (Huntly, Grampian) respectively. Most of the places with less than a fifth of their register unemployed for more than a year were seaside resorts or enjoyed the greatest prosperity (e.g. Watford). Most of the places with over a third out of work for a year were present or former 'assisted areas', having qualified as such by virtue of their aggregate unemployment. The exceptions were Swindon (33 per cent), Kidderminster (34 per cent) and all the statistical areas of the West Midlands Metropolitan County (34–38 per cent). Most distressing of all was the Liverpool 'travel-to-work area', where the figure of 43 per cent (38,400 people) was the second worst in the whole of GB (it was exceeded only by Huntly).

The details of youth unemployment are unexpected. Over one million of the unemployed were aged under 25 at the beginning of 1982, well over 20 per cent of the whole age group. But this is not a new disaster. The share of unemployment borne by this age group had already expanded in the two earlier recessions of the 1970s, and the large increase in numbers between 1976 and 1982 (January data in Table 10.3) represented only a small worsening in the share of the total burden. In January 1982 (a date well removed from the peak of school-leaving in July) this share varied only a little between Regions, between 35.3 per cent in the West Midlands and 40.2 per cent in Scotland. In reading Table 10.3 it should be borne in mind that degrees of under-registration may vary.

Unpublished data for the main 'travel-to-work areas' of GB

Table 10.3: Youth Unemployment and that of Older Workers in Great Britain, 1976–82; Males and Females

January data, Great Britain	Age: Under 25	Age: 55 and over	Total unemployment
1976, thousands	453.6	207.3	1251.8
1982, thousands	1105.3	441.3	2957.3
	%	%	%
1976, per cent of total	36.2	16.6	100.0
1979, per cent of total	35.9	17.0	100.0
1981, per cent of total	38.3	14.8	100.0
1982, per cent of total	37.4	14.9	100.0
January 1982, per cent			
Scotland	40.2	11.1	100.0
Wales	37.5	14.2	100.0
North	38.1	15.1	100.0
North West	38.4	13.2	100.0
Yorks & Humberside	38.1	16.0	100.0
East Midlands	35.8	17.9	100.0
West Midlands	35.3	16.0	100.0
South East	36.8	15.3	100.0
South West	36.1	17.5	100.0
East Anglia	35.7	17.5	100.0

Source: *Employment Gazette*, Table 2.6 (quarterly).

showed a complex range of variation in youth unemployment. The following features are noteworthy:

(1) In the largest cities the proportion of youth on the register tended to correlate with its overall rate. Thus Liverpool (42 per cent) and Glasgow (40 per cent), as centres of longstanding high unemployment, showed two of the highest figures, though they were exceeded in many areas of Scotland (and in a few areas of the South with a small register).

(2) Some of the very lowest are naturally those places heavily affected by adult redundancies, not only, for example, Shotton (29 per cent) but also the West Midlands Metropolitan County (32–36 per cent).

There are several myths about the composition of the

unemployed. One is that in a difficult period men are displacing women from jobs. In fact females represented a successively larger proportion of employees in employment in each year of our study; it is true that they likewise made up an increasing proportion of the unemployed in each year 1976 to 1980, but 1981, the year of most decisive increase in unemployment, showed a clear decline in the female proportion. It may be supposed that redundancy was more concentrated in the largely separate male labour market. A second myth is that white-collar workers have suffered a disproportionate share of the national increase in unemployment. In fact 'managerial and professional workers' have formed a fairly constant proportion of the registered unemployed, 'clerical and related' occupations had a declining share, and it was 'craft and similar' manual occupations which showed the main acceleration of increase.[10]

Finally, it is sometimes held that Commonwealth migrants and their children represent a large proportion of the increase of unemployed. The best official figures, for 'minority group workers', migrants from listed Commonwealth and ex-Commonwealth countries and their children, suffer from under-counting.[11] On this basis the minority groups represent 4.1 per cent of GB unemployed in early 1982, compared with 3.7 per cent two years before. Naturally the figure was somewhat higher in Regions of greater former immigration, chiefly the West Midlands (8.6 per cent) and the South East (7.4 per cent). Unpublished data for all 'travel-to-work areas' of GB, at end-1981, showed the very highest proportions in textile and clothing areas of other Regions (viz. Leicester, 22 per cent of the register; Blackburn, 19 per cent; and Bradford, 16 per cent) with the other high figures in the South East (Slough 17 per cent, and High Wycombe 15 per cent) and the West Midlands (Wolverhampton 15 per cent, and Birmingham 14 per cent). Individual local employment offices in inner Birmingham and inner London recorded much higher figures.

Some Empirical Findings of this Book

A synopsis of our observations is presented here before turning to future possibilities. We have repeatedly found some divergence between different Regions, 1976–9. The poor performance of 'peripheral Regions' was important in accumulating long-term unemployment, particularly in Liverpool and Glasgow. Otherwise the remarkable feature, with formidable implications for any spatial policy, was the *national scope of recession* after 1979. Though it started in individual corporations, industries and Regions, the more diffuse spatial spread of its later phases, finally impinging even on the service sector, affected virtually every aspect of the national economy:

(1) Recession was common to most manufacturing industries, but more intense in metal manufacture and textiles.

(2) Recession has been reflected in the shedding of labour by most leading corporations, but most strongly by BSC, BL, Courtaulds and GKN.

(3) All Regions were affected by recession; for different reasons it was most severe in the West Midlands, Northern Ireland, Wales and the North West.

(4) All the different types of sub-regions – conurbations, urban, semi-rural and rural – were equally affected by the rise in unemployment in 1979–81. It was not obvious that the 'urban problem' had increased in importance *relative* to that of other types of area, or that inner areas were the leading centres of manufacturing closures.

(5) Post-war industrial 'growth areas' were often fully involved in recession; New Towns and Expanded Towns were vulnerable to their general dependence on manufacturing industry.

(6) Registered unemployment among ethnic minority groups increased a little more than average. Outside London, these groups were concentrated in areas vulnerable to recession, mainly in the West Midlands County and in some textiles towns elsewhere in the 'Manufacturing Heartland'.

(7) The proportion of young people on the employment register, already high before this last recession, only worsened slightly.

(8) Unemployment increased among workers of all grades, but manual workers, in particular more skilled workers, suffered a disproportionate increase. The largest group numerically is still the less skilled manual.

(9) By the beginning of 1982 the cumulative impact of recession was most marked in long-term unemployment.

The widespread reduction of economic activity had generated

unemployment even more rapidly than the most pessimistic forecasts.

The Prospects for Employment

In 1982, long-term planning lay in abeyance in corporations, in government and in local authorities. It remained certain that the population of working age would continue to grow rapidly – by over 750,000 in the five years 1981 to 1986. Forecasters agreed that many more people of working age would be forced to leave the labour market altogether, and that registered unemployment would remain at about three million at least until 1985.[12] The recession of 1979–81 would thus produce a fresh 'plateau' in unemployment, at twice the level of that in 1976–9; the prospects of a return to full employment before the 1990s would be remote.

Most industrial job losses in 1979–81 *were independent of the much-heralded 'micro-electronic revolution'*, the application of micro-processors to more routine tasks in offices, factories and workplaces. The effects of that on home and work are yet to come. Many of the different estimates of these effects on employment are contradictory because of varying assumptions and time spans. Some of the most disturbing statements deal in the numbers of existing jobs displaced by the new technology, without much reference to the new tasks, demands and production which it generates itself. Jenkins and Sherman in *The collapse of work*[13] foresaw the loss of 5.2 million jobs over 25 years. A study for the International Labour Office[14] concluded: 'It would seem that a transition is taking place from a society with unemployment to one that no longer needs its full potential labour force to produce the necessary goods and services under current conditions of work'. A more tangible forecast was made by the Manpower Services Commission in 1981, that nearly a million unskilled jobs would disappear from the British labour market by 1985.[15] To Sleigh *et al.*[16] 'the impact upon employment of micro-electronic technology will be gradual rather than revolutionary'. Other writers argued that early British adoption of new technology in a favourable upswing of the economy might forestall its destructive effects, so that new job creation would keep pace with labour displacement.

The full force of developments in micro-electronics is expected to fall on offices and the service sector, including education staff somewhat more readily than health service workers. This could bear heavily on less skilled city workers living in inner areas. Can growth of the service sector offset this displacement? On the USA model 'Some services, such as tourism and entertainment, will undoubtedly increase their activities and possibly the number of their employees, but the question of whether such increases will compensate for losses elsewhere remains open' (Rada, 1980[17]). Sheriff[18] rejects the idea that further specialisation in services could provide a full solution to Britain's problems of 'de-industrialisation', as there is a long way to go before services can replace manufactures in paying for the nation's imports. Some proponents of the 'Long Cycle' argue that a surge of innovations may propel us from the trough into a new long upswing of investment and economic activity. Mensch, 1979[19] identifies the past timing of the deployment of innovations with periods of recovery in the Long Cycle of the international economy. For Ray the microprocessor may be the *Innovation in the Long Cycle*[20] at the centre of economic recovery, and British specialisation in certain products (e.g. instrumentation or aerospace) might yet provide a cure for the economy.

National Palliatives for Unemployment

The EEC in 1979 saw 'work-sharing' and a ban on systematic overtime as the best answers to an expected crisis of employment, but there was no agreement among EEC members. The Socialist government of France has taken some modest steps to reduce the working week, but little work-spreading has occurred in Britain, except for schemes of early retirement in certain organisations. The Labour government of 1974–9 responded to worsening employment conditions partly through 'job creation schemes' (mainly on a national basis, though some were concentrated on 'assisted areas'). Despite the constraints on public expenditure and the 'new broom' approach of the incoming Conservative government of 1979 most schemes continued. By end-August, 1981, no less than 692,000 people were covered by the GB 'special employment and training measures';[21] these included 370,000 on the Temporary Short-Time Working Schemes (TSTWCS), 215,000 on the Youth Opportunities Programme (YOP), 52,000 on the Job Release

Scheme (encouraging early retirement and replacement of staff) and 30,200 on 'Training for Skills'. It was estimated that the direct effect on the unemployment register was to reduce it by about 320,000. This is less than 692,000 for a number of reasons. For instance, the figure given for TSTWCS is the number of people working short time 'in order to avoid redundancies', rather than the number of redundancies averted. New government measures of 1981–2 included a subsidy to employers to take on young people under 18, a further expansion of YOP, and a plan to create by September, 1983 a one-year Youth Training Scheme for all unemployed school-leavers. The evidence, however, was that YOP trainees increasingly returned to the unemployment register after their period of 'training', and that existing and new schemes were merely threatening the interests of established workers, as reflected in trades union opposition to some proposals.

Local Initiatives and Small Firms

'Can we make jobs?' In 1980 and 1981 the sight of mass redundancies in large corporations on the one hand, and the palliative nature of 'job creation schemes' on the other, led to a search for new initiatives at the local level, some of them subsidised by the Community Enterprise Programme, covering 26,500 people in early 1982.

(1) *Voluntary organisations* had for some time used 'job creation schemes' to provide temporary jobs and training (e.g. on community work and landscaping), and had promoted use of existing leisure facilities by the unemployed. 'Job creation schemes' normally excluded the possibility of creating a permanent, profit-making enterprise. However, the idea emerged of 'Community Business Ventures', in which a community group would establish its own business or act as a catalyst for an individual or group to do so (e.g. a co-operative of redundant workers).

(2) *Local authorities* had few powers in this field till the Inner Urban Areas Act 1978 allowed some councils to give direct physical and financial assistance to industry. By 1979 the Royal Town Planning Institute was claiming for local authorities a leading role in *Employment Planning*,[22] providing expertise for small firms, finding ways of averting closures and cutting 'red tape'. Many of the

newly Labour-controlled councils elected in 1981, particularly the West Midlands County and Cleveland County, announced a wide range of initiatives; it was essential for them to be seen to act, but the likely results were of a modest scale, and the role of local authorities was to be curtailed in 1982, except in inner city areas.

(3) Large corporations began to show a concern to promote small industry in areas where they themselves had redundancies. The British Steel Corporation set up its own industrial promotion agency to attract new industry to its closure areas.

(4) The Conservative government from 1979 claimed that economic recovery would come from the growth of small firms, which it ostensibly supported through budget measures, the Small Firms Division of the Department of Industry, and (in England) the existing Council for Small Industry in Rural Areas.

So the urgency of the problem aroused apparent interest from many different parts of the political spectrum, even if many were expressions of concern rather than practical schemes of any size. In North-East England, Price[23] lists no less than 44 organisations, of all the four types above, which provide information and services for small business. This appears to answer the increasingly important objective of 'self-reliant' regional economic growth (see Segal, 1979[24]). At best, it must be said that the 'internal solution' to a Region's economic problems must take many years; at worst there is a danger of proponents of the small firms solution falling victim to their own propaganda. The Conservative government laid stress on the American 'Birch Report',[25] which reported that small firms created 66 per cent of all new jobs in the USA; they apparently missed the point, detected by Fothergill and Gudgin,[26] that only eight per cent are in the manufacturing sector. The same writers demonstrate in the favourable case of the East Midlands that new manufacturing firms managed to increase employment by a mere seven per cent in the seven years to 1975. Storey[27] demonstrates that in Cleveland, wholly new manufacturing firms created around 2,000 jobs between 1965 and 1976: we have reported 11,300 job losses there since 1976 in BSC alone. 'To place exclusive reliance upon small firms risks imposing on this sector greater expectations than are justified by a cool review of its prospects' (Storey). Little data were available as to how small firms performed in the recession itself; one prominent report, based on survey returns from 3,000 firms, found that each small business laid off an average of three workers in 1981 (equivalent to 800,000 nationally).

The suggested solutions are therefore disappointing. In Third World countries one response to a shortage of job opportunities has been the growth of the 'informal sector' of the economy – that is, of people working on their own account often with no premises and few tools. It is suggested that the unemployed do this already in Britain, and that the 'Black Economy' accounts for a significant proportion (six to eight per cent[28]) of total British production. At one stage the International Labour Office saw planning merits in promoting the 'informal sector'; but the consensus is that this was a mistaken view of the prospects.

The Future of Spatial Planning Policies

Early in our period of study the achievements of regional policy were discredited as never before in closures (on Merseyside and Strathclyde etc.) of some of the largest new factories in 'peripheral areas': in the last important work of the 1970s on regional policy, at a time of proposals for devolution and inner cities, Maclennan and Parr conclude[29] by assessing the prospects for a 'more complex' policy. The issue now rather is whether a policy is possible at all. Does the recent failure of many 'regional policy factories' militate against spending further government money on such ventures? We have seen that the majority of such failures after 1979 were principally connected with the national performance of their respective industries, and that the position in 'assisted areas' would have been considerably worse without the 'regional policy factories' that did survive. In logic the case for a regional policy on re-distributive grounds is as strong as ever: in practice the nub is that the opportunities for diverting investments from one Region to another are weaker than at any time since the 1930s. Regional policy had always shown cyclical variations in effectiveness; it depended on there being prosperous Regions (where industrial growth would impose social costs) from which to divert industry. Throughout our period of study unemployment and other factors led governments to refuse very few industrial developments in 'normally prosperous' Regions. Thus the ending of office development permits in August 1979 and of industrial development certificates in December 1981 only set the seal on a change of policy by both parties.

Compared with these factors the precise definition of 'assisted areas' (though it may turn out to be crucial for some towns) is a minor technical issue, which may profit from use of 1981 Census measures and different boundary systems. The Conservatives' reduction in the 'assisted areas' and in financial inducements for industry in them was announced in mid–1979, before national recession was anticipated. The first stage in the downgrading of areas occurred in August 1980 and the second in August 1982 (review as promised). Some areas of redundancy in the steel industry were promoted at intervening dates. As explained at greater length with maps in Townsend, 1980,[30] these geographically complex measures were the end-result of fairly simple financial cuts. The review of 1982 downgradings was announced on 29 June by the Secretary for Industry. The principal feature, long overdue in terms of the impact of recession, was the promotion of Teesside to the status of Special Development Area. An increased use of Enterprise Zones was apparent in statements by the Chancellor on 27 July 1982. Local authorities were invited to apply for a further eleven zones in the UK.

Any new thinking for the UK in a frustrating policy vacuum came principally from the EEC, in its new regional policy guidelines of 1981.[31] The Commission allocated 29 per cent of the quota section of the Regional Fund to parts of the UK 'peripheral Regions', and proposed that a larger 'non-quota section' should be directed, in the EEC at large, to 'areas in which the recession has caused a decline of industry on an alarming scale'. The Commission accepted that it was becoming increasingly difficult for regional policy to rely on new industrial investments by large corporations; it therefore proposed to encourage indigenous development in small and medium-sized businesses, including development of information sources. The most striking feature was that regional development would in future proceed through programme contracts in which regional authorities (which we do not have in England) would be closely involved. It was not difficult to align this approach with possible policies of the Social Democratic and Liberal Parties (with their emphasis on regional devolution and general decentralisation respectively). Hallett[32] does not see the EEC role as very significant – indeed Labour might have us withdraw – and it is essential not to exaggerate the real economic significance of political and administrative devolution. Central methods of decision-making cannot be replaced (though they may be supported) by the apparent institutional solution of creating new agencies, offices or assemblies in the Regions. They will have their place, not least in presenting the needs of their areas to London, but key lessons from the dull history of Regional Economic Planning Councils (1965–79) must also be applied. They cannot work without new legislation and some influence over the allocation of public expenditure in their areas; they cannot contribute to the inter-regional movement of investment. There is perhaps a more marked role than in the past for them to make decisions about intra-regional inequalities, because these have now evolved a sharper substance. For instance, the more prosperous Regions show major differences as between say Bristol and Plymouth, or Cambridgeshire and Norfolk. Indeed, Hall[33] sees the accommodation of growth pressures in the South as an important task for Town and Country Planning. The Labour Party was committed to providing Regions of England with a Development Agency like those of Scotland or Wales, but some of its proposals were for a centralised French-style national ministry which would draw up 'development contracts' with leading corporations in priority sectors.

The Regional Studies Association began a major inquiry into the problem by stressing that it was imperative that 'the old, outworn and costly palliatives of yesterday should not unthinkingly be applied again', but it saw no reason to believe that economic recovery would not leave significant geographical inequalities in its wake. Most academic calculations forecast a consolidation in the 1980s of the regional differences established in the recession. Regular reviews of the position of critical areas such as the West Midlands conurbation will be necessary. Cameron (1980)[34] saw 'every reason to predict an increasing *proportion* of investment decisions favouring non-conurbation locations'. Should these inequalities again be the focus of a national set of spatial policies? It may yet be the case that the 1980s show such high unemployment and such low investment that the opportunities to transfer developments between sub-regions remain minimal: it is politically convenient for everyone to maximise any possibilities that do exist toward an 'internal solution' within different Regions, including more systematic assistance to existing firms.

Our view is that it will remain politically necessary for a British government to have 'a regional policy' and an 'inner city policy' Secondly, existing and future areas of heavy redundancy should receive priority attention. Thirdly, financial inducements in 'assisted areas' should at the very least serve to focus investment from outside the UK (despite recent withdrawals by foreign corporations reported in this volume). This much is probably the 'lowest common denominator' of future inter-party approaches. In the writer's view the situation will require a more imaginative approach to both manufacturing and service industries, including the restoration of physical controls (such as industrial development certificates), and the political courage in due course to use them to transfer industrial developments from prosperous parts of the South East, South West and East Anglia to future 'assisted areas'. This often-tried method dealt with expansions within corporations, but it would also be wise, in view of the far-reaching scope of the 'meso-economic sector', to consider taking some control over corporations' closure plans for different plants (as often happened in the public sector before 1979).

Many will react that planning only works when 'it is cutting with the grain of events', e.g. if it were to support the 'M4 growth axis'. If such critics were ever to visit some of the 'assisted areas' they would realise that the 'residential space preferences' of some corporation executives could be met if certain areas were well marketed. The final suggestion then is that a regional policy is not wholly inconsistent with future employers' preferences. It is certainly possible that there may be, by the late 1980s, a surge of innovative investment in new technology and services. It is accepted that 'more and more, the remaining dynamic parts of the economy are likely to be the high-amenity areas' (Hall, 1981[35]). It is usually accepted both that 'high-amenity' implies a location in the South (often following the concentration of research functions of the national economy in the outer South East), and that it would injure economic growth to 'transfer' them north. On the other hand the present 'assisted areas' will increasingly lose to industrialising countries their chances of attracting less skilled work, but do have sub-regions of very great amenity value, and some precedents in the development of office and research functions. The first priority must be to provide some work in great centres of redundancy such as Consett or Ellesmere Port. Beyond this attention might be focussed on high-amenity areas within travel-to-work influence of the least favoured conurbations and black-spots.

The task must be to concentrate on a tough international marketing operation to scientific industry, based on the image of these higher-amenity areas. The 'assisted areas' of the future can maximise their powers of attraction if they build on and focus around areas such as the Vale of Glamorgan (for the sake of Mid and West Glamorgan), the Chester sub-region (for the sake of Merseyside and Clwyd), Lothian (for the sake of Clydeside and Fife), the mid-Tyne valley (for the sake of Tyneside), or Warwickshire (if Birmingham and Coventry require central government support). This may seem like a late conversion to 'growth area' principles of 1963. It is in fact a deliberate response to evolving location preferences in new types of industry. This type of proposal must however remain of modest importance for the 're-industrialisation' of the worst-hit areas of the UK. In short we may say that local initiatives and small firms policies are insufficient to match the impact of recession, and in turn that regional policy is no substitute for a medium-term upsurge of national investment. This upturn is the first requisite for any success in increasing investment in new plants, and the great question of academic speculation is whether any upturn in the Kondratieff 'Long Cycle' is indeed inevitable.

Notes

1. J. O'Connor, *The Fiscal Crisis of the State* (St. Martin's Press, New York, 1973).
2. R. Parry, 'The Territorial Dimension in United Kingdom Public Employment', *Studies in Public Policy* No. 65 (University of Strathclyde, Glasgow, 1980).
3. Joint Manpower Watch Group, Quarterly returns for England and Wales, issued as Department of Environment Press Notices.
4. *Financial Times*, 8 Sept. 1981.
5. *Financial Times*, 11 Nov. 1981.
6. *Financial Times*, 2 Feb. 1982.
7. Produced by P. Dodds and R. Nelson, University of Durham, as part of a joint project with University of Newcastle, 'Integration and Presentation of Manpower Data for Travel-to-Work Areas'.
8. H.S.E. Gravelle, 'Mortality and Unemployment', *The Lancet*, 26 Sept. 1981, pp. 625–9.
9. H. Brenner, *Mental Illness and the Economy* (Harvard University Press, Cambridge, Mass., 1973).
10. *Employment Gazette*, Table 2.11 (monthly).
11. *Employment Gazette*, Table 2.17 (quarterly).
12. *Financial Times*, 1 March 1982; for 1985 the London Business School were then forecasting a level of 3.1m., and the NIESR one of 3.3m.
13. C. Jenkins and B. Sherman, *The Collapse of Work* (Eyre Methuen, London, 1979).
14. J. Rada, *The Impact of Micro-electronics* (ILO, Geneva, 1980), p. 105.
15. *Employment Gazette*, vol. 89, no. 10 (1981), p. 419.

16. J. Sleigh, B. Boatwright, P. Irwin and R. Stanyon, *The Manpower Implications of Micro-Electronic Technology* (HMSO, London, 1979), p. 109.

17. Rada, *The Impact of Micro-electronics*, pp. 36–7.

18. T. Sheriff, 'A De-industrialised Britain?', *Fabian Research Series* 341 (1979), p. 15.

19. G. Mensch, *Stalemate in technology* (Ballinger, Cambridge, Mass., 1979).

20. G. Ray, 'Innovation in the Long Cycle', *Lloyds Bank Review*, no. 135 (1980), pp. 14–28.

21. *Employment Gazette*, vol. 89, no. 10 (1981), p.419.

22. Royal Town Planning Institute, *Employment Planning: a Consultation Document* (RTPI, London, 1979).

23. K. Price, 'Help for Small Businesses in the North East', *Northern Economic Review*, no. 2 (1982), pp. 25–32.

24. N. Segal, 'The Limits and Means of "Self-Reliant" Regional Economic Growth', in D. Maclennan and J.B. Parr (eds.), *Regional Policy, Past Experience and New Directions* (Martin Robertson, Oxford, 1979), pp. 212–24.

25. D.L. Birch, *The Job Generation Process* (MIT, Cambridge, Mass., 1979).

26. S. Fothergill and G. Gudgin, 'The Job Generation Process in Britain', *Centre for Environmental Studies Research Series 32* (CES, London, 1979).

27. D. Storey, 'Small Firms and Economic Recovery', *Northern Economic Review*, no. 2 (1982), pp. 14–20.

28. Chairman of the Board of Inland Revenue, *Financial Times*, 29 April 1982.

29. D. Maclennan and J.B. Parr (eds.), *Regional Policy, Past Experience and New Directions* (Martin Robertson, Oxford, 1979), pp. 328–9.

30. A.R. Townsend, 'Unemployment Geography and the New Government's "Regional" Aid', *Area*, vol. 12, no. 1 (1981), pp. 13–18.

31. 'Reform of the Community's Regional Policy', *Bulletin of the European Communities Commission*, 10 (1981).

32. G. Hallett, *Second Thoughts on Regional Policy* (Centre for Policy Studies, London, 1981).

33. P. Hall, 'Issues for the Eighties', *The Planner* (1981), pp. 4–5.

34. G. Cameron (ed.), *The Future of the British Conurbation* (Longman, London, 1980).

35. Hall, 'Issues for the Eighties', p. 5.

SELECT BIBLIOGRAPHY

Bacon, R. and Eltis, W. *Britain's Economic Problem: Too Few Producers* (Macmillan, London, 1976)

Bell, D. *The Coming of Post-Industrial Society, A Venture in Social Forecasting* (Heinemann, London, 1974)

Blackaby, F. (ed.), *De-industrialisation* (Heinemann, London, 1979)

Brown, W. (ed.), *The Changing Contours of British Industrial Relations. A Survey of Manufacturing Industry* (Blackwell, Oxford, 1981)

Carney, J., Hudson, R. and Lewis, J. (eds.), *Regions in Crisis* (Croom Helm, London, 1980)

Chisholm, M. 'Regional Policies in an Era of Slow Population Growth and Higher Unemployment', *Regional Studies*, vol. 10, no. 2 (1976), pp. 201–13.

Creedy, J. (ed.), *The Economics of Unemployment in Britain* (Butterworths, London, 1981)

Cross, M. *New Firm Formation and Regional Development* (Gower, Farnborough, 1981)

Dennis, R. 'The Decline of Manufacturing Employment in Greater London, 1966–74', *Urban Studies*, vol. 15, no. 1 (1978), pp. 63–73

Dunford, M., Geddes, M. and Perrons, D. 'Regional Policy and the Crisis in the UK: a Long-run Perspective', *International Journal of Urban and Regional Research*, vol. 5, no. 3 (1981)

Dunnett, P.J.S. *The Decline of the British Motor Industry* (Croom Helm, London, 1980)

Fothergill, S. and Gudgin, G. 'Regional Employment Change: a Sub-regional Explanation', *Progress in Planning*, vol. 12, part 3 (1979), pp. 155–219

——— *Unequal Growth: Urban and Regional Employment Change in the UK* (Heinemann, London, 1982)

Frank, A.G. *Reflections on the World Economic Crisis* (Hutchinson, London, 1981)

Froebel, F., Heinrichs, J. and Kreye, O. *The New International Division of Labour* (Cambridge University Press, Cambridge, English translation 1980)

Frost, M. and Spence, N. 'The Timing of Unemployment Response in British Regional Labour Markets, 1963–1976', in Martin, R.L. (ed.), *Regional Wage Inflation and Unemployment* (Pion, London, 1981)

Garfield, W.R. *The Measurement of Unemployment* (Blackwell, Oxford, 1980)

Gillespie, A.E. and Owen, D.W. 'Unemployment Trends in the Current Recession', *Area*, vol. 13, no. 3 (1981), pp. 189–96.

Goddard, J.B. 'Office Development and Urban and Regional Development in Britain', in Daniels, P.W. (ed.), *Spatial Patterns of Office Growth and Location* (Wiley, Chichester, 1979), p. 43.

Gudgin, G. *Industrial Location Processes and Regional Employment Growth* (Saxon House, Farnborough, 1978)

Hall, P. 'The Geographer and Society', *The Geographical Journal*, vol. 147, pt. 2 (1981), p. 151

Hart, P.E. and Clarke, R. *Concentration in British Industry, 1935–75* (Cambridge University Press, Cambridge, 1980)

Hawkins, K. *Unemployment* (Penguin, Harmondsworth, 1979)

Healey, M.J. 'Plant Closures in Multi-Plant Enterprises – the case of a Declining Industrial Sector', *Regional Studies*, vol. 16, no. 1 (1982), pp. 37–51

Henderson, R.A. 'An Analysis of Closures among Scottish Manufacturing Plants', *ESU Discussion, Paper 3* (Scottish Economic Planning Department, Edinburgh, 1979)

Hughes, J. *Britain in Crisis* (Spokesman, Nottingham, 1981)

Jordan, B. *Mass Unemployment and the Future of Britain* (Basil Blackwell, Oxford, 1982)

Keeble, D. *Industrial Location and Planning in the United Kingdom* (Methuen, London, 1976)

———— 'Industrial Decline in the Inner City and Conurbation', *Transactions of the Institute of British Geographers*, New Series vol. 3, no. 1 (1978), pp. 101–114

———— 'Industrial Decline, Regional Policy, and the Urban-rural Manufacturing Shift in the United Kingdom', *Environment and Planning A*, vol. 12, no. 8 (1980), pp. 945–62

Kondratieff, N.D. (translated by W.F. Stolper, 1935, and abbreviated), 'The Long Waves in Economic Life', *Lloyds Bank Review*, no. 129 (1978), pp. 41–60.

Lever, H. and Edwards, G. *Banking on Britain, Reversing Britain's Economic Decline* (Sunday Times reprint of six

articles, London, 1981)
Lever, W.F. 'The Inner-City Employment Problem in Great Britain since 1952: A Shift-Share Approach', in Rees, J., Hewings, G.J.D. and Stafford, H.A. (eds.) *Industrial Location and Regional Systems* (Croom Helm, London, 1981)
Lloyd, P.E. and Dicken, P. *Modern Western Society: a Geographical Perspective on Work, Home and Wellbeing* (Harper & Row, London, 1981)
Maclennan, D. and Parr, J.B. (eds.) *Regional Policy, Past Experience and New Directions* (Martin Robertson, Oxford, 1979)
Mandel, E. (translated by J. Rothschild), *The Second Slump, A Marxist Analysis of Recession in the Seventies*, (New Left Books, London, 1978)
Manners, G., Keeble, D., Rodgers, B. and Warren, K. *Regional Development in Britain* (Wiley, London, 1972)
Manners, G. 'Reinterpreting the Regional Problem', *The Three Banks Review*, no.111 (1976), pp. 33–5.
Marquand, J. 'Measuring the Effects and Costs of Regional Incentives', *Government Economic Service Working Paper No. 32* (Department of Industry, London, 1980)
Martin, R.L. 'Labour Shake-out and the Regional Incidence of Redundancy in the Current Recession', *Cambridge Journal of Economics* (1982 forthcoming)
Massey, D.B. and Meegan, R.A. 'Industrial Restructuring versus the Cities', *Urban Studies*, vol. 15, no. 3 (1978)
Massey, D. 'In What Sense a Regional Problem?', *Regional Studies*, vol. 13, no. 2 (1979)
——— and Meegan, R.A. *The Anatomy of Job Loss* (Methuen, London, 1982)
Moore, B., Rhodes, J. and Tyler, P. 'The Impact of Regional Policy in the 1970s', *CES Review*, Vol. 1 (1977), pp. 67–77.
Norton, R.D. and Rees, J. 'The Product Cycle and the Spatial Decentralization of American Manufacturing', *Regional Studies*, vol. 13, no. 2 (1979), pp. 141–51
O'Connor, J. *The Fiscal Crisis of the State* (St Martin's Press, New York, 1973)
O'Farrell, P. 'An Analysis of Industrial Closures: the Irish Experience, 1960–73', *Regional Studies*, vol. 10, no. 4 (1976), pp. 433–48.
Ogilvy, A.A. 'Population Migration Between the Regions of

Great Britain, 1971–9', *Regional Studies*, vol. 16, no. 1 (1982), pp. 65–73.

Reddaway, W.B. 'The Economic Consequences of Zero Population Growth', *Lloyds Bank Review*, no. 124 (1977), pp. 14–30.

Short, J. 'Defence Spending in the U.K. Regions', *Regional Studies*, vol. 15, no. 2 (1981), pp. 101–110

Sinfield, A. *What Unemployment Means* (Martin Robertson, Oxford, 1981)

Singh, A. 'UK industry and the World Economy; a Case of De-industrialisation?', *Cambridge Journal of Economics*, vol. 1, no. 2 (1977)

Sleigh, J., Boatwright, B., Irwin, P. and Stanyor, R. *The Manpower implications of micro-electronics technology* (HMSO, London, 1979)

Townsend, A.R. 'The relationship of Inner City problems to Regional Policy', *Regional Studies*, vol. 11, no. 4 (1977), pp. 225–51.

———, Smith, E. and Johnson, M.R.D. 'Employees' Experience of New Factories in North East England; Survey Evidence on some Implications of British Regional Policy', *Environment and Planning A*, vol. 10, no. 12 (1978), pp.1345–62

——— 'Geographical Perspectives on major job losses in the UK, 1977–80', *Area*, vol. 13, no. 1 (1981), pp. 31–8.

——— 'Unemployment geography and the new government's "regional" aid', *Area*, vol. 12, No. 1 (1980), pp. 9–18.

——— 'Recession and the Regions in Great Britain, 1976–80: Analyses of Redundancy Data', *Environment and Planning A*, vol. 14 (1982 forthcoming)

Watts, H.D. *The Large Industrial Enterprise* (Croom Helm, London, 1980)

Wood, P.A. *Industrial Britain, The West Midlands* (David & Charles, London, 1976)

INDEX

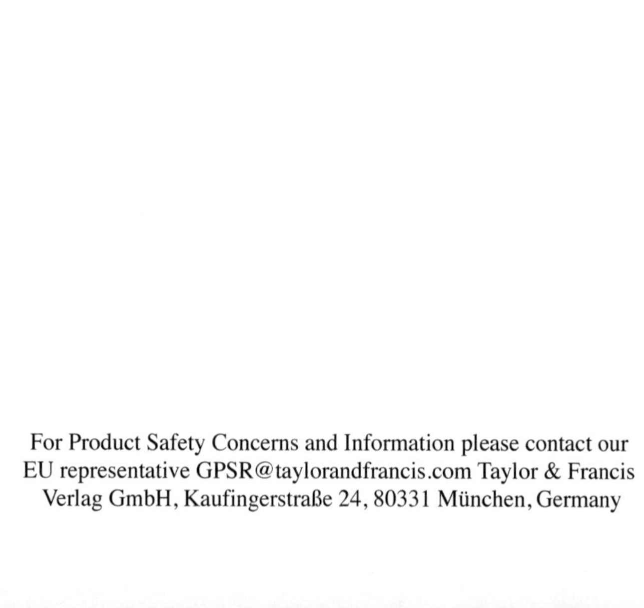